Secrets of Fat-Free Desserts

Secrets of Fat-Free Desserts

Over 150 low-fat and fat-free recipes for scrumptious and simple-to-make cakes, cobblers, cookies, crisps, pies, puddings, trifles, & other tasty goodies

Sandra Woodruff, RD

Avery Publishing Group
Garden City Park, New York

Text Illustrator: John Wincek
Interior Color Photographs: Victor Giordano
Photo Food Styling: BC Giordano
Front Cover Photograph: John Strange
Back Cover Photographs: Victor Giordano
Cover Design: William Gonzalez
Typesetting: Elaine V. McCaw
In-House Editor: Joanne Abrams

Avery Publishing Group
120 Old Broadway
Garden City Park, NY 11040
1-800-548-5757

Library of Congress Cataloging-in-Publication Data

Woodruff, Sandra L.
    Secrets of fat-free desserts: over 150 low-fat and fat-free
recipes for scrumptious, simple-to-make cakes, cobblers, cookies,
crisps, pies, puddings, trifles, and other tasty goodies / Sandra
Woodruff.
        p. cm.
    Includes index.
    ISBN 0-89529-824-4
    1. Low-fat diet—Recipes. 2. Desserts. I. Title.
RM237.7.W663 1998
641.5'638—dc21   97-29864
                                                 CIP

Contents

Acknowledgments,   vii

Preface,   ix

Introduction,   1

1. Having Your Cake and Eating It, Too,   3
2. Cool and Creamy Cheesecakes,   19
3. Creative Cakes,   43
4. Pleasing Pies, Tarts, and Pastries,   69
5. Creamy Puddings, Mousses, and Trifles,   97
6. Colossal Cookies,   121
7. Refreshing Frozen Desserts,   145
8. Crisps, Cobblers, and Other Fabulous Fruit Desserts,   163
9. Delightful Dessert Breads,   187

Resource List,   209

Metric Conversion Tables,   211

Index,   213

This book is dedicated to my favorite taste testers, Wiley and C.D.

Acknowledgments

I am very grateful to have had the opportunity to do work that I love *and* to work with great people while doing it. It has been a tremendous pleasure to produce this book with the talented and dedicated professionals at Avery Publishing Group, who lend their support and creativity at every stage of production. Special thanks go to Rudy Shur and Ken Rajman for providing the opportunity to publish this book, and to my editor, Joanne Abrams, whose hard work, diligent attention to detail, and endless patience have added so much.

Thanks also go to my husband, Tom, and to my dear friends and family members for their long-term support and encouragement. And last but not least, I would like to express my gratitude to my clients and coworkers, whose questions and ideas keep me learning and experimenting with new things.

Preface

As a nutritionist, I have long been aware of the need to help people trim the fat from their diet. I also know the importance of creating nutrient-rich foods made with whole grains and other ingredients that are as close as possible to their natural state. But I also know that foods must be more than just healthy. They must be visually appealing and absolutely delicious, and they must be simple to prepare. If they are not the former, people simply will not eat them. If they are not the latter, people simply will not make them.

Having worked closely with clients for well over a decade, I have witnessed firsthand the dramatic changes that occur when people modify their diets for the better—reduced body fat and weight loss, lower blood cholesterol and blood pressure, and greatly enhanced energy levels and feelings of well-being. People are usually surprised to find just how painless the process of adopting a healthy diet can be. They are equally surprised to learn that with just a little fore-thought, they can have their cake and eat it, too. After all, no one wants to give up dessert!

Secrets of Fat-Free Desserts is the perfect book for people who want to reduce the fat in their diet, control calories, maximize their nutrition, and still enjoy great-tasting sweet treats. From Royal Raspberry Cake, to Apricot Custard Tart, to Triple Chocolate Biscotti, every recipe has been designed to eliminate or greatly reduce fat, to keep sugar within reasonable limits, and, whenever possible, to increase fiber and boost nutrition. Just as important, every recipe has been kitchen-tested to make sure that you enjoy success each and every time you make it, and people-tested to make sure that every treat you create is a hit.

The first chapter of *Secrets of Fat-Free Desserts* begins by explaining just why dietary fat should be reduced, and just how much fat is allowable in a healthy diet. It also provides a wealth of information about the flours, sweeteners, dairy products, fat substitutes, and other no- and low-fat cooking ingredients that will help you slash fat and improve the nutritional value of your home-made desserts. The remainder of the book presents a fabulous collection of recipes for delectable cakes, pies, puddings, cookies, cobblers, crisps, dessert breads, and other sweet treats, each made with little or no added fat, and often with less sugar than that used in most traditional desserts.

In addition to including tried-and-true recipes, *Secrets of Fat-Free Desserts* provides a wealth of tips designed to guide you in creating more healthful versions of your own favorite confections. Within these pages, you will discover how to replace unhealthy fats with natural fat substitutes, how to cook with many of the new reduced-fat and nonfat products, and how to bake with healthful whole grain flours. These simple tips will make modifying your own recipes a breeze.

So get out your spatula, and get ready to learn just how healthy and delicious dessert can be. It is my hope that *Secrets of Fat-Free Desserts* will prove to you that treats do not have to be full of fat, calories, and sugar, and that wholesome goodies can be satisfying and delicious.

Introduction

Everyone loves dessert. But let's face it. Most of the ingredients that make up traditional desserts—cups of butter, margarine, and other fats; gobs of full-fat cream cheese, sour cream, and whipping cream; and generous amounts of chocolate, sugar, and refined flours—just don't fit into today's recommendations for healthful eating. Fortunately, you don't have to give up dessert to adopt a healthy lifestyle. Cookies fresh from the oven, bubbling cobblers and fruit crisps, warm and yeasty coffee cakes, sweet quick breads, velvety cheesecakes, cool and creamy puddings and frozen treats, and delicious cakes and pies can all be yours—once you know the secrets of fat-free desserts.

Secrets of Fat-Free Desserts was written to guide you in creating sweet treats that will not blow your fat budget. Just as important, unlike many other low-fat dessert books, this book goes beyond the goal of cutting down on fat. Because so many low-fat desserts compensate for the loss of fat by adding extra sugar, they are surprisingly high in calories. But by keeping sugar within reason, the desserts in this collection keep calories in rein—a boon for everyone who's watching their weight.

As a nutritionist and teacher, and as a person who loves good food, I began looking for ways to reduce or totally eliminate the fat in foods long before anyone ever heard the term "fat-free." At the same time, though, I discovered that many of the natural fat substitutes and wholesome flours I used also reduced the need for sugar. As a result of years of experimentation and kitchen testing, and of many helpful suggestions from clients and students, I developed ways to make moist and flavorful cakes, cookies, pies, cobblers, puddings, and other treats with little or no added fat, and, quite often, with less sugar. These are the discoveries that I am sharing in this book. Besides eliminating or reducing fat and sugar, I have further improved the nutritional value of many of these sweet treats by using whole grain flours and other wholesome ingredients, such as fruits and fruit juices. The result? Great-tasting desserts that can be easily incorporated into a healthful diet.

One of the nicest features of this book is the simplicity of the recipes. Every effort has been made to keep the number of ingredients to a minimum, and to utilize as few pots, pans, utensils, and other equipment as possible. Many of the recipes can be easily mixed by hand in only one bowl. This will save you time and make cleanup a breeze—important considerations for most people today.

As you will see, watching your fat intake does not have to mean dieting and deprivation. This book is filled with easy-to-follow recipes for delightful desserts that your whole family will enjoy, as well as plenty of ideas for getting the fat out of your own favorite recipes. I wish you the best of luck and health with all your fat-free cooking.

1

Having Your Cake and Eating It, Too

Sometimes you can have your cake and eat it too . . . and your pies, cobblers, crisps, puddings, cookies, and many other treats. This book presents a variety of confections—velvety smooth cheesecakes, spicy crisps, creamy puddings, and more—that are totally fat-free or greatly reduced in fat. In addition, most contain 25 to 50 percent fewer calories than traditional desserts. Experienced cooks and novices alike will be amazed by the number of creative and healthful ways in which fat and calories can be trimmed from baked goods and other sweet treats. They will also be delighted to discover that these tantalizing creations are as easy to make as they are easy to love.

This chapter will begin by explaining why dietary fat should be decreased, and will guide you in budgeting your fat intake. In addition, you will learn about the various healthful ingredients used throughout this book—ingredients that may be old friends, or may become new additions to your pantry.

BIG FAT PROBLEMS

There are plenty of reasons to trim the fat from your diet, but the most common one is the desire to lose weight. How does reducing your fat intake help with weight loss? With more than twice the calories of carbohydrate or protein, fat is the most concentrated source of calories there is. Compare a cup of butter or margarine (almost pure fat) with a cup of flour (almost pure carbohydrate). The butter has 1,600 calories, while the flour has only 400. It's easy to see where most of our calories come from.

Besides being high in calories, fat is also readily converted into body fat when eaten in excess. Carbohydrate-rich foods eaten in excess are also stored as fat, but they must first be converted into fat—a process that burns up some of the carbohydrates. The bottom line is that a high-fat diet will cause 20 percent more weight gain than will a high-carbohydrate diet, even when the two diets contain the same number of calories. So a high-fat diet is a double-edged sword for the weight-conscious person. It is high in calories, and it is the kind of nutrient that is most readily stored as body fat.

But high-fat diets pose a threat to much more than our weight. When fatty diets lead to obesity, diseases like diabetes and high blood pressure can result. And specific types of fats present their own unique problems. For example, eating too much saturated fat—found in meat, butter, and high-fat dairy products, among other foods—raises blood cholesterol levels, setting the stage for heart disease. Polyunsaturated fat, once thought to be the solution to heart disease, can also be harmful when eaten in excess. A diet overly rich in certain vegetable oils—sunflower, safflower, and corn oils, and products made from these oils—can alter body chemistry to favor the development of blood clots, high blood pressure, and inflammatory diseases. Too much polyunsaturated fat can also promote free radical damage to cells, contributing to heart disease and cancer.

Where do monounsaturated fats fit in? These fats—abundant in canola oil, olive oil, cashews, almonds, peanuts, and avocados—have no known harmful effects other than being a concentrated source of calories, like all fats.

One other kind of fat needs to be considered—especially if you are concerned about heart disease. Trans-fatty acids, also called trans fats, are chemically altered fats that are produced by adding hydrogen to liquid vegetable oils. This process, called hydrogenation, transforms the liquid vegetable oils into solid margarines and shortenings, giving these products a butter-like consistency. While hydrogenation improves the cooking and baking qualities of oils, and extends their shelf life as well, it also creates trans fats. And researchers have discovered that trans fats act much like saturated fats to raise lev-

els of LDL, or "bad" cholesterol, and at the same time lower levels of HDL, or "good" cholesterol.

Considering the problems caused by excess fat, you may think it would be best to completely eliminate fat from your diet. But the fact is that we do need some dietary fat. For instance, linoleic acid, a polyunsaturated fat naturally abundant in oils such as corn, soy, and safflower, and in walnuts, pine nuts, sunflower seeds, and sesame seeds, is essential for life. The average adult needs a minimum of 3 to 6 grams of linoleic acid per day—the amount present in one to two teaspoons of polyunsaturated vegetable oil or one to two tablespoons of nuts or seeds. Linolenic acid, a fat present in fish, flax seeds, and green plants, is also essential for good health. Some fat is also needed in the diet so that we may absorb fat-soluble nutrients like vitamin E.

Unfortunately, many people are getting too much of a good thing. The liberal use of margarine, cooking oils, mayonnaise, and oily salad dressings has created an unhealthy overdose of linoleic acid in the American diet. And, of course, most people also eat far too much saturated fat. How can we correct this? It's very simple. We can limit the fats that we use for baking and cooking, as well as fats that are added at the table. We can choose nonfat and low-fat dairy products and lean meats. And we can build our diets on a base of whole grains, legumes, vegetables, and fruits.

FIGHTING FAT

Now that you understand some of the reasons you should get the fat out of your diet, it's time to do just that. In the remainder of this chapter, you will discover how to develop your own personal fat budget, and you will become acquainted with some of the ingredients that will help you prune the fat and maximize the nutrition in your favorite treats. Throughout the rest of the book, you will learn how to use these ingredients to create delicious desserts that you will be proud to serve, and that family and friends will love to eat.

Budgeting Your Fat

For most Americans, about 34 percent of the calories in their diet come from fat. However, currently it is recommended that fat calories constitute no more than 30 percent of the diet, and, in fact, 20 to 25 percent would be even better in most cases. So the amount of fat you should eat every day is based on the number of calories you need.

Because people's calorie needs depend on their weight, age, gender, activity level, and metabolic rate, these needs vary greatly from person to person. Most adults, though, must consume 13 to 15 calories per pound each day to maintain their weight. Of course, some people need even fewer calories, while very physically active people need more.

Once you have determined your calorie requirements, you can estimate a fat budget for yourself. Suppose you are a moderately active person who weighs 150 pounds. You will probably need about 15 calories per pound to maintain your weight, or about 2,250 calories per day. To limit your fat intake to 20 percent of your calorie intake, you can eat no more than 450 calories derived from fat per day (2,250 x .20 = 450). To convert this to grams of fat, divide by 9, as one gram of fat has 9 calories. Therefore, you should limit yourself to 50 grams of fat per day (450 ÷ 9 = 50 fat grams).

The following table shows two maximum daily fat budgets—one based on 20 percent of calorie intake, and one based on 25 percent of calorie intake. If you are overweight, go by the weight you would like to be. This will allow you to gradually reach your goal weight. And keep in mind that although you have budgeted X amount of fat grams per day, you don't have to eat that amount of fat—you just have to avoid going over budget.

Recommended Maximum Daily Calorie and Fat Intakes

Weight (pounds)	Recommended Daily Calorie Intake (13–15 calories per pound)	Daily Fat-Gram Intake (20% of Calorie Intake)	Daily Fat-Gram Intake (25% of Calorie Intake)
100	1,300–1,500	29–33	36–42
110	1,430–1,650	32–37	40–46
120	1,560–1,800	34–40	43–50
130	1,690–1,950	38–43	47–54
140	1,820–2,100	40–46	51–58
150	1,950–2,250	43–50	54–62
160	2,080–2,400	46–53	58–67
170	2,210–2,550	49–57	61–71
180	2,340–2,700	52–60	65–75
190	2,470–2,850	55–63	69–79
200	2,600–3,000	58–66	72–83

How Low Should You Go?

If you are like most people, you have discovered that for maximum health, you must reduce your daily fat intake. How low should you go? As discussed earlier, some fat is necessary for good health. Therefore you should try not to consume less than 20 grams of fat per day. Of course, if you eat a balanced diet containing plenty of whole, natural foods, it would be impossible to eat less than this, anyway. On the other hand, if you eat a diet rich in fat-free refined and processed foods, you could be at risk for a deficiency of essential fats, as well as deficiencies of other nutrients.

Realize, too, that a very low-fat diet is not for everyone. If you have a specific medical problem, be sure to check with your physician or nutritionist before making any dramatic dietary changes.

Remember That Calories Count, Too

As you know by now, weight loss is the number-one reason that most people are trying to reduce their fat intake. And over the past decade, Americans have been able to reduce their fat consumption from 40 percent of calories down to about 34 percent. Yet during this same time, the rate of obesity has actually increased. Now, one out of three Americans is considered obese, compared with one out of four in 1980. How can this be? It's simple. People tend to forget that calories count too. The fact is that people now eat more calories than they did a decade ago—and exercise less.

In a way, the fat-free food frenzy has contributed to an expanding national waistline by creating a false sense of security. Many people mistakenly think that if a food is low in fat or fat-free, they can consume unlimited quantities of it. They may start their day with a couple of fat-free toaster pastries, keep a jar of jelly beans on their desk to nibble on throughout the day, snack on fat-free cookies at break time, and eat a bowl of fat-free ice cream for an evening snack. Although all of these foods are better choices than their full-fat counterparts, they are loaded with sugar and provide few or no nutrients. Moreover, some of these items have just as many calories as the full-fat versions. The truth is that any foods eaten in excess of calories burned in a day will be converted to body fat. And this is just as true of fat-free foods as it is of high-fat foods.

Does this mean that you should forget about using fat-free foods to lose weight? Not by any means. Chosen wisely, these foods can help you reach and maintain a healthy body weight. Setting up a fat budget is the place to start, since a low-fat diet is generally low in calories, too—unless you eat too many fat-free junk foods. So if you are trying to lose weight, stay within the bounds of your fat budget and choose mostly nutrient-rich foods. By doing this, you should be able to reach your weight-management goals. But if you have trouble losing or maintaining your weight, you must consider whether you are staying within the bounds of your calorie budget, as well.

ABOUT THE INGREDIENTS

The recipes in this book will allow you to make goodies that not only are delicious, but also will fit into your low-fat lifestyle. In the pages that follow, we'll take a look at the wholesome dairy products, grains, flours, sweeteners, and other ingredients that can help trim the fat, but not the flavor, from virtually any dessert.

Low-Fat and Nonfat Dairy Products

A wide range of low-fat and nonfat dairy products are available, making it possible to create deceptively rich-tasting cheesecakes, parfaits, puddings, and dessert fillings. Here are some of the dairy products used throughout this book.

Buttermilk. Used for generations to add rich flavor to baked goods such as muffins, quick breads, and cakes, buttermilk is a must-have staple in the fat-free kitchen. The acid in buttermilk tenderizes the gluten in batters that contain wheat flour, reducing the need for fat. This thick and tangy beverage also lends a rich and "cheesy" taste to puddings, fillings, sherbets, and frozen desserts.

But isn't buttermilk high in fat? Contrary to what its name implies, most buttermilk is quite low in fat. Originally a by-product of butter making, buttermilk should perhaps be called "butterless" milk. Brands of 1-percent buttermilk are widely available in grocery stores, and many stores offer nonfat brands, as well. Choose these for your low-fat cooking needs.

If you do not have buttermilk on hand, a good substitute can be made by mixing equal parts of nonfat yogurt and skim milk. Alternatively, place a tablespoon of vinegar or lemon juice in a one-cup measure, and fill to the one-cup mark with skim milk. Let the mixture sit for five minutes to thicken before using.

Cottage Cheese. Although often thought of as a diet food, full-fat cottage cheese has 5 grams of fat per 4-ounce serving, making it far from diet fare. Instead, choose nonfat or low-fat cottage cheese. These healthful products add richness and body to cheesecakes, puddings, toppings, fillings, and many other recipes.

When purchasing your cottage cheese, select brands with 1 percent or less milkfat, such as Breakstone's Free and Light n' Lively nonfat. Most brands of cottage cheese are quite high in sodium, with about 400 milligrams per half-cup, so it is best to avoid adding salt whenever this cheese is a recipe ingredient. As an alternative, use unsalted cottage cheese, which is available in some stores. Another option is to buy dry curd cottage cheese. This nonfat version is made without the "dressing" or creaming mixture. Minus the dressing, cottage cheese has a drier consistency; hence its name, dry curd. Unlike most cottage cheese, dry curd is very low in sodium. This product can be substituted cup for cup for nonfat or low-fat cottage cheese in your favorite recipes. (In some cases, you might need to add a tablespoon or two of milk to the recipe to compensate for the drier consistency.) Look for brands like Breakstone's Dry Curd.

Cream Cheese. This product adds creamy richness to cheesecakes, fillings, frostings, and many other desserts. But with 10 grams

of fat per ounce, this popular spread can blow your fat budget in a hurry. In fact, just one block of full-fat cream cheese contains 80 grams of fat—the equivalent of a stick of butter! But don't fear; many lower-fat alternatives are now available. Neufchâtel cheese, with 6 grams of fat per ounce, was once the only lower-fat alternative—and is still a good choice. But these days, a variety of light brands with 3 to 5 grams of fat per ounce are also sold in grocery stores. Better still are the many brands of nonfat cream cheese, such as Philadelphia Free and Healthy Choice. Most grocery stores also sell their own brand of nonfat cream cheese.

When using nonfat cream cheese in your recipes, keep in mind that this product— especially the soft tub type—has a higher moisture content than its reduced-fat and full-fat counterparts. For this reason, cheesecakes made with nonfat brands may have a softer, more pudding-like texture, and frostings and fillings made with fat-free cream cheese may become runny. Fortunately, these problems can be prevented by using the firmer block-style cheese rather than the soft tub cream cheese, and by following the tips presented on pages 28 and 34.

Evaporated Skimmed Milk. This ingredient can be substituted for cream in custards, puddings, and many other dishes, where it will add creamy richness and nutrients, but no fat.

Milk. Whole milk, the highest-fat milk available, is 3.5 percent fat by weight and has 8 grams of fat per cup. Instead choose skim (also called fat-free or nonfat) milk, which, with all but a trace of fat removed, has only about 0.5 gram of fat per cup. Another good choice is 1-percent low-fat or light milk, which, as the name implies, is 1-percent fat by weight and contains about 2 grams of fat per cup. Be aware that with 5 grams of fat per cup, 2-percent milk is not considered a low-fat product.

Nonfat Dry Milk. Like evaporated skimmed milk, nonfat dry milk powder adds a creamy richness to custards and puddings while boosting nutritional value. One cup of skim mixed with one-third cup of nonfat dry milk powder can replace cream in most recipes. This ingredient may also be stirred into fat-free and low-fat baked goods to add richness and promote browning. Be sure to use *instant* nonfat dry milk powder for the easiest mixing.

Ricotta Cheese. Ricotta is a mild, slightly sweet, creamy cheese that may be used in cheesecakes, mousses, frostings, and dessert fillings. As the name implies, nonfat ricotta contains no fat at all. Low-fat and light brands of ricotta, on the other hand, have 1 to 3 grams of fat per ounce, while whole-milk ricotta has 4 grams of fat per ounce.

Soft Curd Farmer Cheese. This soft white cheese makes a good low-fat substitute for cream cheese. Brands made with skim milk have about 3 grams of fat per ounce, compared with cream cheese's 10 grams. Nonfat brands are also available in some grocery stores and specialty shops. Soft curd farmer cheese may be used in cheesecakes, fillings, and frostings. Some brands are made with whole milk, so read the label before you buy. Look for a brand like Friendship Farmer Cheese.

Sour Cream. As calorie- and fat-conscious people know, full-fat sour cream can contain almost 500 calories and 48 grams of fat per cup! Use nonfat sour cream, though, and you'll save 320 calories and 48 grams of fat. Made from cultured nonfat milk thickened with vegetable gums, this product beautifully

replaces its fatty counterpart in any dish. Plain nonfat yogurt can also be substituted for sour cream in many recipes.

Sweetened Condensed Milk. Sweet and creamy, this convenient product has long been a favorite addition to pies, frozen desserts, puddings, and many other treats. Fat-conscious cooks will be happy to know that fat-free and low-fat brands—made from evaporated skimmed or low-fat milk—are now sold alongside the traditional product, which is made from evaporated whole milk. Eagle Brand Fat Free Sweetened Condensed Skimmed Milk is one brand that is widely available.

Yogurt. Plain or flavored yogurts can replace part or all of the liquid in many baked goods, adding tenderness, creamy richness, and flavor. Flavored yogurts can also be combined with nonfat whipped toppings to make creamy frostings and fillings, and they can star in puddings, parfaits, and other desserts that do not require cooking. In your low-fat cooking, select brands with 1 percent or less milkfat.

Yogurt Cheese. This thick, creamy product results when the whey, or watery portion, of the yogurt is drained from the solids. An excellent substitute for cream cheese in cheesecakes, frostings, and fillings, yogurt cheese can easily be made at home with many different flavors of yogurt. For complete directions on making yogurt cheese, see the inset on page 23.

Butter, Margarine, Oil, and Fat Substitutes

Most people are surprised to learn that fats like butter, margarine, and oil usually contribute more calories to desserts than sugar does. So the best way to cut calories in desserts is to cut the fat. Unfortunately, when many dessert recipes eliminate the fat, they simultaneously increase the sugar, offsetting much of the calorie savings. Why do they do this? In the case of baked goods like cakes, quick breads, and cookies, both sugar and fat add tenderness. You see, wheat flour contains proteins that, when mixed with liquid into a batter, form tough strands called gluten. Fat tenderizes baked goods by interfering with this process. This is why removing the fat from baked goods often makes them tough or rubbery. Since sugar also interferes with gluten formation, many fat-free recipes solve this problem by adding extra sugar. The recipes in this book offer a better solution. They use low-gluten flours, wholesome fat substitutes, and creative cooking techniques—all of which will produce the texture you love, minus the fat.

Most of the recipes in this book do not contain any added fats at all. Instead they are made with the wholesome fat substitutes that you will read about below. Some of the recipes, though, do include small amounts of reduced-fat margarine, light butter, or vegetable oil—products that can be useful for those treats that are difficult to make completely fat-free. Let's learn a little more about these fat-saving products.

Fat Substitutes for Baking. Almost any moist ingredient can replace part or all of the fat in cakes, cookies, brownies, breads, and other baked goods. The recipes in this book use a variety of fat substitutes. All of these substitutes, including applesauce, fruit purées, fruit juices, nonfat buttermilk, nonfat yogurt, mashed cooked pumpkin, and commercial fat substitutes made from prunes, are

Using Purées as Fat Substitutes

Looking for a healthful and delicious way to get the fat out of your favorite baked goods? Think fruit. By now, nearly everyone has heard about using applesauce as a fat substitute, but a variety of other fruit products—including puréed pears, peaches, and apricots, as well as mashed bananas and Prune Purée (page 131)—can also replace part or all of the fat in quick breads, cakes, and other baked goods, lending versatility and extra flavor to your recipes.

How do fruit purées work? Fat performs many vital functions in baking, some of which can be duplicated by fruit purées. For instance, fat adds moistness and flavor, imparts tenderness, and promotes browning. Fruit purées reduce the need for fat because their fiber and naturally occurring sugars hold moisture into baked goods. The fiber, sugar, and mild acids in fruit purées also help tenderize baked goods, while fruit sugars help promote browning.

When substituting fruit purées for fat, be sure to choose a purée that complements your recipe. In some cases this is easy, as many recipes already contain a fat substitute. For instance, when making banana bread, simply replace the fat with extra bananas. When you want a fat substitute that will not alter the color or flavor of your recipe, use applesauce. Puréed canned pears also have a very mild flavor that will not interfere with the taste of the finished product. When you want to add a fruity flavor to a recipe, try puréed canned peaches or apricots. And to complement the flavor of chocolate, use applesauce, puréed pears, mashed bananas, or Prune Purée.

How do you go about substituting fruit purées and other ingredients for the fat in your recipes? Throughout this book, you'll find helpful insets that will guide you in using these great fat-saving ingredients in a variety of baked goods.

readily available in grocery stores. One additional fat substitute—Prune Purée—can also be easily made at home using the recipe found in the inset on page 131. (To learn more about using fruit purées as fat substitutes, see the inset on page 9.)

Light Butter. Contrary to popular belief, you *can* bake with light butter. By doing this, you can cut fat by more than half without greatly affecting taste or texture. Because this product is diluted with water, however, it cannot be substituted for a full-fat product on a one-for-one basis. The inset on page 51 provides complete directions for using light butter in your favorite baked goods. Just be sure not to confuse whipped butter—butter that has had air whipped into it—with light butter.

Nonfat Margarine. Since nonfat margarine is mostly water, it generally cannot be used in most desserts. However, a few of the recipes in this book—such as the crumb crusts and crumb toppings—do call for this fat-free ingredient, as they were specifically developed for its use.

Nonfat margarine is available in tub, liquid (squeeze bottle), and spray forms. The recipes in this book call for tub-style nonfat margarine, as this form has the thickest consistency and performs best in recipes. Look for brands like Fleischmann's nonfat, Promise Ultra fat-free, and I Can't Believe It's Not Butter! fat-free.

Oil. Oil is pure fat and loaded with calories. In fact, just one tablespoon of any oil contains 120 calories and 13.6 grams of fat. For this reason, oil, like other fats, should be used only in small amounts. For baking, try a flavorful oil like unrefined corn oil. Unlike the tasteless refined oils commonly sold in grocery stores, unrefined corn oil has a golden amber color and a delicious buttery flavor. It

also retains much of the oil's natural nutritional value. Just a little bit adds wonderful flavor to your recipe. Look for this product in health food stores and some grocery stores. Another flavorful option is walnut oil. Widely sold in grocery stores, this oil is less refined than most vegetable oils and has a delightful nutty flavor. Another oil to choose for baking is canola oil, which is available in grocery stores. Be aware, though, that canola oil will add no flavor to your recipe.

When using unrefined oils, keep in mind that they will turn rancid quickly if stored at room temperature. For this reason, it is wise to purchase small bottles. (You will not be using much oil, anyway.) After opening the bottle, store the oil in the refrigerator.

Reduced-Fat Margarine. Like light butter, reduced-fat margarine can be substituted for regular butter using the guidelines on page 51.

Egg Whites and Egg Substitutes

Everyone who cooks knows the value of eggs. Eggs are star ingredients in puddings and custards. They add body to cheesecakes, lightness to mousses, and are indispensable in a wide range of baked goods, from breads to cakes to cookies. Of course, eggs are also loaded with cholesterol and contain some fat as well. For this reason, the recipes in this book call for fat-free egg substitutes or egg whites. Just how great are your savings in cholesterol and fat when whole eggs are replaced with one of these ingredients? One large egg contains 80 calories, 5 grams of fat, and 210 milligrams of cholesterol. The equivalent amount of egg white or fat-free egg substitute—3 tablespoons—contains 20 to 30 calories, no fat, and no cholesterol. The benefits of these substitute ingredients are clear.

You may wonder why some of the recipes in

this book call for egg whites while others call for egg substitute. In some cases, one ingredient does, in fact, work better than the other. For instance, egg substitute is the best choice when making puddings and custards. On the other hand, when recipes require whipped egg whites, egg substitutes will not work.

In most recipes, egg whites and egg substitutes can be used interchangeably. Yet, even in these recipes, one may sometimes be listed instead of the other due to ease of measuring. For example, while a cake made with 3 tablespoons of fat-free egg substitute would turn out just as well if made with 3 tablespoons of egg whites, this would require you to use one and a half large egg whites, making measuring something of a nuisance.

Whenever a recipe calls for egg whites, use large egg whites. When selecting an egg substitute, look for a fat-free brand like Egg Beaters, Scramblers, or Better'n Eggs. Most grocery stores also carry their own brand of fat-free egg substitute. A few brands of egg substitutes contain vegetable oil, so read the label to make sure that your product is fat-free. When replacing egg whites with an egg substitute, or whole eggs with egg whites or an egg substitute, use the following guidelines:

1 large egg = 1½ large egg whites	
1 large egg = 3 tablespoons egg substitute	
1 large egg white = 2 tablespoons egg substitute	

Grains and Flours

Just because a food is low in fat or fat-free does not mean it is good for you. Fat-free treats made from refined white flour provide few nutrients, and can actually deplete nutrient stores if eaten in excess. Whole grains and whole grain flours, on the other hand, contain a multitude of nutrients, including folate, vitamin B_6, vitamin E, chromium, cop-

per, magnesium, potassium, zinc, fiber, and a whole range of health-promoting phytochemicals. For this reason, many of the recipes in this book include ingredients like whole wheat flour, oat flour, oats, oat bran, wheat germ, and whole grain cereals. These products not only add vitamins, minerals, and fiber, but also provide great taste. In fact, once accustomed to the heartier taste and texture of whole grains, most people prefer whole grains to refined products.

Aside from the health benefits of whole grains, these products offer an additional advantage to the low-fat cook. As previously mentioned, wheat flour contains proteins that, when mixed with liquid into a batter, form tough strands called gluten. One function of both fat and sugar is to interfere with gluten development, and thus add tenderness to baked goods. Whole grains are naturally lower in gluten-forming proteins than is refined wheat flour. In addition, the fiber in whole grains interferes with the development of gluten. This means that baking with whole grains reduces the need for both fat and sugar.

Clearly, whole grains provide a wealth of benefits and should be enjoyed often. Following is a description of some of the wholesome grains and flours used throughout this book. Many of these products are readily available in grocery stores, while others may be found in health foods stores and gourmet shops. If you are unable to locate a particular grain or flour, the manufacturer can probably tell where to find it in your area. Alternatively, it may be available by mail order. See the Resource List on page 209.

Barley Flour. This flour, made from ground barley kernels, is rich in cholesterol-lowering soluble fiber. Slightly sweet tasting, barley flour adds a cake-like texture to baked goods, and can be used interchangeably with oat flour in recipes.

Brown Rice Flour. Brown rice flour is simply finely ground brown rice. It has a texture similar to that of cornmeal, and adds a mildly sweet flavor to baked goods. Use it in cookies for a crisp and crunchy texture.

Cornmeal. This grain adds a sweet flavor, a lovely golden color, and a crunchy texture to baked goods. Select whole grain (unbolted) cornmeal for the most nutrition. Next in line is bolted cornmeal, which is nearly whole grain. Degermed cornmeal is the most refined, and therefore the least desirable.

Oat Bran. Made of the outer part of the oat kernel, oat bran has a sweet, mild flavor and is a concentrated source of cholesterol-lowering soluble fiber. Oat bran helps retain moisture in baked goods, making it a natural for fat-free and low-fat baking. Look for it in the hot cereal section of your grocery store, and choose the softer, more finely ground products, like Quaker Oat Bran. Coarsely ground oat bran makes excellent hot cereal, but is not the best choice for baking purposes.

Oat Flour. This mildly sweet flour is perfect for use in cakes, muffins, and other baked goods. Like oat bran, oat flour is especially effective at retaining moisture in baked goods, and thus reducing the need for fat. Available in health foods stores and many grocery stores, oat flour can also be made at home by finely grinding quick-cooking oats in a blender or food processor.

Oats. Loaded with cholesterol-lowering soluble fiber, oats add a chewy texture and sweet flavor to quick breads, cookies, and crumb toppings. The recipes in this book use quick-cooking rolled oats—the kind that cook in one minute.

Unbleached Flour. This is refined white flour that has not been subjected to a bleaching process. Unbleached white flour lacks signif-

Measuring Ingredients

Because different measuring techniques can result in varying amounts of an ingredient being added to a recipe—and, in some cases, in dramatically different results—proper measuring is critical to the success of your fat-free cooking and baking endeavors. The recipes in this book were developed using the following measuring methods. By using the same techniques carefully and consistently in your own kitchen, you will enjoy greater success when using the recipes in this book.

Measuring Dry Ingredients. When measuring flour, sugar, and other dry ingredients, use a dry measuring cup that has the exact capacity you wish to measure. Scoop the ingredient directly from the canister, bin, or bag; then level the top off with the back of a knife. Do not pack any dry ingredients except for brown sugar.

Measuring Liquid Ingredients. Use a clear glass or plastic measuring cup to measure liquids. Place the cup on a level surface, and bend down so that the mark you wish to read is at eye level. Then fill the cup to that mark. If your recipe calls for more than one liquid ingredient to be added at the same time, you can place them all in the same cup. For instance, if your recipe calls for $\frac{3}{4}$ cup of milk and $\frac{1}{4}$ cup of egg substitute, first fill the cup to the $\frac{3}{4}$-cup mark with the milk. Then add enough egg substitute to reach the 1-cup mark.

Measuring Semisolid Ingredients. When measuring ingredients like fruit purées, applesauce, and yogurt, use a dry measuring cup that has the exact capacity you wish to measure. Spoon the ingredient into the cup; then level the top off with the back of a knife.

icant amounts of nutrients compared with whole wheat flour, but does contain more vitamin E than bleached flour.

The unbleached flour that is widely available in supermarkets is a presifted multipurpose flour that can be used in a variety of baked goods recipes, including any recipes in this book that call for unbleached flour. If you can find an unbleached pastry flour, it will produce even better results in your low-fat and fat-free cakes, pie crusts, cookies, quick breads, and muffin recipes—although you will need to substitute it for regular flour by using the guidelines found below. Made from a softer (lower-protein) wheat, unbleached pastry flour will produce a softer, more tender texture in baked goods than will regular unbleached flour. Unfortunately, unbleached pastry flour is not widely available. It can, however, be purchased by mail order.

You may have noticed that many fat-free and low-fat recipes include **cake flour**, a finely ground low-protein flour that is widely available in grocery stores. While cake flour does perform well in baking, it is a highly refined product that has been bleached with chlorine gas. Unbleached pastry flour is a much more wholesome choice.

Whole Wheat Flour.   This flour, made by grinding whole grain wheat kernels, includes the grain's nutrient-rich bran and germ. Nutritionally speaking, whole wheat flour is far superior to refined flour. Sadly, most people grew up eating white bread and other white flour products, and find whole wheat flour too heavy for their taste. A good way to learn to enjoy whole grain flours is to use part whole wheat and part unbleached flour in recipes, and gradually increase the amount of whole wheat used over time.

Several kinds of whole wheat flour are available, each with different characteristics, making some better choices than others for your fat-free desserts. The very best kind of whole wheat flour to use in fat-free desserts is **whole wheat pastry flour**, also called **whole grain pastry flour.** Made from a softer (lower-protein) wheat, whole wheat pastry flour produces lighter, softer-textured baked goods than regular whole wheat flour. Whole wheat pastry flour also has a milder, sweeter flavor than regular whole wheat flour, making it a natural choice for fat-free desserts. Whole wheat pastry flour is widely available in natural foods stores and many grocery stores. One nationally available brand is Arrowhead Mills. And since most major grocery chains carry Arrowhead Mills products, they should be able to order it for you if they do not already carry it.

White whole wheat flour is another option for making baked goods and fat-free desserts. Made from hard white wheat instead of the hard red wheat used to make regular whole wheat flour, white whole wheat flour is sweeter and lighter tasting than its red wheat counterpart. White whole wheat flour is available in many grocery stores and by mail order.

As you can see, there is a wide variety of flours available for use in baking. Experiment with various flours too see which kinds you like best. Here are some guidelines that will allow you to substitute various flours for refined wheat flour in your own favorite recipes:

1 cup refined wheat flour equals:

☐ 1 cup unbleached flour

☐ 1 cup plus 2 tablespoons unbleached pastry flour

☐ 1 cup plus 2 tablespoons cake flour

☐ 1 cup whole wheat pastry flour

☐ 1 cup minus 1 tablespoon white whole wheat flour

☐ 1 cup minus 2 tablespoons regular whole wheat flour

☐ 1 cup brown rice flour

☐ 1 cup barley flour

☐ 1 cup oat flour

Sweeteners

Refined white sugar contains no nutrients. In fact, when eaten in excess, refined sugar can actually deplete the body's stores of essential nutrients like chromium and the B vitamins. Of course, a moderate amount of sugar is usually not a problem for people who eat an otherwise healthy diet. What is moderate? No more than 10 percent of your daily intake of calories should come from sugar. For an individual who needs 2,000 calories to maintain his or her weight, this amounts to an upper limit of 12.5 teaspoons (about $1/4$ cup) of sugar a day. Naturally, a diet that is lower in sugar is even better.

Most of the recipes in this book contain 25 to 50 percent less sugar than traditional recipes do. Ingredients like fruit juices, fruit purées, and dried fruits; flavorings and spices like vanilla extract, nutmeg, and cinnamon; and mildly sweet grains such as whole wheat pastry flour, oats, and oat bran have often been used to reduce the need for sugar.

The recipes in this book call for moderate amounts of white sugar, brown sugar, and different liquid sweeteners. However, a large number of sweeteners are now available, and you should feel free to substitute one sweetener for another, using your own tastes, your desire for high-nutrient ingredients, and your pocketbook as a guide. (Some of the newer less-refined sweeteners are far more expensive than traditional sweeteners.) For best results, replace granular sweeteners with other granular sweeteners, and substitute liquid sweeteners for other liquid sweeteners.

You can, of course, replace a liquid with granules, or vice versa, but adjustments in other recipe ingredients will have to be made. (For each cup of liquid sweetener substituted for a granulated sweetener, reduce the liquid by $1/4$ to $1/3$ cup.) Also be aware that each sweetener has its own unique flavor and its own degree of sweetness, making some sweeteners better suited to particular recipes.

Following is a description of some of the sweeteners commonly available in grocery stores, health foods stores, and gourmet shops. Those sweeteners that can't be found in local stores can usually be ordered by mail. (See the Resource List on page 209.)

Apple Butter. Sweet and thick, apple butter is made by cooking down apples with apple juice and spices. Many brands also contain added sugar, but some are sweetened only with juice. Use apple butter as you would honey to sweeten products in which a little spice will enhance flavor. Spice cakes, bran muffins, and oatmeal cookies are all delicious when made with apple butter.

Brown Rice Syrup. Commonly available in health foods stores, brown rice syrup is made by converting the starch in brown rice into sugar. This syrup is mildly sweet—about 30 to 60 percent as sweet as sugar, depending on the brand—and has a delicate malt flavor. Perhaps most important, brown rice syrup retains most of the nutrients found in the rice from which it was made. This sweetener is a good substitute for honey or other liquid sweeteners whenever you want to tone down the sweetness of a recipe.

Brown Sugar. This granulated sweetener is simply refined white sugar that has been coated with a thin film of molasses. Light brown sugar is lighter in color than regular brown sugar, but not lower in calories, as the name might imply. Because this sweetener contains some molasses, brown sugar has more calcium, iron, and potassium than white sugar. But like most sugars, brown sugar is no nutritional powerhouse. The advantage of using this sweetener instead of white sugar is that it is more flavorful and so often can be used in smaller quantities.

Date Sugar. Made from ground dried dates, date sugar provides copper, magnesium, iron, and B vitamins. With a distinct date flavor, date sugar is delicious in breads, cakes, and muffins. Because it does not dissolve as readily as white sugar does, it is best to mix date sugar with the recipe's liquid ingredients and let it sit for a few minutes before proceeding with the recipe. Date sugar is less dense than white sugar, and so is only about two-thirds as sweet. However, date sugar is more flavorful, and so can often be substituted for white sugar on a cup-for-cup basis.

Fruit Juice Concentrates. Frozen juice concentrates add sweetness and flavor to baked goods while enhancing nutritional value. Use the concentrates as you would honey or other liquid sweeteners, but beware—too much will be overpowering. Always keep cans of frozen orange and apple juice concentrate in the freezer just for cooking and baking. Pineapple and tropical fruit blends also make good sweeteners, and white grape juice is ideal when you want a more neutral flavor.

Fruit Source. Made from white grape juice and brown rice, this sweetener has a rather neutral flavor and is about as sweet as white sugar. Fruit Source is available in both granular and liquid forms. Use the liquid as you would honey, and the granules as you would sugar. The granules do not dissolve as readily as sugar does, so mix Fruit Source with the recipe's liquid ingredients and let it sit for a few minutes before proceeding with the recipe.

Fruit Spreads, Jams, and Preserves. Available in a variety of flavors, these products make delicious sweeteners. For best flavor and nutrition, choose a brand made from fruits and fruit juice concentrate, with little or no added sugar, and select a flavor that is compatible with the baked goods you're making. Use as you would any liquid sweetener.

Honey. Contrary to popular belief, honey is not significantly more nutritious than sugar, but it does add a nice flavor to baked goods. It also adds moistness, reducing the need for fat. The sweetest of the liquid sweeteners, honey is generally 20 to 30 percent sweeter than sugar. Be sure to consider this when making substitutions.

Maple Sugar. Made from dehydrated maple syrup, granulated maple sugar adds a distinct maple flavor to baked goods. Powdered maple sugar is also available, and can be used to replace powdered white sugar in glazes.

Maple Syrup. The boiled-down sap of sugar maple trees, maple syrup adds delicious flavor to all baked goods, and also provides some potassium and other nutrients. Use it as you would honey or molasses.

Molasses. Light, or Barbados, molasses is pure sugar cane juice boiled down into a thick syrup. Light molasses provides some calcium, potassium, and iron, and is delicious in spice cakes, muffins, breads, and cookies. Blackstrap molasses is a by-product of the sugar-refining process. Very rich in calcium, potassium, and iron, it has a slightly bitter, strong flavor, and is half as sweet as refined sugar. Because of its distinctive taste, more than a few tablespoons of blackstrap in a recipe is overwhelming.

Sucanat. Granules of evaporated sugar cane juice, Sucanat tastes similar to brown sugar. This sweetener provides small amounts of potassium, chromium, calcium, iron, and vitamins A and C. Use it as you would any other granulated sugar.

Sugarcane Syrup. The process used to make sugarcane syrup is similar to that of making light molasses. Consequently, the syrup has a molasses-like flavor and is nutritionally comparable to the other sweetener.

Comparing Sweeteners

Sweetener (¼ cup)	Calories	Calcium (mg)	Iron (mg)	Potassium (mg)
Apple Butter	130	10	0.5	176
Brown Rice Syrup	256	3	0.1	140
Brown Sugar	205	47	1.2	189
Date Sugar	88	10	0.4	209
Fruit Juice Concentrate (apple)	116	14	0.6	315
Fruit Juice Concentrate (orange)	113	23	0.3	479
Fruit Source (granules)	192	16	0.4	142
Fruit Source (syrup)	176	15	0.4	138
Fruit Spreads	216	8	0	12
Honey	240	0	0.5	27
Maple Sugar	176	45	0.8	137
Maple Syrup	202	83	1.0	141
Molasses, Blackstrap	170	548	20.2	2,342
Molasses, Light	172	132	4.3	732
Sucanat	164	48	0.8	240
Sugar Cane Syrup	210	48	2.9	340
White Sugar	192	1	0	2

Throughout our discussion of sweeteners, we have mentioned that some sweeteners are higher in nutrients than others. Just how much variation is there among sweeteners? The table on this page compares the amounts of selected nutrients found in one quarter cup of different sweeteners. Pay special attention to how the sweeteners compare with white sugar, the most refined of all the sweeteners.

Other Ingredients

Aside from the ingredients already discussed, a few more items may prove useful as you venture into fat-free and low-fat dessert-making. Some ingredients may already be familiar to you, while others may fast become staples that you find yourself using again and again.

Barley Nugget Cereal. Crunchy, nutty cereals, like Grape-Nuts nuggets, make a nice addition to crumb toppings, cookies, muffins, and other sweet treats whenever you want to reduce or eliminate the use of high-fat nuts.

Dried Fruits. A wide variety of dried fruits are available for your cooking pleasure. Dried pineapples, apricots, peaches, cranberries, prunes, dates, and currants can be found in most grocery stores, while health foods stores and gourmet shops often carry dried mangoes, papayas, cherries, and blueberries. These foods add bursts of natural sweetness, as well as flavor and texture, to breads, cookies, puddings, pies, and many other desserts—without adding fat. If you cannot find the type of dried fruit called for in a recipe, feel free to substitute another type.

Fat-Free Granola. Like barley nugget cereals, fat-free granola can add crunch and flavor to recipes when you wish to reduce or eliminate nuts. Many low-fat granolas are also available, offering other good options.

Look for brands with no more than 2 grams of fat per ounce.

Gelatin Mixes. Available in a variety of flavors, in both sugar-free and sugar-sweetened versions, gelatin mixes have always been fat-free. These handy mixes can serve as the base for delightful pie fillings, puddings, mousses, and many other creations.

Low-Fat Graham Crackers. Graham crackers have always been one of the lowest-fat cookie choices. Now several low-fat brands are widely available, in both regular and chocolate flavors, making these versatile crackers an even better option. Use low-fat graham crackers in crumb crusts, crumb toppings, parfaits, and many other treats.

Nonfat Whipped Topping. With just 15 calories and less than half a gram of fat per 2-tablespoon serving, nonfat whipped toppings make it possible to create ultra-light and creamy frostings, fillings, mousses, and other sweet delights. Light whipped toppings, with 20 calories and 1 gram of fat per serving, are your next best bet. How do these products stack up to whipped cream? For each 2-tablespoon serving, you will save 36 calories and 5 grams of fat by replacing full-fat whipped cream with its nonfat counterpart, making your savings substantial. Look for brands like Cool Whip Free and Cool Whip Light. Many grocery stores now also carry their own brands of nonfat and light whipped toppings.

Nuts. It may surprise you to learn that the recipes in this book sometimes include nuts as an ingredient, or suggest them as an optional addition. True, nuts are high in fat. But when used in small amounts, these tasty morsels will not blow your fat budget, and will provide some of the fats, vitamins, and minerals that are essential for good health. Read

more about using nuts in low-fat cooking on page 167.

Pie Fillings. Canned pie fillings make convenient fillings and toppings for parfaits, cheesecakes, pastries, and many other goodies. Most fruit-based pie fillings have always been fat-free. Light varieties are also available, with about a third less sugar and calories. Look for brands like Comstock Light, Lucky Leaf Lite, and Thank You Light.

Pudding Mixes. Fat-free pudding mixes are now available in a range of flavors, in both sugar-free and regular versions, and in cook-and-serve and instant varieties. While the directions on regular pudding mixes usually warn against preparing the product with skim milk, as this will result in a thin mixture, fat-free pudding mixes are meant especially for use with skim milk, and mix up into a thick, rich-tasting treat. These convenient mixes can form the base for fillings, frostings, mousses, trifles, and many other sweet creations.

Wheat Germ. This ingredient adds crunch and nutty flavor to baked goods, crumb crusts, crumb toppings, and many other delightful desserts. A super-nutritious food, wheat germ is loaded with B vitamins, vitamin E, zinc, magnesium, and many other nutrients. Two kinds of wheat germ are commonly available in the cereal section of grocery stores—plain toasted and honey crunch. Try substituting toasted wheat germ for part of the flour in quick breads, muffins, and coffee cakes. Honey crunch wheat germ has a more nugget-like texture than toasted wheat germ. Use it as a substitute for chopped nuts, and cut the fat by 90 percent!

A Word About Salt

Salt, a combination of sodium and chloride,

enhances the flavors of many foods. A little salt added to a cookie, cake, or other dessert recipe can reduce the need for sugar. Salt is also a necessary ingredient in yeast breads, as it controls the rising of the yeast. For this reason, a few recipes in this book call for a small amount of salt, or may suggest it as an optional ingredient. However, with the exception of the yeast-risen dessert breads in Chapter 9, any of the recipes in this book can be made with no added salt at all.

How much sodium is too much? Most health experts recommend an upper limit of 2,400 milligrams per day, the equivalent of about one teaspoonful.

ABOUT THE NUTRITIONAL ANALYSIS

The Food Processor II (ESHA Research) computer nutrition analysis system, along with product information from manufacturers, was used to calculate the nutritional information for the recipes in this book. Nutrients are always listed per one piece, one cookie, one serving, etc.

Sometimes recipes give you options regarding ingredients. For instance, you might be able to choose between wheat germ and nuts, nonfat cream cheese or low-fat farmer cheese, or two different frostings. This will help you create desserts that suit your tastes. Just keep in mind that the nutritional analysis is based on the first ingredient listed.

The nutritional analysis for each recipe also provides an estimate of the calories and fat grams you will save by using and low- and no-fat products. This analysis is based on a comparison of the low-fat recipe with a standard recipe that uses full-fat ingredients. In some cases, the calorie savings also reflect a reduced amount of sugar. The comparison becomes even more meaningful when you consider that for every one hundred calories that you trim from your diet on a daily basis, you can lose ten pounds in a year!

WHERE DOES THE FAT COME FROM IN FAT-FREE RECIPES?

You may notice that even though a recipe may contain no oil, butter, margarine, chocolate chips, nuts, or other fatty ingredients, it still contains a small amount (less than one gram) of fat. In some cases, the fat in no-added-fat recipes comes from whole grains, such as oats, oat bran, whole wheat flour, and wheat germ. All whole grains naturally contain a small amount of oil, which is stored in the germ, or center part of the grain. The oil in whole grains is beneficial because it is rich in essential fatty acids and contains vitamin E. Whole grains also provide a wealth of vitamins and minerals that refined grains do not.

Ingredients like nonfat margarine and nonfat whipped toppings also add a trace amount of fat to recipes. Though labeled fat-free, these products can legally contain up to 0.49 gram of fat per serving, while claiming 0 gram of fat in the Nutrition Facts portion of the package label. Whenever possible, the nutritional analysis of the recipes in this book reflects the actual fat content of products like these, rather than rounding down to zero.

Other ingredients, such as low-fat graham crackers and small amounts of nuts or chocolate chips, also add some fat to the recipes in this book. However, because these recipes use high-fat ingredients very sparingly, the amount of fat in the total recipe is still well within the bounds of a healthful low-fat diet. In fact, the majority of the desserts in this book contain less than 2 grams of fat per serving.

This book is filled with creative desserts and other sweet treats that can make any day special. The recipes not only are simple, satisfying, and delicious, but also are treats that you can feel good about serving to your family and friends. So get ready to create some new family favorites and to experience the pleasures and rewards of fat-free desserts!

2

Cool and Creamy Cheesecakes

There's something about cheesecake that can turn even the most humdrum meal into a special event. The cool, creamy, undeniably satisfying texture of cheesecake makes it an undisputed favorite. Unfortunately, all of these attributes also make it one of the world's richest and most fattening desserts. And if you look at the ingredients in a typical cheesecake recipe, it's easy to see where all the fat comes from.

For starters, there's the cream cheese. Just one 8-ounce block contains 800 calories and 80 grams of fat—the equivalent of a stick of butter! Of course, most cheesecakes call for *several blocks* of cream cheese, along with several whole eggs and perhaps some sour cream. And don't forget about the graham cracker crust, which is held together by a generous amount of butter or margarine. The result? Just one small slice of traditional cheesecake can deliver well over 400 calories and 30 grams of fat!

But don't fear, for cheesecake is also one of the most easily slimmed-down of all desserts. The recipes in this chapter make good use of the creamy nonfat cheeses that are now available. These cheeses are combined with fat-free egg substitutes, pure vanilla extract, liqueurs, and other sweet flavorings into smooth, luxurious fillings. Finally, the fillings are complemented by low- or no-fat crusts and crowned with tantalizing toppings.

So whether you like your cheesecake blanketed with fresh berries; swirled with chocolate; bursting with the juice of tangy limes; or flavored with a hint of cinnamon, coffee, or cocoa, you will find a dessert sure to make any occasion special. And, as you will see, these deceptively decadent confections contain only about half the calories and practically none of the fat found in traditional versions. What greater reason do you need to celebrate?

Lite and Luscious Lemon Cheesecake

Yield: *10 servings*

CRUST

6 large (2 1/2-x-5-inch) reduced-fat graham crackers

2 tablespoons sugar

1 tablespoon tub-style nonfat margarine, or 1 tablespoon plus 1 1/2 teaspoons reduced-fat margarine

2 tablespoons honey crunch wheat germ

FILLING

2 blocks (8 ounces each) nonfat cream cheese, softened to room temperature

1 1/2 teaspoons vanilla extract

3 tablespoons cornstarch

1 can (14 ounces) fat-free sweetened condensed milk

1/2 cup plus 2 tablespoons fat-free egg substitute

1/3 cup lemon juice

1 1/2 teaspoons freshly grated lemon rind, or 1/2 teaspoon dried

TOPPING

2 1/2 cups fresh raspberries or sliced fresh strawberries

1. To make the crust, break the graham crackers into pieces, place in the bowl of a food processor, and process into fine crumbs. Measure the crumbs. There should be 3/4 cup. (Adjust the amount if needed.)

2. Return the crumbs to the food processor, add the sugar, and process for a few seconds to mix well. Add the margarine, and process for about 20 seconds, or until moist and crumbly. Add the wheat germ, and process for a few seconds to mix well.

3. Coat a 9-inch springform pan with nonstick cooking spray, and use the back of a spoon to press the crumb mixture against the bottom and sides of the pan, forming an even crust. (Periodically dip the spoon in sugar, if necessary, to prevent sticking.) Then use your fingers to finish pressing the crust firmly against the bottom and sides of the pan.

4. Bake at 350°F for about 8 minutes, or until the edges feel firm and dry. Set aside to cool to room temperature before filling.

5. To make the filling, place the cream cheese and vanilla extract in a large bowl, and beat with an electric mixer until smooth. Sprinkle the cornstarch over the cheese mixture, and beat until smooth. Add the sweetened condensed milk, and beat to mix well. Add the egg substitute, and beat to mix well. Finally, add the lemon juice and lemon rind, and beat to mix well.

6. Spread the cheesecake batter evenly over the crust, and bake at 325°F for about 50 minutes, or until the center is firm to the touch. (If you use a dark pan instead of a shiny one, reduce the oven temperature to 300°F.) Turn the oven off, and allow the cake to cool in the oven with the door ajar for 1 hour. Remove the cake from the oven, cover, and chill for at least 8 hours, or until firm.

7. Run a knife between the cheesecake and the collar of the pan, and remove the collar just before slicing and serving. Top individual servings with some of the fresh berries, and serve.

NUTRITIONAL FACTS (PER SERVING)

Calories: 234   Carbohydrates: 43 g   Cholesterol: 6 mg
Fat: 0.9 g   Fiber: 1.5 g   Protein: 13.1 g   Sodium: 312 mg

You Save: Calories: 202   Fat: 25.6 g

Apple-Topped Cheesecake

1. To make the crust, break the graham crackers into pieces, place in the bowl of a food processor, and process into fine crumbs. Measure the crumbs. There should be ¾ cup. (Adjust the amount if needed.)

2. Return the crumbs to the food processor, add the brown sugar, and process for a few seconds to mix well. Add the margarine, and process for about 20 seconds, or until moist and crumbly. Add the wheat germ or pecans, and process for a few seconds to mix well.

3. Coat a 9-inch springform pan with nonstick cooking spray, and use the back of a spoon to press the crumb mixture against the bottom and sides of the pan, forming an even crust. (Periodically dip the spoon in sugar, if necessary, to prevent sticking.) Then use your fingers to finish pressing the crust firmly against the bottom and sides of the pan.

4. Bake at 350°F for about 8 minutes, or until the edges feel firm and dry. Set aside to cool to room temperature before filling.

5. To make the filling, place the cottage cheese in a large wire (fine mesh) strainer, and rinse with cool running water until all of the creaming mixture has been rinsed away. Using the bottom of a glass, push the curds against the bottom of the strainer to press out as much of the water as possible, leaving just the dry curds in the strainer.

6. Place the dry cottage cheese curds, cream cheese, vanilla extract, sugar, and cornstarch in the bowl of a food processor, and process until smooth. Add the egg substitute, and process to mix well.

7. Spread the batter over the crust, and bake at 325°F for 1 hour and 5 minutes, or until the center is firm to the touch. (If you use a dark pan instead of a shiny one, reduce the temperature to 300°F.) To minimize cracking, run a sharp, thin-bladed knife between the cheesecake and the collar of the pan. Turn the oven off, and allow the cake to cool in the oven with the door ajar for 1 hour. Remove the cake from the oven, cover, and chill for 6 hours, or until firm.

8. Spread the pie filling over the top of the cheesecake, extending the filling to the edge of the cake, and chill for at least 2 additional hours. Remove the collar of the pan just before serving.

Yield: *12 servings*

CRUST

6 large (2½-x-5-inch) reduced-fat graham crackers

2 tablespoons light brown sugar

1 tablespoon tub-style nonfat margarine, or 1 tablespoon plus 1½ teaspoons reduced-fat margarine

2 tablespoons honey crunch wheat germ or finely chopped toasted pecans (page 167)

FILLING

2½ cups nonfat cottage cheese

2 blocks (8 ounces each) nonfat cream cheese, softened to room temperature

2 teaspoons vanilla extract

¾ cup plus 2 tablespoons sugar

3 tablespoons cornstarch

¾ cup fat-free egg substitute

TOPPING

1 can (20 ounces) light (reduced-sugar) apple pie filling

NUTRITIONAL FACTS (PER SERVING)
Calories: 208　Carbohydrates: 37g　Cholesterol: 6 mg
Fat: 0.9g　Fiber: 0.6g　Protein 13g　Sodium: 308 mg

You Save: Calories: 238　Fat: 30.2g

Vanilla Yogurt Cheesecake

Yield: *8 servings*

1 1/2 large (2 1/2-x-5-inch) reduced-fat graham crackers

FILLING

1 1/2 blocks (8 ounces each) nonfat cream cheese, softened to room temperature

1 teaspoon vanilla extract

1/2 cup sugar

2 tablespoons cornstarch

1/4 cup plus 2 tablespoons fat-free egg substitute

1 1/2 cups vanilla yogurt cheese (page 23)

TOPPING

1 cup plus 2 tablespoons canned blueberry pie filling

For variety, substitute lemon yogurt cheese for the vanilla yogurt cheese.

1. Break the graham cracker into pieces, place in the bowl of a food processor, and process into fine crumbs. Measure the crumbs. There should be 3 tablespoons. (Adjust the amount if needed.)

2. Coat a 9-inch glass pie pan with nonstick cooking spray. Place the graham cracker crumbs in the pan, and tilt the pan to coat the bottom and sides with the crumbs. Set aside.

3. To make the filling, place the cream cheese and vanilla extract in a large bowl, and beat with an electric mixer until smooth. Add the sugar, and beat to mix well. Sprinkle the cornstarch over the cheese mixture, and beat to mix well. Add the egg substitute, and beat to mix well. Finally, add the yogurt cheese, and beat just until well mixed.

4. Spread the batter evenly in the pan, and bake at 300°F for 45 to 50 minutes, or until the center is firm to the touch. Turn the oven off, and allow the cake to cool in the oven with the door ajar for 1 hour. Remove the cake from the oven, cover, and chill for at least 6 hours, or until firm.

5. Spread the pie filling over the top of the cheesecake to within 1/2 inch of the edge. Chill for an additional 2 hours before slicing and serving.

NUTRITIONAL FACTS (PER SERVING)

Calories: 181   Carbohydrates: 33 g   Cholesterol: 4 mg
Fat: 0.4 g   Fiber: 0.7 g   Protein: 11 g   Sodium: 272 mg

You Save: Calories: 240   Fat: 30.9 g

Making and Using Yogurt Cheese

Yogurt cheese—a great substitute for cream cheese—is a wonderfully versatile food that can be used in dessert frostings and fillings, as a base for puddings and mousses, and, of course, in creamy cheesecakes.

To make yogurt cheese, start with any brand of fat-free or low-fat plain or flavored yogurt that does not contain gelatin, modified food starch, or vegetable gums like carrageenan and guar gum. These ingredients will prevent the yogurt from draining properly. Yogurts that contain pectin will drain nicely and can be used for making cheese.

Simply place the yogurt in a funnel lined with cheesecloth or a coffee filter, and allow it to drain into a jar in the refrigerator for at least 8 hours or overnight. Special funnels designed just for making yogurt cheese are also available in cooking shops. When the yogurt is reduced by half, it is ready to use. The whey that collects in the jar may be used in bread and muffin recipes, in place of the listed liquid.

When making baked cheesecakes, substitute yogurt cheese for cream cheese on a cup-for-cup basis, adding 1 to 1½ tablespoons of flour or 1½ to 2 teaspoons of cornstarch to the batter for each cup of yogurt cheese used. This will insure a firm-textured yet creamy cake. For best results, avoid using a blender or food processor for mixing, as this can cause the yogurt cheese to become thin. Instead, mix this ingredient into your batter with a spoon, wire whisk, or electric mixer.

Busy Day Strawberry Cheesecake

Yield: 8 servings

1½ large (2½-x-5-inch)
    reduced-fat graham crackers

FILLING

1½ blocks (8 ounces each)
    nonfat cream cheese,
    softened to room temperature

1½ cups nonfat cottage cheese

⅔ cup sugar

¼ cup unbleached flour

¼ cup plus 2 tablespoons fat-
    free egg substitute

1½ teaspoons vanilla extract

TOPPING

2 cups sliced fresh strawberries

½ cup ready-made strawberry
    pie glaze

1. Break the graham cracker into pieces, place in the bowl of a food processor, and process into fine crumbs. Measure the crumbs. There should be 3 tablespoons. (Adjust the amount if needed.)

2. Coat a 9-inch glass pie pan with nonstick cooking spray. Place the graham cracker crumbs in the pan, and tilt the pan to coat the bottom and sides with the crumbs. Set aside.

3. To make the filling, place the cream cheese, cottage cheese, and sugar in the bowl of a food processor, and process until smooth. Add the flour, egg substitute, and vanilla extract, and process until smooth.

4. Spread the batter evenly in the pan, and bake at 300°F for about 50 minutes, or until the center is firm to the touch. Turn the oven off, and allow the cake to cool in the oven with the door ajar for 1 hour. Remove the cake from the oven, cover, and chill for at least 6 hours, or until firm.

5. To make the topping, combine the strawberries and glaze in a medium-sized bowl, and toss to coat the berries with the glaze. Spread the glazed berries over the top of the cheesecake to within 1 inch of the edge. Cover and chill for at least 2 hours before slicing and serving.

NUTRITIONAL FACTS (PER SERVING)

Calories: 175   Carbohydrates: 33 g   Cholesterol: 4 mg
Fat: 0.3 g   Fiber: 0.8 g   Protein: 10.2 g   Sodium: 245 mg

You Save: Calories: 228 Fat: 31 g

No-Bake Pineapple Cheesecake

Yield: *8 servings*

1. To make the filling, place the pineapple juice in a 1-quart pot. Sprinkle the gelatin over the juice and allow to sit for 2 minutes to soften.

2. Place the pot over low heat, and cook, stirring constantly, for a minute or 2, or until the gelatin is completely dissolved. Do not allow the juice to boil. Remove the pot from the heat and set aside for about 15 minutes, or until the juice cools to room temperature.

3. Place the cream cheese and vanilla extract in a large bowl, and beat with an electric mixer until smooth. Slowly add the sugar, a tablespoon at a time, beating constantly. Add the yogurt cheese and sour cream, and beat to mix well.

4. Slowly pour the pineapple juice-gelatin mixture into the cheese mixture, beating constantly with an electric mixer until smooth and creamy. Spread the cheese mixture evenly in the crust, cover, and chill for at least 3 hours, or until firm.

5. To make the topping, place the pineapple with its juice in a 1-quart pot. Add the cornstarch and sugar, and stir to dissolve the cornstarch. Place the pot over medium heat, and cook, stirring constantly, for several minutes, or until the mixture is thickened and bubbly. Remove the pot from the heat, and allow to cool to room temperature.

6. Gently fold the whipped topping into the cooled pineapple mixture. Spread the topping over the cheesecake, and chill for at least 1 additional hour before slicing and serving.

1 prebaked Lite Graham Cracker Pie Crust (page 70) made with plain graham crackers

FILLING

1/2 cup unsweetened pineapple juice

1 1/2 teaspoons unflavored gelatin

1 1/2 blocks (8 ounces each) nonfat cream cheese, softened to room temperature

1 teaspoon vanilla extract

1/2 cup sugar

1/2 cup vanilla yogurt cheese (page 23)

1/4 cup nonfat sour cream

TOPPING

1 can (8 ounces) crushed pineapple in juice, undrained

1 tablespoon cornstarch

1 tablespoon sugar

1 cup nonfat or light whipped topping

NUTRITIONAL FACTS (PER SERVING)

Calories: 237 Carbohydrates: 46 g Cholesterol: 3 mg
Fat: 1.4 g Fiber: 0.6 g Protein: 10.3 g Sodium: 338 mg

You Save: Calories: 165 Fat: 19.9 g

Citrus Chiffon Cheesecake

Yield: *8 servings*

1 prebaked Lite Graham Cracker Pie Crust (page 70) made with plain graham crackers

FILLING

2 tablespoons lemon juice

2 tablespoons water

1 1/2 teaspoons unflavored gelatin

1/4 cup frozen orange juice concentrate, thawed

1 1/2 blocks (8 ounces each) nonfat cream cheese, softened to room temperature

1/2 teaspoon vanilla extract

1/4 cup plus 3 tablespoons sugar

3/4 cup vanilla yogurt cheese (page 23)

TOPPING

1 1/4 cups fresh or frozen (unthawed) blueberries or raspberries

1/4 cup orange marmalade

2 tablespoons orange juice

2 1/2 teaspoons cornstarch

1. To make the filling, place the lemon juice and water in a 1-quart pot. Place over medium heat, and cook for a minute or 2, or until the mixture comes to a boil.

2. Remove the pot from the heat, and sprinkle the gelatin over the juice mixture. Stir for about 1 minute, or until the gelatin is completely dissolved. Stir in the juice concentrate, and set aside for about 10 minutes, or until the mixture reaches room temperature.

3. Place the cream cheese and vanilla extract in a large bowl, and beat with an electric mixer until smooth. Slowly add the sugar, a tablespoon at a time, beating constantly. Add the yogurt cheese, and continue to beat to mix well.

4. Using clean beaters, beat the cooled gelatin mixture for about 3 minutes, or until light and fluffy. Add the whipped gelatin mixture to the cheese mixture, and beat to mix well.

5. Spread the cheese mixture evenly in the crust. Cover and chill for at least 3 hours, or until firm.

6. To make the topping, place the berries and marmalade in a 1-quart pot, and stir to mix well. Place the pot over medium heat, and cook, stirring occasionally, for about 5 minutes, or until hot and bubbly.

7. Place the orange juice in a small bowl, add the cornstarch, and stir to dissolve the cornstarch. Add the juice mixture to the berry mixture, and cook, stirring constantly, for a minute or 2, or until thickened and bubbly. Allow the topping to cool to room temperature.

8. Spread the topping over the top of the cheesecake to within 1 inch of the edge. Chill for 1 additional hour before slicing and serving.

NUTRITIONAL FACTS (PER SERVING)
Calories: 229 Carbohydrates: 45 g Cholesterol: 4 mg
Fat: 1.1 g Fiber: 1.1 g Protein: 20.1 g Sodium: 337 mg

You Save: Calories: 237 Fat: 27.3 g

Classic Berry-Topped Cheesecake

Yield: *12 servings*

1. To make the crust, break the graham crackers into pieces, place in the bowl of a food processor, and process into fine crumbs. Measure the crumbs. There should be ¾ cup. (Adjust the amount if needed.)

2. Return the crumbs to the food processor, add the sugar, and process for a few seconds to mix well. Add the margarine, and process for about 20 seconds, or until moist and crumbly. Add the wheat germ, and process for a few seconds to mix well.

3. Coat a 9-inch springform pan with nonstick cooking spray, and use the back of a spoon to press the crumb mixture against the bottom and sides of the pan, forming an even crust. (Periodically dip the spoon in sugar, if necessary, to prevent sticking.) Then use your fingers to finish pressing the crust firmly against the bottom and sides of the pan.

4. Bake at 350°F for about 8 minutes, or until the edges feel firm and dry. Set aside to cool to room temperature before filling.

5. To make the filling, place the cream cheese and vanilla extract in a large bowl, and beat with an electric mixer until smooth. Sprinkle the cornstarch and lemon rind over the cheese mixture, and beat until smooth. Add the sweetened condensed milk, and beat until smooth. Add the egg substitute, and beat until smooth. Finally, add the yogurt cheese, and beat until smooth.

6. Spread the batter evenly over the crust, and bake at 325°F for about 1 hour, or until the center is firm to the touch. (If you use a dark pan instead of a shiny one, reduce the oven temperature to 300°F.) Turn the oven off, and allow the cake to cool in the oven with the door ajar for 1 hour. Remove the cake from the oven, cover, and chill for at least 6 hours, or until firm.

7. Arrange the berries in concentric circles over the top of the cheesecake. Place the jam in a small pot, and place over medium heat. Cook, stirring constantly, for about 1 minute, or until the jam is runny. Drizzle the jam over the berries, and chill for at least 2 additional hours. Remove the collar of the pan just before slicing and serving.

CRUST

6 large (2½-x-5-inch) reduced-fat graham crackers

2 tablespoons sugar

1 tablespoon tub-style nonfat margarine, or 1 tablespoon plus 1½ teaspoons reduced-fat margarine

2 tablespoons honey crunch wheat germ

FILLING

2 blocks (8 ounces each) nonfat cream cheese, softened to room temperature

2 teaspoons vanilla extract

2 tablespoons plus 1 teaspoon cornstarch

1 teaspoon dried grated lemon rind, or 1 tablespoon fresh

1 can (14 ounces) fat-free sweetened condensed milk

½ cup plus 2 tablespoons fat-free egg substitute

1 cup vanilla yogurt cheese (page 23)

TOPPING

2 cups fresh strawberry halves or fresh whole raspberries

¼ cup plus 2 tablespoons seedless strawberry or raspberry jam

---

NUTRITIONAL FACTS (PER SERVING)

Calories: 226 Carbohydrates: 42 g Cholesterol: 6 mg
Fat: 0.7 g Fiber: 0.7 g Protein: 12.3 g Sodium: 314 mg

You Save: Calories: 227 Fat: 28 g

Tips for Making Perfect Fat-Free Cheesecakes

Cheesecake lovers rejoice! With the wide variety of slimmed-down creamy cheeses now available, it is finally possible to have your cheesecake and eat it, too. Here are a few basic tips that will insure the best possible success when making the ultra-light cheesecakes in this chapter, as well as when lightening up your own recipes.

☐ Unless otherwise directed, turn the oven off when the center of your fat-free cheesecake is set, or firm to the touch. If you stop baking your cheesecake before it reaches this point, it will most likely be soft and pudding-like in the center. Note that this test for doneness is different from that recommended in most traditional recipes, which direct you to stop baking the cake when it is still soft or "jiggly" in the center.

☐ Be aware that the kind of springform pan that you use to bake cheesecakes—shiny versus dark—can produce dramatic differences in baking times. The baking times and temperatures for the recipes in this chapter are based on using a shiny springform pan. If you use a dark pan, which absorbs heat more readily, reduce the oven temperature by 25°F. This will allow you to follow the baking times specified in the recipe.

☐ Keep in mind, too, that almost all cheesecakes—including high-fat and low-fat recipes—tend to crack on top as they cool. This is probably why most cheesecakes include toppings, as they cover up the cracks. You can minimize cracking by cooling the cheesecake in the oven with the door ajar. This prevents the rapid temperature changes that can exacerbate cracking. If you know that a particular cake is especially prone to cracking, run a sharp, thin-bladed knife between the cake and the collar of the pan as soon as it is done baking. This will minimize cracking as the cake cools and shrinks from the sides of the pan.

☐ See the inset on page 34 for tips on substituting low- and no-fat cheeses for the full-fat cheese in your favorite cheesecake recipe.

PEACH-AMARETTO CHEESECAKE

1. To make the crust, break the graham crackers into pieces, place in the bowl of a food processor, and process into fine crumbs. Measure the crumbs. There should be ¾ cup. (Adjust the amount if needed.)

2. Return the crumbs to the food processor and add the brown sugar. Process for a few seconds to mix well. Add the margarine, and process for about 20 seconds, or until moist and crumbly. Add the wheat germ or almonds, and process for a few seconds to mix well.

3. Coat a 9-inch springform pan with nonstick cooking spray, and use the back of a spoon to press the crumb mixture against the bottom and sides of the pan, forming an even crust. (Periodically dip the spoon in sugar, if necessary, to prevent sticking.) Then use your fingers to finish pressing the crust firmly against the bottom and sides of the pan.

4. Bake at 350°F for about 8 minutes, or until the edges feel firm and dry. Set aside to cool to room temperature before filling.

5. To make the filling, place the cream cheese and vanilla extract in a large bowl, and beat with an electric mixer until smooth. Sprinkle the cornstarch over the cheese, and beat to mix well. Add the sweetened condensed milk, and beat to mix well. Beat in first the liqueur and then the egg substitute. Finally, add the yogurt cheese, and beat to mix well.

6. Spread the batter over the crust, and bake at 325°F for 1 hour, or until the center is firm to the touch. (If you use a dark pan instead of a shiny one, reduce the temperature to 300°F.) Turn the oven off, and allow the cake to cool in the oven with the door ajar for 1 hour. Remove the cake from the oven, cover, and chill for 8 hours, or until firm.

7. To make the topping, place ¾ cup of the peaches and the brown sugar and liqueur in a blender or food processor, and process until smooth. Place the remaining peaches in a medium-sized bowl, add the puréed mixture, and mix well. Chill for at least 2 hours.

8. When ready to serve, run a sharp, thin-bladed knife between the cheesecake and the collar of the pan and remove the collar. Top each serving with a heaping tablespoon of the topping, and serve.

NUTRITIONAL FACTS (PER SERVING)
Calories: 235 Carbohydrates: 43 g Cholesterol: 6 mg
Fat: 0.7 g Fiber: 1 g Protein: 12.4 g Sodium: 276 mg

You Save: Calories: 227 Fat: 29.7 g

Yield: *12 servings*

CRUST

6 large (2½-x-5-inch) reduced-fat graham crackers

2 tablespoons light brown sugar

1 tablespoon tub-style nonfat margarine, or 1 tablespoon plus 1½ teaspoons reduced-fat margarine

2 tablespoons honey crunch wheat germ or finely chopped toasted almonds (page 167)

FILLING

2 blocks (8 ounces each) nonfat cream cheese, softened to room temperature

2 teaspoons vanilla extract

2 tablespoons plus 2 teaspoons cornstarch

1 can (14 ounces) fat-free sweetened condensed milk

2 tablespoons amaretto liqueur

½ cup plus 2 tablespoons fat-free egg substitute

1 cup vanilla yogurt cheese (page 23)

TOPPING

3 cups diced peeled fresh peaches, divided (about 4 medium)

2 tablespoons light brown sugar

2 tablespoons amaretto liqueur

Coconut-Key Lime Cheesecake

Yield: *10 servings*

CRUST

6 large (2½-x-5-inch) reduced-fat graham crackers

2 tablespoons light brown sugar

1 tablespoon tub-style nonfat margarine, or 1 tablespoon plus 1½ teaspoons reduced-fat margarine

¼ teaspoon coconut-flavored extract

¼ cup shredded sweetened coconut

FILLING

2 blocks (8 ounces each) nonfat cream cheese, softened to room temperature

1½ teaspoons vanilla extract

3 tablespoons cornstarch

1 can (14 ounces) fat-free sweetened condensed milk

½ cup plus 2 tablespoons fat-free egg substitute

⅓ cup key lime juice

TOPPING

2 cups sliced fresh strawberries

2 tablespoons sugar

1. To make the crust, break the graham crackers into pieces, place in a food processor, and process into fine crumbs. Measure the crumbs. There should be ¾ cup. (Adjust the amount if needed.)

2. Return the crumbs to the food processor, add the brown sugar, and process for a few seconds to mix well. Add the margarine and coconut extract, and process for about 20 seconds, or until moist and crumbly. Add the coconut, and process for a few seconds to mix well.

3. Coat a 9-inch springform pan with nonstick cooking spray, and use the back of a spoon to press the mixture against the bottom and sides of the pan, forming an even crust. (Periodically dip the spoon in sugar, if necessary, to prevent sticking.) Then use your fingers to finish pressing the crust firmly against the bottom and sides of the pan.

4. Bake at 350°F for about 8 minutes, or until the edges feel firm and dry. Set aside to cool to room temperature before filling.

5. To make the filling, place the cream cheese and vanilla in a large bowl, and beat with an electric mixer until smooth. Sprinkle the cornstarch over the cheese mixture, and beat until smooth. Add the condensed milk, and beat to mix well. Add the egg substitute, and beat to mix well. Finally, add the lime juice, and beat to mix well.

6. Spread the batter evenly over the crust, and bake at 325°F for about 50 minutes, or until the center is firm to the touch. (If you use a dark pan instead of a shiny one, reduce the oven temperature to 300°F.) Turn the oven off, and allow the cake to cool in the oven with the door ajar for 1 hour. Remove the cake from the oven, cover, and chill for at least 8 hours, or until firm.

7. To make the topping, place the strawberries and sugar in a medium-sized bowl, and stir to mix well. Cover and chill for at least 2 hours.

8. When ready to serve, run a sharp, thin-bladed knife between the cheesecake and the collar of the pan. Remove the collar, and cut the cheesecake into wedges. Top each serving with some of the strawberry topping, and serve.

NUTRITIONAL FACTS (PER SERVING)
Calories: 241 Carbohydrates: 44 g Cholesterol: 6 mg
Fat: 1.5 g Fiber: 0.8 g Protein: 12.8 g Sodium: 361 mg

You Save: Calories: 220 Fat: 27 g

Using Coconut in Low-Fat Recipes

Loaded with saturated fat, coconut oil has long been strictly off limits in heart-healthy diets. Does this mean that the meat of the coconut is also taboo? Not necessarily. While coconut does contain coconut oil—one cup of shredded sweetened coconut contains about 33 grams of fat, or about 7 teaspoons of oil—small amounts of coconut may be added to recipes, especially if the recipe contains little or no other added fat.

For example, the recipe for Coconut-Key Lime Cheesecake (page 30) contains ¼ cup of coconut in the whole cake. This means that each serving contains just over one teaspoon of coconut, or 0.8 gram of coconut oil. This small amount of fat combined with trace amounts from the cake's other ingredients brings the total fat count to a mere 1.5 grams per serving. Not a high price to pay for the exotic sweetness of coconut!

When reducing the fat in your own recipes, try to decrease the amount of coconut used instead of totally eliminating this flavorful ingredient. For example, rather than thickly covering a cake's frosting with coconut, sprinkle the coconut sparingly over the top or just around the edge of the cake. This will enhance the flavor and appearance of the cake without adding too much fat. A little coconut-flavored extract added to batters, frostings, and fillings will also reduce the amount of coconut needed.

Chocolate Swirl Cheesecake

Yield: *12 servings*

CRUST

6 large (2^1/$_2$-x-5-inch) reduced-fat chocolate graham crackers

2 tablespoons sugar

1 tablespoon tub-style nonfat margarine, or 1 tablespoon plus 1 ^{1}/$_2$ teaspoons reduced-fat margarine

2 tablespoons honey crunch wheat germ or finely chopped toasted almonds (page 167)

FILLING

3 blocks (8 ounces each) nonfat cream cheese, softened to room temperature

2 teaspoons vanilla extract

1 cup nonfat ricotta cheese

3 tablespoons plus 1 teaspoon cornstarch

^{3}/$_4$ cup plus 2 tablespoons sugar

^{1}/$_2$ cup fat-free egg substitute

CHOCOLATE SWIRL

2 tablespoons Dutch processed cocoa powder

^{1}/$_4$ cup sugar

^{1}/$_2$ teaspoon vanilla extract

1. To make the crust, break the graham crackers into pieces, place in the bowl of a food processor, and process into fine crumbs. Measure the crumbs. There should be ^{3}/$_4$ cup. (Adjust the amount if needed.)

2. Return the crumbs to the food processor, add the sugar, and process for a few seconds to mix well. Add the margarine, and process for about 20 seconds, or until moist and crumbly. Add the wheat germ or almonds, and process for a few seconds to mix well.

3. Coat a 9-inch springform pan with nonstick cooking spray, and use the back of a spoon to press the crumb mixture against the bottom and sides of the pan, forming an even crust. (Periodically dip the spoon in sugar, if necessary, to prevent sticking.) Then use your fingers to finish pressing the crust firmly against the bottom and sides of the pan.

4. Bake at 350°F for about 8 minutes, or until the edges feel firm and dry. Set aside to cool to room temperature before filling.

5. To make the filling, place the cream cheese and vanilla extract in a large bowl, and beat with an electric mixer until smooth. Add the ricotta, and beat for about 2 minutes, or until light, creamy, and smooth. Sprinkle the cornstarch over the cheese mixture, and beat until smooth. Add the sugar, and beat to mix well. Finally, add the egg substitute, and beat just enough to mix well.

6. To make the chocolate swirl, place 1½ cups of the cheese filling in a medium-sized bowl. Add the cocoa powder, sugar, and vanilla extract, and beat with an electric mixer to mix well.

7. Spread half of the plain cheesecake batter evenly over the crust. Spoon half of the cocoa batter randomly over the plain batter. Repeat the layers. Then draw a knife through the batter to produce a marbled effect.

8. Bake at 325°F for about 1 hour and 10 minutes, or until the center is firm to the touch. Note that sometimes cheesecakes made with ricotta will puff up during baking, making it difficult to tell if the center is firm. In this case, bake until the cake is just beginning to brown around the edges. (If you use a dark pan instead of a shiny one, reduce the oven temperature to 300°F.)

9. Run a sharp, thin-bladed knife between the cheesecake and the collar of the pan. (This will minimize cracking as the cake cools.) Turn the oven off, and allow the cake to cool in the oven with the door ajar for 1 hour. Remove the cake from the oven, cover, and chill for at least 8 hours, or until firm. Remove the collar of the pan just before slicing and serving.

NUTRITIONAL FACTS (PER SERVING)

Calories: 202 Carbohydrates: 35 g Cholesterol: 6 mg
Fat: 1 g Fiber: 0.5 g Protein: 13.9 g Sodium: 365 mg

You Save: Calories: 323 Fat: 31.5 g

Getting the Fat Out of Your Favorite Cheesecake Recipes

By far, most of the fat in cheesecake comes from the cream cheese that forms the base of its batter. Just one 8-ounce block of cream cheese contains 800 calories and 80 grams of fat—the equivalent of a stick of butter! Fortunately, a variety of creamy nonfat and low-fat cheeses can successfully replace the full-fat cream cheese in all your favorite cheesecake recipes, slashing calories and almost completely eliminating the fat. You'll note that many of the recipes in this chapter blend nonfat cream cheese with other low- or no-fat cheeses, as this results in a more traditional flavor and texture than you would get by using only nonfat cream cheese. The following table presents the healthful cheeses used in this chapter, looks at the fat and calorie savings offered by these great products, and gives you tips for using them successfully in your own recipes.

Using Nonfat and Low-Fat Cheeses in Cheesecakes

Cheese	Savings Per Cup When Substituted for Full-Fat Cream Cheese	Special Considerations
Neufchâtel (reduced-fat) cream cheese	230 calories 32 g fat	Substitute cup-for-cup for full-fat cream cheese. No adjustments are usually required.
Nonfat cottage cheese	640 calories 80 g fat	Substitute cup-for-cup for full-fat cream cheese. In baked cheesecakes, add 1 to $1\frac{1}{2}$ tablespoons flour or $1\frac{1}{2}$ to 2 teaspoons cornstarch per cup of nonfat cottage cheese to insure a firm texture. Some recipes instruct you to rinse the creaming mixture off of the cottage cheese and press out any excess liquid, leaving just the dry curds. This also helps insure a firm texture.
Nonfat cream cheese	560 calories 80 g fat	Substitute cup-for-cup for full-fat cream cheese, and use the block-style cream cheese for best results. In baked cheesecakes, add 1 to $1\frac{1}{2}$ tablespoons flour or $1\frac{1}{2}$ to 2 teaspoons cornstarch per cup of nonfat cream cheese to insure a firm texture.
Nonfat ricotta cheese	560 calories 80 g fat	Substitute cup-for-cup for full-fat cream cheese. If any liquid has separated from the cheese, drain it off before using. In baked cheesecakes, add 1 to $1\frac{1}{2}$ tablespoons flour or $1\frac{1}{2}$ to 2 teaspoons cornstarch per cup of nonfat ricotta cheese to insure a firm texture.

Cheese	Savings Per Cup When Substituted for Full-Fat Cream Cheese	Special Considerations
Soft curd farmer cheese	400 calories 60 g fat	Substitute cup-for-cup for full-fat cream cheese. In baked cheesecakes, add 1 to $1\frac{1}{2}$ tablespoons flour or $1\frac{1}{2}$ to 2 teaspoons cornstarch per cup of farmer cheese to insure a firm texture.
Yogurt cheese (page 23)	630 calories 80 g fat	Substitute cup-for-cup for full-fat cream cheese. In baked cheesecakes, add 1 to $1\frac{1}{2}$ tablespoons flour or $1\frac{1}{2}$ to 2 teaspoons cornstarch per cup of yogurt cheese to insure a firm texture.

No-Bake Cherry Cheesecake

Yield: *8 servings*

1 prebaked Lite Graham Cracker Pie Crust (page 70) made with plain or chocolate graham crackers

FILLING

2 blocks (8 ounces each) nonfat cream cheese or soft curd farmer cheese, softened to room temperature

$1/2$ cup sugar

1 teaspoon vanilla extract

1 tablespoon plus 1 teaspoon lemon juice

1 teaspoon unflavored gelatin

TOPPING

1 can (20 ounces) light (reduced-sugar) cherry pie filling

1. To make the filling, place the cream cheese or farmer cheese, sugar, and vanilla extract in the bowl of a food processor, and process until smooth. Set aside.

2. If using a microwave oven, place the lemon juice in a small microwave-safe bowl, and microwave at high power for about 30 seconds, or until the juice comes to a boil. If using a stovetop, place the juice in a small pot, and place over medium heat for about 30 seconds, or until it comes to a boil. Remove the pot from the heat. Sprinkle the gelatin over the lemon juice and stir for about 1 minute, or until the gelatin is completely dissolved.

3. Add the gelatin mixture to the cheese mixture, and process until well mixed. Spread the cheese filling evenly over the crust, cover, and chill for at least 3 hours, or until set.

4. Spread the cherry pie filling over the top of the cheesecake, extending it all the way to the edges of the cake. Chill for at least 1 additional hour before slicing and serving.

NUTRITIONAL FACTS (PER SERVING)

Calories: 233 Carbohydrates: 46 g Cholesterol: 4 mg
Fat: 1 g Fiber: 1.2 g Protein: 9.9 g Sodium: 430 mg

You Save: Calories: 227 Fat: 26 g

Top Left: *Apple-Topped Cheesecake (page 21)*
Center Right: *No-Bake Cherry Cheesecake (page 36)*
Bottom Left: *Cappuccino Cheesecake (page 38)*

Top Right: Royal Raspberry Cake (page 54)
Center Left: Sour Cream-Coconut Bundt Cake (page 47)
Bottom Right: Cranberry-Pear Coffee Cake (page 57)

No-Bake Mocha Mousse Cheesecake

1. To make the filling, place ¼ cup of the coffee in a blender. Sprinkle the gelatin over the top, and set aside for 2 minutes to allow the gelatin to soften.

2. Place the remaining ¼ cup of coffee in a small pot, and bring to a boil over medium-high heat. Pour the boiling hot coffee into the blender, cover with the lid, and blend at low speed for about 2 minutes, or until the gelatin is completely dissolved. Allow the mixture to sit for about 20 minutes, or until it has cooled to room temperature.

3. Add the cream cheese, ricotta, brown sugar, cocoa, liqueur, and vanilla extract to the blender, and blend until smooth. Transfer the mixture to a large bowl, cover, and chill for at least 4 hours, or until firm.

4. When the gelatin mixture has become firm, beat it with an electric mixer until it is the consistency of pudding. Gently fold in the whipped topping.

5. Spread the filling in the cooled crust, swirling the top with a knife. Cover and chill for at least 4 hours, or until set, before slicing and serving.

Yield: *8 servings*

1 prebaked Lite Graham Cracker Pie Crust (page 70) made with chocolate graham crackers

FILLING

½ cup coffee, cooled to room temperature, divided

1 envelope (¼ ounce) unflavored gelatin

1 block (8 ounces) nonfat cream cheese, softened to room temperature

1 cup nonfat ricotta cheese

½ cup light brown sugar

2 tablespoons Dutch processed cocoa powder

2 tablespoons coffee liqueur

1½ teaspoons vanilla extract

1¼ cups nonfat or light whipped topping

NUTRITIONAL FACTS (PER SERVING)
Calories: 205 Carbohydrates: 36 g Cholesterol: 4 mg
Fat: 1.5 g Fiber: 0.8 g Protein: 11.3 g Sodium: 263 mg

You Save: Calories: 259 Fat: 33.8 g

Cappuccino Cheesecake

Yield: *12 servings*

CRUST

6 large (2 1/2-x-5-inch) reduced-fat chocolate graham crackers

2 tablespoons sugar

1 tablespoon tub-style nonfat margarine, or 1 tablespoon plus 1 1/2 teaspoons reduced-fat margarine

2 tablespoons honey crunch wheat germ or finely chopped almonds

FILLING

2 blocks (8 ounces each) nonfat cream cheese, softened to room temperature

2 teaspoons vanilla extract

2 tablespoons coffee liqueur

3/4 teaspoon instant coffee granules

2 tablespoons plus 2 teaspoons cornstarch

1 tablespoon cocoa powder

1/4 teaspoon ground cinnamon

1 can (14 ounces) fat-free sweetened condensed milk

1/2 cup plus 2 tablespoons fat-free egg substitute

1 cup vanilla yogurt cheese (page 23)

1. To make the crust, break the graham crackers into pieces, place in the bowl of a food processor, and process into fine crumbs. Measure the crumbs. There should be 3/4 cup. (Adjust the amount if needed.)

2. Return the crumbs to the food processor, and add the sugar. Process for a few seconds to mix well. Add the margarine, and process for about 20 seconds, or until moist and crumbly. Add the wheat germ or almonds, and process for a few seconds to mix well.

3. Coat a 9-inch springform pan with nonstick cooking spray, and use the back of a spoon to press the mixture against the bottom and sides of the pan, forming an even crust. (Periodically dip the spoon in sugar, if necessary, to prevent sticking.) Then use your fingers to finish pressing the crust firmly against the bottom and sides of the pan.

4. Bake at 350°F for about 8 minutes, or until the edges feel firm and dry. Set aside to cool to room temperature before filling.

5. To make the filling, place the cream cheese and vanilla extract in a large bowl, and beat with an electric mixer until smooth.

6. Place the liqueur and coffee granules in a small bowl, and stir to dissolve the coffee granules. Add the liqueur mixture to the cream cheese mixture, and beat to mix well.

7. Sprinkle the cornstarch over the cheese mixture, and beat to mix well. Sprinkle the cocoa and cinnamon over the cheese mixture, and beat to mix well. Add the sweetened condensed milk, and beat to mix well. Add the egg substitute, and beat to mix well. Finally, add the yogurt cheese, and beat to mix well.

8. Spread the cheesecake batter evenly over the crust, and bake at 325°F for about 1 hour, or until the center is firm to the touch. (If you use a dark pan instead of a shiny one, reduce the oven temperature to 300°F.) Turn the oven off, and allow the cake to cool in the oven with the door ajar for 1 hour. Remove the cake from the oven, cover, and chill for at least 8 hours, or until firm.

9. When ready to serve, run a sharp, thin-bladed knife between the cheesecake and the collar of the pan. Remove the collar, and cut the cheesecake into wedges. Top each serving with ¼ cup of the berries. Then drizzle 1½ teaspoons of the chocolate syrup over the top, and serve.

TOPPING

3 cups fresh raspberries or sliced fresh strawberries

¼ cup plus 2 tablespoons chocolate syrup

NUTRITIONAL FACTS (PER SERVING)

Calories: 241 Carbohydrates: 44 g Cholesterol: 6 mg
Fat: 1.3 g Fiber: 1.7 g Protein: 12.7 g Sodium: 281 mg

You Save: Calories: 226 Fat: 29 g

Blueberry Swirl Cheesecake

Yield: *12 servings*

CRUST

6 large (2$\frac{1}{2}$-x-5-inch) reduced-
fat graham crackers

2 tablespoons sugar

1 tablespoon tub-style nonfat
margarine, or 1 tablespoon
plus 1$\frac{1}{2}$ teaspoons reduced-
fat margarine

2 tablespoons honey crunch
wheat germ

FILLING

2$\frac{1}{2}$ cups nonfat cottage cheese

2 blocks (8 ounces each) nonfat
cream cheese, softened to
room temperature

2$\frac{1}{2}$ teaspoons vanilla extract

$\frac{1}{4}$ cup plus 2 tablespoons
unbleached flour

$\frac{1}{2}$ teaspoon dried grated
lemon rind, or 1$\frac{1}{2}$
teaspoons fresh

$\frac{3}{4}$ cup plus 2 tablespoons
sugar

$\frac{3}{4}$ cup fat-free egg substitute

$\frac{3}{4}$ cup canned blueberry pie
filling

1. To make the crust, break the graham crackers into pieces, place in the bowl of a food processor, and process into fine crumbs. Measure the crumbs. There should be $\frac{3}{4}$ cup. (Adjust the amount if needed.)

2. Return the crumbs to the food processor, add the sugar, and process for a few seconds to mix well. Add the margarine, and process for about 20 seconds, or until moist and crumbly. Add the wheat germ, and process for a few seconds to mix well.

3. Coat a 9-inch springform pan with nonstick cooking spray, and use the back of a spoon to press the mixture against the bottom and sides of the pan, forming an even crust. (Periodically dip the spoon in sugar, if necessary, to prevent sticking.) Then use your fingers to finish pressing the crust firmly against the bottom and sides of the pan.

4. Bake at 350°F for about 8 minutes, or until the edges feel firm and dry. Set aside to cool to room temperature before filling.

5. To make the filling, place the cottage cheese in a large wire (fine mesh) strainer, and rinse with cool running water until all of the creaming mixture has been rinsed away. Using the bottom of a glass, push the curds against the bottom of the strainer to press out as much of the water as possible, leaving just the dry curds in the strainer. Place the dry curds in a food processor, and process until smooth. Set aside.

6. Place the cream cheese and vanilla extract in a large bowl, and beat with an electric mixer until smooth. Add the puréed cottage cheese, and beat for about 2 minutes, or until light, creamy, and smooth. Sprinkle the flour and lemon rind over the mixture, and beat until smooth. Add the sugar, and beat to mix well. Finally, add the egg substitute, and beat just until well mixed.

7. Spread half of the cheesecake batter evenly over the crust. Then spoon the blueberry pie filling randomly over the batter. Top with the remaining batter, and draw a knife through the batter to produce a marbled effect.

8. Bake at 325°F for about 1 hour and 5 minutes, or until the center is firm to the touch. (If you use a dark pan instead of a shiny one, reduce the oven temperature to 300°F.) Run a sharp, thin-bladed knife between the cheesecake and the collar of the pan. (This will minimize cracking as the cake cools.) Turn the oven off, and allow the cake to cool in the oven with the door ajar for 1 hour.

9. Remove the cake from the oven, cover, and chill for at least 8 hours, or until firm before slicing and serving.

NUTRITIONAL FACTS (PER SERVING)

Calories: 193 Carbohydrates: 33 g Cholesterol: 6 mg
Fat: 0.5 g Fiber: 0.4 g Protein: 13.4 g Sodium: 303 mg

You Save: Calories: 259 Fat: 32.8 g

3

Creative Cakes

If you have ever tried to make a cake without fat, you understand the importance of this ingredient. Besides adding moistness and flavor, fat inhibits the development of gluten, a protein in flour that causes baked goods to become tough. Sugar does the same thing, which is why so many fat-free cakes contain additional sugar—as well as all the calories that go along with it.

Fortunately, there are better ways to reduce the fat in cakes and still maintain a pleasing texture. The secret? Include some healthful whole grain flours in your recipe. These are naturally lower in gluten than refined flours. With their mildly sweet flavor, oat flour and oat bran work especially well in no- and low-fat baked goods. Another excellent option is whole wheat pastry flour—a versatile product that will help you make the lightest, most tender cakes possible.

A variety of other products also help slash fat and add flavor in these recipes. Ingredients like applesauce and fruit purées, nonfat buttermilk, nonfat yogurt, and nonfat sour cream reduce the need for fat by adding moistness and richness to batters. Fat-free egg substitutes save more fat and cholesterol. And nonfat cream cheese, yogurt, and whipped toppings form the base of delightfully light and creamy fillings and frostings.

In a hurry? Busy cooks will be happy to know that cake mixes are easily prepared with no added fat. This chapter presents a variety of super-moist, meltingly tender made-from-mix treats with only a couple of grams of fat per serving.

So whether you are looking for a grand finale to an elegant meal or for a simple coffee cake for a casual get-together, you need look no further. With a little creativity, you and your family will be delighted to find that you can have your cake and eat it, too.

Black Forest Crumb Cake

Yield: *8 servings*

1/2 cup unbleached flour

1/4 cup plus 2 tablespoons oat flour

1/4 cup plus 2 tablespoons cocoa powder

3/4 cup sugar

3/4 teaspoon baking soda

1/8 teaspoon salt

1 1/2 cups halved frozen pitted dark sweet cherries, thawed

1/2 cup plain nonfat yogurt

1 teaspoon vanilla extract

TOPPING

1/4 cup honey crunch wheat germ, finely chopped walnuts, or finely chopped almonds

2 tablespoons whole wheat pastry flour

2 tablespoons cocoa powder

1/4 cup light brown sugar

1 tablespoon plus 2 teaspoons chocolate syrup

1. To make the topping, place the wheat germ or nuts, flour, cocoa, and brown sugar in a small bowl, and stir to mix well. Add the chocolate syrup, and stir until the mixture looks like moist and crumbly cookie dough. Add a little more chocolate syrup if needed. Set aside.

2. Place the flours, cocoa, sugar, baking soda, and salt in a medium-sized bowl, and stir to mix well. Add the cherries (including the juice that accumulates during thawing), yogurt, and vanilla extract, and stir to mix well.

3. Coat a 9-inch round cake pan with nonstick cooking spray, and spread the batter evenly in the pan. Sprinkle the topping over the batter. If necessary, use your fingers to break the topping into smaller pieces.

4. Bake at 325°F for about 35 minutes, or just until the top springs back when lightly touched. Be careful not to overbake. Remove the cake from the oven, and allow it to cool to room temperature before cutting into wedges and serving.

NUTRITIONAL FACTS (PER SERVING)

Calories: 204 Carbohydrates: 46 g Cholesterol: 0 mg
Fat: 1.4 g Fiber: 3.7 g Protein: 4.6 g Sodium: 169 mg

You Save: Calories: 118 Fat: 14.3 g

Variation

To make Banana-Fudge Crumb Cake, substitute 3/4 cup mashed very ripe banana (about 1 1/2 large) for the cherries.

NUTRITIONAL FACTS (PER SERVING)

Calories: 201 Carbohydrates: 46 g Cholesterol: 0 mg
Fat: 1.4 g Fiber: 3.4 g Protein: 4.5 g Sodium: 170 mg

You Save: Calories: 121 Fat: 14.3 g

Glazed Pineapple Cake

1. Place the flours, sugar, milk powder, and baking soda in a large bowl, and stir to mix well. Add the pineapple with its juice and the egg substitute and vanilla extract, and stir just until well mixed.

2. Coat a 9-x-13-inch pan with nonstick cooking spray, and spread the mixture evenly in the pan. Bake at 325°F for about 40 minutes, or just until the top springs back when lightly touched and a wooden toothpick inserted in the center of the cake comes out clean. Allow the cake to cool for 20 minutes at room temperature.

3. While the cake is cooling, place all of the glaze ingredients in a small bowl, and stir to mix well. Spread the glaze in a thin layer over the top of the warm cake. Allow the cake to cool to room temperature before cutting into squares and serving.

Yield: 16 servings

1 cup unbleached flour

1 cup oat flour or whole wheat pastry flour

1 1/2 cups sugar

1/4 cup instant nonfat dry milk powder

1 teaspoon baking soda

1 can (20 ounces) crushed pineapple in juice, undrained

1/4 cup plus 2 tablespoons fat-free egg substitute

1 1/2 teaspoons vanilla extract

GLAZE

1 1/4 cups powdered sugar

2 tablespoons skim milk or pineapple juice

3/4 teaspoon almond extract

NUTRITIONAL FACTS (PER SERVING)

Calories: 190 Carbohydrates: 43 g Cholesterol: 0 mg
Fat: 0.6 g Fiber: 1.3 g Protein: 3 g Sodium: 96 mg

You Save: Calories: 163 Fat: 10.2 g

Citrus Carrot Cake

Yield: *18 servings*

3 cups unbleached flour

1½ cups sugar

2 teaspoons baking soda

2 teaspoons baking powder

¼ teaspoon salt

2 teaspoons ground cinnamon

1⅓ cups orange juice

¾ cup fat-free egg substitute

2 teaspoons vanilla extract

4 cups (packed) grated carrots (about 8 large)

½ cup golden or dark raisins

½ cup chopped toasted pecans or walnuts (page 167) (optional)

1 recipe Fluffy Cream Cheese Frosting (page 48)

1. Place the flour, sugar, baking soda, baking powder, salt, and cinnamon in a large bowl, and stir to mix well. Stir in the juice, egg substitute, and vanilla extract. Fold in the carrots, raisins, and, if desired, the nuts.

2. Coat a 9-x-13-inch pan with nonstick cooking spray, and spread the mixture evenly in the pan. Bake at 300°F for about 55 minutes, or just until the top springs back when lightly touched and a wooden toothpick inserted in the center of the cake comes out clean. Allow to cool to room temperature.

3. Spread the frosting over the cooled cake and refrigerate for at least 2 hours before cutting into squares and serving.

NUTRITIONAL FACTS (PER SERVING)

Calories: 211 Carbohydrates: 45 g Cholesterol: 1 mg
Fat: 0.5 g Fiber: 1.5 g Protein: 6.5 g Sodium: 327 mg

You Save: Calories: 220 Fat: 23.5 g

The Finishing Touch

Usually when you think of topping cakes, you think of frostings and icings. And certainly it is possible to make icings and frostings that are not only luscious enough to satisfy any sweet tooth, but also low in fat and calories. (See the inset on page 48.) But sometimes a simpler topping—rather than a conventional frosting—can lend the perfect finishing touch to your low-fat cake. Here are some ideas.

☐ Dust the top of your cake with a few tablespoons of powdered sugar instead of adding a gooey icing. Try sifting some powdered maple sugar over the tops of spice, banana, and applesauce cakes.

☐ Spread a thin layer of low-sugar fruit spread or jam over the top of your cake. Try raspberry spread on chocolate cake, pineapple spread on banana cake, and apricot or peach spread on spice cake.

☐ Spread your cake with yogurt cheese—a sweet, creamy spread made by draining the whey from yogurt (page 23). To cover a 9-x-13-inch cake, use 2 cups of yogurt cheese, which is made from about 4 cups of yogurt. Try vanilla, coffee, or raspberry yogurt cheese on chocolate cake; vanilla, pineapple, or banana yogurt cheese on banana cake; and lemon or vanilla yogurt cheese on lemon or carrot cake.

SOUR CREAM-COCONUT BUNDT CAKE

1. Place the cake mix and pudding mix in a large bowl, and stir to mix well. Add the egg substitute, water, and sour cream, and beat with an electric mixer for about 2 minutes, or until well mixed.

2. Coat a 12-cup bundt pan with nonstick cooking spray, and spread the batter evenly in the pan. Bake at 350°F for 40 to 45 minutes, or just until the top springs back when lightly touched and a wooden toothpick inserted in the center of the cake comes out clean. Be careful not to overbake.

3. Allow the cake to cool in the pan for 45 minutes. Then invert onto a serving platter and cool to room temperature.

4. To make the glaze, place the powdered sugar, sour cream, and coconut extract in a small bowl, and stir to mix well. If using a microwave oven, microwave on high power for 30 seconds, or until hot and runny. If using a stovetop, place the glaze in a small pot and cook over medium heat, stirring constantly, for about 30 seconds, or until hot and runny.

5. Drizzle the hot glaze over the cake, and sprinkle the glaze with the coconut. Allow the cake to sit for at least 15 minutes before slicing and serving.

Yield: *16 servings*

1 box (1 pound, 2.25 ounces) reduced-fat or regular yellow, white, or chocolate cake mix

1 package (4-serving size) fat-free or regular instant toasted coconut pudding mix*

1 cup fat-free egg substitute

3/4 cup water

3/4 cup nonfat sour cream

GLAZE

1/2 cup powdered sugar

1 tablespoon plus 1 teaspoon nonfat sour cream

1/2 teaspoon coconut-flavored extract

2 tablespoons shredded sweetened coconut

* If you cannot find toasted coconut pudding mix, substitute 1 package instant vanilla pudding mix plus 3/4 teaspoon coconut-flavored extract and 2 tablespoons finely shredded toasted coconut.

NUTRITIONAL FACTS (PER SERVING)
Calories: 188 Carbohydrates: 38.4 g Cholesterol: 0 mg
Fat: 2 g Fiber: 0.5 g Protein: 3 g Sodium: 281 mg

You Save: Calories: 106 Fat: 14 g

Variation

For a denser pound cake-like texture, reduce the water in the recipe to 1/2 cup, and bake for 35 to 40 minutes.

The Frosting on the Cake

Traditionally, recipes for cake frostings have often called for up to 3 cups of powdered sugar and a stick of butter. But is there an alternative that not only is lower in sugar and fat, but also satisfies everyone's expectations of a sweet and creamy topping? Of course there is! Instead of being laden with fat, the icings and frostings in this book are made from ingredients like nonfat cream cheese, nonfat whipped topping, and nonfat yogurt. Just as important, they contain just a fraction of the sugar found in traditional recipes. Enjoy the following three frostings on your own favorite cakes, as well as on the cakes in this chapter. (For more ideas on topping cakes, see the inset on page 46.)

Fluffy Cream Cheese Frosting

Yield: *about 3 cups, enough for a 9-x-13-inch cake or a 9-inch double layer cake*

1½ blocks (8 ounces each) nonfat cream cheese, softened to room temperature

1½ teaspoons vanilla extract

¼ cup plus 2 tablespoons sugar

1½ cups nonfat or light whipped topping

1. Place the cream cheese and vanilla extract in a large bowl, and beat with an electric mixer until smooth. Slowly add the sugar, a tablespoon at a time, beating constantly, until smooth and creamy.

2. Gently fold the whipped topping into the cream cheese mixture, and immediately spread the frosting over the cake.

NUTRITIONAL FACTS (PER 3-TABLESPOON SERVING)
Calories: 49 Carbohydrates: 8 g Cholesterol: 1 mg
Fat: 0.2 g Fiber: 0 g Protein: 3 g Sodium: 106 mg

You Save: Calories: 82 Fat: 11.3 g

Yogurt Fluff Frosting

Yield: *about 3 cups, enough for a 9-x-13-inch cake or a 9-inch double layer cake*

2¼ cups nonfat or light whipped topping

¾ cup nonfat yogurt, any flavor

1. Place the whipped topping in a medium-sized bowl. Gently fold in the yogurt, and immediately spread over the cake.

NUTRITIONAL FACTS (PER 3-TABLESPOON SERVING)
Calories: 29 Carbohydrates: 6 g Cholesterol: 0 mg
Fat: 0.3 g Fiber: 0 g Protein: 0.5 g Sodium: 14 mg

You Save: Calories: 53 Fat: 8 g

Pudding Perfection Frosting

1. Place the pudding mix and milk in a large bowl, and whisk with a wire whip for about 2 minutes, or until thick.

2. Gently fold the whipped topping into the pudding mixture, and immediately spread the frosting over the cake.

Yield: *about 3 cups, enough for a 9-x-13-inch cake or a 9-inch double layer cake*

1 box (4-serving size) fat-free or regular instant pudding mix, any flavor

1 cup skim milk

2 cups nonfat or light whipped topping

NUTRITIONAL FACTS (PER 3-TABLESPOON SERVING)

Calories: 43 Carbohydrates: 10 g Cholesterol: 0 mg
Fat: 0.3 g Fiber: 0 g Protein: 0.5 g Sodium: 104 mg

You Save: Calories: 40 Fat: 5.4 g

Cinnamon-Mocha Fudge Cake

Yield: *16 servings*

1 box (1 pound, 2.25 ounces) reduced-fat or regular devil's food or chocolate cake mix

1 package (4-serving size) fat-free or regular instant chocolate pudding mix

1/2 teaspoon ground cinnamon

1 cup fat-free egg substitute

3/4 cup coffee, cooled to room temperature

1/2 cup unsweetened applesauce

GLAZE

1/2 cup powdered sugar

1 tablespoon cocoa powder

1 tablespoon coffee, cooled to room temperature

1. Place the cake mix, pudding mix, and cinnamon in a large bowl, and stir to mix well. Add the egg substitute, coffee, and applesauce, and beat with an electric mixer for about 2 minutes, or until well mixed.

2. Coat a 12-cup bundt pan with nonstick cooking spray, and spread the batter evenly in the pan. Bake at 350°F for about 40 minutes, or just until the top springs back when lightly touched and a wooden toothpick inserted in the center of the cake comes out clean. Be careful not to overbake.

3. Allow the cake to cool in the pan for 45 minutes. Then invert onto a serving platter, and cool to room temperature.

4. To make the glaze, place all of the glaze ingredients in a small bowl, and stir to mix well. If using a microwave oven, microwave on high power for 25 seconds, or until hot and runny. If using a stovetop, place the glaze in a small pot and cook over medium heat, stirring constantly, for about 30 seconds, or until hot and runny.

5. Drizzle the hot glaze over the cake. Allow the cake sit for at least 15 minutes before slicing and serving.

NUTRITIONAL FACTS (PER SERVING)
Calories: 175 Carbohydrates: 36 g Cholesterol: 0 mg
Fat: 2.3 g Fiber: 1 g Protein: 3 g Sodium: 372 mg

You Save: Calories: 137 Fat: 14.5 g

Citrus Pound Cake

For variety, add 2 tablespoons of poppy seeds to the batter.

Yield: *16 servings*

1. Place the cake mix and pudding mix in a large bowl, and stir to mix well. Add the mandarin oranges with their liquid and the egg substitute, and beat with an electric mixer for about 2 minutes, or until the ingredients are well mixed and the oranges are pulverized.

2. Coat a 12-cup bundt pan with nonstick cooking spray, and spread the batter evenly in the pan. Bake at 350°F for about 40 minutes, or just until the top springs back when lightly touched and a wooden toothpick inserted in the center of the cake comes out clean. Be careful not to overbake.

3. Allow the cake to cool in the pan for 45 minutes. Then invert onto a serving platter and cool to room temperature. If desired, sift the powdered sugar over the top just before slicing and serving.

1 box (1 pound, 2.25 ounces) reduced-fat or regular lemon or yellow cake mix

1 box (4-serving size) fat-free or regular instant lemon pudding mix

1 can (11 ounces) mandarin oranges, undrained

¾ cup fat-free egg substitute

3 tablespoons powdered sugar (optional)

NUTRITIONAL FACTS (PER SERVING)

Calories: 168 Carbohydrates: 36 g Cholesterol: 0 mg
Fat: 1.5 g Fiber: 0.4 g Protein: 2 g Sodium: 306 mg

You Save: Calories: 106 Fat: 13.2 g

Baking with Reduced-Fat Margarine and Light Butter

Contrary to popular belief, you *can* bake with reduced-fat margarine and light butter. These products make it possible to reduce fat by more than half and still enjoy light, tender, buttery-tasting cakes; crisp cookies; flaky pie crusts; and other goodies that are not easily made fat-free.

The secret to using these reduced-fat products successfully in your baked goods is to substitute three-fourths as much of the light product for the full-fat butter or margarine. This will compensate for the extra water that the reduced-fat products contain. For example, if a cake recipe calls for 1 cup of butter, substitute ¾ cup of light butter. And be sure to choose brands that contain 5 to 6 grams of fat and 50 calories per tablespoon. (Full-fat brands contain 11 grams of fat and 100 calories per tablespoon.) Brands with less fat than this do not generally work well in baking.

Be careful not to overbake your reduced-fat creations, as they can become dry. Bake cakes and quick breads at 325°F to 350°F, and biscuits and scones at 375°F to 400°F. Check the product for doneness a few minutes before the end of the usual baking time. Then enjoy! (For tips on using reduced-fat margarine and light butter in cookies, see the inset on page 125.)

Piña Colada Cake

Yield: *16 servings*

1 box (1 pound, 2.25 ounces) reduced-fat or regular yellow cake mix

1 package (4-serving size) fat-free or regular instant toasted coconut pudding mix*

1 can (8 ounces) crushed pineapple, undrained

1 cup nonfat sour cream

1 cup fat-free egg substitute

1/4 cup water

SYRUP

1/2 cup fat-free sweetened condensed milk

1/4 cup light rum

3/4 teaspoon coconut-flavored extract

FROSTING

2 cups nonfat or light whipped topping

1 cup piña colada or coconut-flavored nonfat yogurt, regular or sugar-free

1/4 cup shredded sweetened coconut (optional)

*If you cannot find toasted coconut pudding mix, substitute 1 package instant vanilla pudding mix plus 3/4 teaspoon coconut-flavored extract and 2 tablespoons finely shredded toasted coconut.

1. Place the cake mix and pudding mix in a large bowl, and stir to mix well. Add the pineapple with its liquid and the sour cream, egg substitute, and water, and beat with an electric mixer for about 2 minutes, or until well mixed.

2. Coat a 9-x-13-inch pan with nonstick cooking spray, and spread the batter evenly in the pan. Bake at 350°F for about 35 minutes, or just until the top springs back when lightly touched and a wooden toothpick inserted in the center of the cake comes out clean. Be careful not to overbake.

3. Allow the cake to cool in the pan for 20 minutes. Using a small knife, poke holes in the cake at 1/2-inch intervals.

4. Place all of the syrup ingredients in a small bowl, and stir to mix well. Slowly pour the syrup over the cake, allowing it to be absorbed into the cake. Allow the cake to cool to room temperature.

5. To make the frosting, place the whipped topping in a medium-sized bowl, and gently fold in the yogurt. Spread the mixture over the cake, swirling the top with a knife. Sprinkle the coconut over the top, if desired. Cover and refrigerate for at least 3 hours before cutting into squares and serving.

NUTRITIONAL FACTS (PER SERVING)

Calories: 235 Carbohydrates: 46 g Cholesterol: 0 mg
Fat: 2.1 g Fiber: 0.5 g Protein: 4.8 g Sodium: 305 mg

You Save: Calories: 124 Fat: 18.5 g

LEMON CREAM CAKE

1. Place the cake mix and pudding mix in a large bowl, and stir to mix well. Add the sour cream, egg substitute, water, and lemon juice, and beat with an electric mixer for about 2 minutes, or until well mixed.

2. Coat a 12-cup bundt pan with nonstick cooking spray, and spread the batter evenly in the pan. Bake at 350°F for 40 to 45 minutes, or just until the top springs back when lightly touched and a wooden toothpick inserted in the center of the cake comes out clean. Be careful not to overbake.

3. Allow the cake to cool in the pan for 45 minutes. Then invert onto a serving platter and cool to room temperature.

4. To make the glaze, place the powdered sugar, lemon juice, and sour cream in a small bowl, and stir to mix well. If using a microwave oven, microwave on high power for 25 seconds, or until hot and runny. If using a stovetop, place the glaze in a small pot and cook over medium heat, stirring constantly, for about 25 seconds, or until hot and runny.

5. Drizzle the hot glaze over the cake. Allow the cake to sit for at least 15 minutes before slicing and serving.

Yield: *16 servings*

1 box (1 pound, 2.25 ounces) reduced-fat or regular lemon or yellow cake mix

1 package (4-serving size) fat-free or regular instant lemon pudding mix

1 cup nonfat sour cream

1 cup fat-free egg substitute

$1/2$ cup water

3 tablespoons lemon juice

GLAZE

$1/2$ cup powdered sugar

$1 1/2$ teaspoons lemon juice

$1 1/2$ teaspoons nonfat sour cream

NUTRITIONAL FACTS (PER SERVING)

Calories: 188 Carbohydrates: 39 g Cholesterol: 0 mg
Fat: 1.5 g Fiber: 0.4 g Protein: 3.1 g Sodium: 323 mg

You Save: Calories: 102 Fat: 12.5 g

Royal Raspberry Cake

Yield: *16 servings*

1 box (1 pound, 2.25 ounces) white cake mix

1 package (4-serving size) fat-free or regular instant white chocolate pudding mix

1 1/4 cups water

1/2 cup nonfat sour cream

3 egg whites

FILLING

1 package (10 ounces) frozen sweetened raspberries, thawed

1 1/2 teaspoons cornstarch

2 tablespoons raspberry or amaretto liqueur

TOPPING

1 recipe Yogurt Fluff Frosting (page 48) made with vanilla or raspberry yogurt

For variety, substitute chocolate or lemon cake and pudding mix for the white cake mix and the white chocolate pudding mix. Use chocolate or lemon yogurt in the frosting.

1. Place the cake mix and pudding mix in a large bowl, and stir to mix well. Add the water, sour cream, and egg whites, and beat with an electric mixer for 2 minutes, or until well mixed.

2. Coat three 9-inch round cake pans with nonstick cooking spray, and divide the batter among the pans, spreading it evenly. Bake at 325°F for about 25 minutes, or just until the tops spring back when lightly touched. Allow the cakes to cool to room temperature in the pans. Be careful not to overbake.

3. To make the filling, transfer 1 tablespoon of the juice from the raspberries to a small bowl. Stir in the cornstarch, and set aside.

4. Place the berries and the remaining juice in a 1-quart pot, and place the pot over medium heat. Cook, stirring frequently, until the mixture comes to a boil and the berries begin to break down. Stir in the cornstarch mixture, and cook for another minute or 2, or until thickened and bubbly. Stir in the liqueur, remove from the heat, and allow to cool to room temperature.

5. To assemble the cake, place one layer, with the top side down, on a serving plate. Spread half of the raspberry filling over the cake layer. Place a second layer over the first, top side down, and spread with the remaining raspberry filling. Place the third layer on the cake, top side up.

6. Spread the frosting over the top and sides of the cake, swirling the frosting with a knife. Cover and refrigerate for at least 2 hours before serving.

NUTRITIONAL FACTS (PER SERVING)
Calories: 213 Carbohydrates: 43 g Cholesterol: 0 mg
Fat: 3 g Fiber: 1.2 g Protein: 2.3 g Sodium: 289 mg

You Save: Calories: 172 Fat: 17 g

Caramel-Apple Coffee Cake

1. To make the topping, place the flour, sugar, and wheat germ or pecans in a small bowl, and stir to mix well. Add the juice concentrate, and stir until the mixture is moist and crumbly. Add a little more juice concentrate if needed. Set aside.

2. Place the flours, brown sugar, and cinnamon in a medium-sized bowl, and stir to mix well, using the back of a spoon to press out any lumps in the brown sugar. Add the baking soda, and stir to mix well.

3. Add the buttermilk, egg substitute, vanilla extract, and apples to the flour mixture, and stir to mix well. (The batter will be thick.)

4. Coat a 9-inch round cake pan with nonstick cooking spray, and spread the batter evenly in the pan. Sprinkle the topping over the batter.

5. Bake at 325°F for 35 to 40 minutes, or just until the top springs back when lightly touched and a wooden toothpick inserted in the center of the cake comes out clean. Be careful not to overbake.

6. Allow the cake to cool at room temperature for at least 30 minutes before cutting into wedges and serving. Serve warm or at room temperature.

Yield: *8 servings*

1/2 cup plus 2 tablespoons unbleached flour

1/2 cup whole wheat pastry flour

3/4 cup light brown sugar

1/2 teaspoon ground cinnamon

3/4 teaspoon baking soda

1/4 cup plus 2 tablespoons non-fat or low-fat buttermilk

1/4 cup fat-free egg substitute

1 teaspoon vanilla extract

2 1/2 cups peeled Granny Smith or Rome apples diced into 1/3-inch pieces (about 3 medium)

TOPPING

1/4 cup whole wheat pastry flour

1/4 cup light brown sugar

1/3 cup honey crunch wheat germ or chopped toasted pecans (page 167)

1 tablespoon plus 1 teaspoon frozen apple juice concentrate, thawed

---

NUTRITIONAL FACTS (PER SERVING)
Calories: 192 Carbohydrates: 43 g Cholesterol: 0 mg
Fat: 0.9 g Fiber: 2.6 g Protein: 4.7 g Sodium: 151 mg

You Save: Calories: 119 Fat: 12.5 g

SOUR CREAM FUDGE CAKE

Yield: *16 servings*

1 1/2 cups unbleached flour

3/4 cup oat flour

1 1/2 cups sugar

3/4 cup cocoa powder

2 teaspoons baking soda

1/4 teaspoon salt

1 cup coffee, cooled to room temperature

1 cup unsweetened applesauce

1/2 cup nonfat sour cream

1/4 cup fat-free egg substitute, or 2 egg whites, lightly beaten

2 teaspoons vanilla extract

GLAZE

1 1/4 cups powdered sugar

1/4 cup nonfat sour cream

2 tablespoons cocoa powder

1 teaspoon vanilla extract

1. Place the flours, sugar, cocoa, baking soda, and salt in a large bowl, and stir to mix well.

2. Place the coffee, applesauce, sour cream, egg substitute, and vanilla extract in a medium-sized bowl, and stir with a whisk to mix well. Add the coffee mixture to the flour mixture, and whisk to mix well.

3. Coat a 9-x-13-inch pan with nonstick cooking spray, and pour the batter into the pan. Bake at 325°F for about 35 minutes, or just until the top springs back when lightly touched and a wooden toothpick inserted in the center of the cake comes out clean. Be careful not to overbake. Remove the cake from the oven, and set aside.

4. To make the glaze, place all of the glaze ingredients in a small bowl, and stir until smooth. Add a little more sour cream if needed to make a thick frosting. Spread the glaze over the hot cake.

5. Allow the cake to cool to room temperature before cutting into squares and serving.

NUTRITIONAL FACTS (PER SERVING)

Calories: 194 Carbohydrates: 46 g Cholesterol: 0 mg
Fat: 1 g Fiber: 2.7 g Protein: 4 g Sodium: 200 mg

You Save: Calories: 98 Fat: 11.6 g

Slashing Fat in Half

Looking for a simple way to slash the fat in cakes and other baked goods? Try replacing the butter, margarine, or other solid shortening in cakes, muffins, quick breads, cookies, and other treats with half as much oil. For instance, if a recipe calls for 1/2 cup of butter, use 1/4 cup of oil instead. Bake as usual, checking the product for doneness a few minutes before the end of the usual baking time. This technique makes it possible to produce moist and tender cakes, breads, and biscuits; crisp cookies; and tender pie crusts—all with about half the original fat.

Cranberry-Pear Coffee Cake

1. To make the topping, place the sugar and wheat germ or nuts in a small bowl, and stir to mix well. Set aside.

2. Place the flours, sugar, and baking soda in a medium-sized bowl, and stir to mix well. Add the orange juice, pears, and vanilla extract, and stir to mix well. (The batter will be thick.) Stir in the cranberries.

3. Coat an 8-inch square cake pan with nonstick cooking spray, and spread the batter evenly in the pan. Sprinkle the topping over the batter.

4. Bake at 325°F for about 30 minutes, or just until the top springs back when lightly touched and a wooden toothpick inserted in the center of the cake comes out clean. Be careful not to overbake.

5. Allow the cake to cool at room temperature for at least 30 minutes before cutting into squares and serving. Serve warm or at room temperature.

NUTRITIONAL FACTS (PER SERVING)

Calories: 174 Carbohydrates: 41 g Cholesterol: 0 mg
Fat: 0.6 g Fiber: 2.4 g Protein: 3.1 g Sodium: 120 mg

You Save: Calories: 117 Fat: 11.4 g

Yield: *8 servings*

³⁄₄ cup unbleached flour

¹⁄₂ cup whole wheat pastry flour

¹⁄₂ cup sugar

³⁄₄ teaspoon baking soda

¹⁄₂ cup plus 1 tablespoon orange juice

1¹⁄₂ cups finely chopped peeled pears (about 1¹⁄₂ medium)

1 teaspoon vanilla extract

¹⁄₃ cup dried cranberries

TOPPING

2 tablespoons light brown sugar

2 tablespoons honey crunch wheat germ or ground pecans, almonds, or walnuts

HEAVENLY LEMON CAKE

Yield: *12 servings*

1 angel food cake (1 pound)

FILLING

2/3 cup sugar

1/4 cup cornstarch

1 3/4 cups skim milk

1/4 cup fat-free egg substitute

1 tablespoon freshly grated lemon rind, or 1 teaspoon dried

1/2 cup lemon juice

FROSTING

2 cups nonfat or light whipped topping

3/4 cup nonfat or low-fat lemon yogurt

1. To make the filling, place the sugar and cornstarch in a 2-quart pot, and stir to mix well. Slowly add the milk while stirring constantly to dissolve the cornstarch and sugar.

2. Place the pot over medium heat, and bring the mixture to a boil, stirring constantly with a wire whisk. Continue to cook and stir for 1 minute, or until the mixture is thickened and bubbly.

3. Reduce the heat under the pot to low. Place the egg substitute in a small dish, and stir in 1/4 cup of the hot milk mixture. Return the mixture to the pot while whisking constantly. Cook and stir for about 2 minutes, or until the mixture is thickened and bubbly.

4. Remove the pot from the heat, and whisk in the lemon rind. Slowly whisk in the lemon juice. Allow the mixture to sit for 20 minutes to cool slightly. Then stir, and pour into a medium-sized bowl. Cover the bowl and refrigerate for several hours, or until well chilled and thickened.

5. To assemble the cake, using a serrated knife, remove a 3/4-inch-thick slice from the top of the cake, and set aside. Cut out the center of the cake, leaving a 3/4-inch-thick shell on the bottom and sides. Place the hollowed out cake on a serving platter. Stir the lemon mixture; then spoon it into the hollow in the cake. Place the top back on the cake.

6. To make the frosting, place the whipped topping in a medium-sized bowl, and gently fold in the yogurt. Spread the frosting over the top and sides of the cake. Cover and refrigerate for at least 3 hours before slicing and serving.

NUTRITIONAL FACTS (PER SERVING)
Calories: 184 Carbohydrates: 40 g Cholesterol: 0 mg
Fat: 0.8 g Fiber: 0.5 g Protein: 4.6 g Sodium: 293 mg

You Save: Calories: 100 Fat: 13.4 g

Tunnel of Fudge Cake

For variety, substitute white chocolate or vanilla pudding mix for the chocolate or devil's food pudding mix.

Yield: *20 servings*

1. To make the filling, place the milk and pudding mix in a small bowl, and stir with a wire whisk for a minute or 2, or until well mixed and thickened. Set the mixture aside for at least 5 minutes. (It will thicken a bit more during this time.)

2. Place the flours, cocoa, sugar, baking soda, and salt in a large bowl, and stir to mix well. Add the buttermilk, egg substitute, oil, and vanilla extract, and stir just enough to mix well.

3. Coat a 12-cup bundt plan with nonstick cooking spray, and spread the batter evenly in the pan. Spoon the filling in a ring over the center of the batter. (The filling will sink into the batter as the cake bakes.)

4. Bake at 350°F for about 45 minutes, or just until a wooden toothpick inserted on either side of the filling comes out clean. Cool the cake in the pan for 45 minutes. Then invert onto a serving platter and set aside while your prepare the glaze.

5. To make the glaze, place the powdered sugar and cocoa in a small bowl, and stir to mix well. Stir in the vanilla extract and just enough of the milk to make a thick but pourable glaze. Drizzle the glaze over the cake and, if desired, sprinkle with the walnuts.

6. Let the cake cool completely before slicing and serving. Refrigerate any leftovers.

2 cups unbleached flour

½ cup oat flour

½ cup Dutch processed cocoa powder

1½ cups sugar

1¼ teaspoons baking soda

¼ teaspoon salt

1 cup plus 2 tablespoons nonfat or low-fat buttermilk

¼ cup plus 2 tablespoons fat-free egg substitute

¼ cup walnut or canola oil

2 teaspoons vanilla extract

FUDGE FILLING

1¼ cups skim or 1% low-fat milk

1 box (4-serving size) fat-free instant chocolate or devil's food pudding mix

GLAZE

½ cup powdered sugar

1 tablespoon Dutch processed cocoa powder

½ teaspoon vanilla extract

1 tablespoon skim milk

1 tablespoon chopped walnuts (optional)

NUTRITIONAL FACTS (PER SERVING)
Calories: 182 Carbohydrates: 36 g Cholesterol: 1 mg
Fat: 3.1 g Fiber: 1.3 g Protein: 3.6 g Sodium: 213 mg

You Save: Calories: 102 Fat: 11 g

Mocha-Zucchini Snack Cake

Yield: *8 servings*

3/4 cup plus 3 tablespoons unbleached flour

1/4 cup plus 2 tablespoons cocoa powder

3/4 cup sugar

1 teaspoon baking powder

1/4 teaspoon baking soda

1/4 teaspoon salt

3/4 teaspoon ground cinnamon

3/4 teaspoon instant coffee granules

1/2 cup unsweetened applesauce

1 cup grated unpeeled zucchini (about 1 medium)

1/4 cup fat-free egg substitute, or 2 egg whites, lightly beaten

1 teaspoon vanilla extract

1/4 cup dark raisins

1/4 cup chopped toasted pecans or walnuts (page 167) (optional)

GLAZE

1 tablespoon plus 1/2 teaspoon skim milk

1/4 teaspoon instant coffee granules

1/2 cup powdered sugar

1 tablespoon cocoa powder

1. Place the flour, cocoa, sugar, baking powder, baking soda, salt, cinnamon, and coffee granules in a medium-sized bowl, and stir to mix well. Add the applesauce, zucchini, egg substitute or egg whites, and vanilla extract, and stir just until moistened. Fold in the raisins and, if desired, the nuts.

2. Coat an 8-inch square pan with nonstick cooking spray, and spread the mixture evenly in the pan. Bake at 325°F for 30 to 35 minutes, or just until the top springs back when lightly touched and a wooden toothpick inserted in the center of the cake comes out clean. Remove the cake from the oven, and set aside.

3. To make the glaze, place the milk and coffee granules in a small bowl, and stir to dissolve the coffee granules. Add the powdered sugar and cocoa, and stir until smooth. Spread the glaze over the hot cake.

4. Allow the cake to cool to room temperature before cutting into squares and serving.

NUTRITIONAL FACTS (PER SERVING)
Calories: 186 Carbohydrates: 41 g Cholesterol: 0 mg
Fat: 0.8 g Fiber: 2.6 g Protein: 3.6 g Sodium: 183 mg

You Save: Calories: 126 Fat: 13.7 g

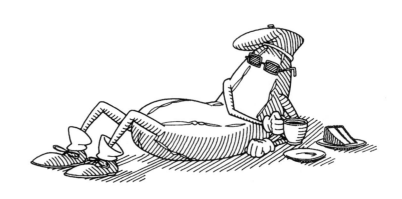

Applesauce-Spice Snack Cake

1. Place the flours, sugar, baking soda, and spices in a medium-sized bowl, and stir to mix well. Add the applesauce, molasses or honey, and egg substitute, and stir just until moistened. Fold in the raisins and, if desired, the walnuts.

2. Coat an 8-inch square pan with nonstick cooking spray, and spread the mixture evenly in the pan. Bake at 325°F for 30 to 35 minutes, or just until the top springs back when lightly touched and a wooden toothpick inserted in the center of the cake comes out clean. Be careful not to overbake.

3. Allow the cake to cool to room temperature. Then cover the pan with foil or plastic wrap, and set aside for at least 6 hours. (This will produce a softer, moister crust.) If desired, sift the powdered sugar over the top just before cutting into squares and serving.

Yield: *8 servings*

3/4 cup unbleached flour

1/2 cup whole wheat pastry flour

1/3 cup sugar

1 teaspoon baking soda

1/2 teaspoon ground cinnamon

1/2 teaspoon ground ginger

1/2 teaspoon ground allspice

3/4 cup unsweetened applesauce

1/2 cup molasses or honey

3 tablespoons fat-free egg substitute

1/3 cup dark or golden raisins

1/4 cup chopped walnuts (optional)

2 tablespoons powdered sugar (optional)

NUTRITIONAL FACTS (PER SERVING)
Calories: 179 Carbohydrates: 43 g Cholesterol: 0 mg
Fat: 0.2 g Fiber: 1.6 g Protein: 3 g Sodium: 175 mg

You Save: Calories: 129 Fat: 14.9 g

Using Fat-Free Cream Cheese in Frostings and Fillings

If you've ever tried to defat a cream cheese frosting recipe by substituting fat-free cream cheese for the full-fat product, you probably ended up with a runny, watery mess. Why? Fat-free cream cheese has a higher water content than full-fat cream cheese. When more than a couple of tablespoons of sugar is added to the fat-free product, water is released from the cheese, resulting in a runny glaze.

The solution? Use a low-sugar frosting, like Fluffy Cream Cheese Frosting (page 48). Or beat a tablespoon or two of instant vanilla pudding mix into your fat-free frosting. This will thicken the mixture to the desired consistency. As another option, make the frosting with Neufchâtel—a reduced-fat cream cheese that has a relatively low water content.

Chocolate Cream Cake Roll

Yield: *12 servings*

1 1/3 cups unbleached flour

1 cup sugar

1/3 cup cocoa powder

1 teaspoon baking soda

3/4 cup unsweetened applesauce

1/2 cup fat-free egg substitute

1/4 cup skim milk

1 teaspoon vanilla extract

FILLING

1 package (4-serving size) fat-free instant chocolate, white chocolate, vanilla, or pistachio pudding mix

1 cup skim milk

1 1/4 cups nonfat or light whipped topping

GLAZE

3/4 cup powdered sugar

1 tablespoon cocoa powder

1 tablespoon plus 1/2 teaspoon skim milk

1/2 teaspoon vanilla extract

1. Line a 15 1/4-x-10 1/4-inch jelly roll pan with waxed paper by laying a 16-inch piece of waxed paper in the pan, and folding up the sides so that the paper covers the bottom and sides. Spray the waxed paper with nonstick cooking spray, and set aside.

2. Place the flour, sugar, cocoa, and baking soda in a medium-sized bowl, and stir to mix well. Add the applesauce, egg substitute, milk, and vanilla extract, and stir to mix well.

3. Spread the batter evenly in the waxed paper-lined pan, and bake at 350°F for 12 minutes, or just until the cake springs back when lightly touched in the center. Be careful not to overbake.

4. While the cake is baking, lay a clean kitchen towel out on a work surface. Remove the cake from the oven, and immediately invert it onto the towel. Peel off the waxed paper. Starting at the short end, loosely roll the cake and towel up together. (There should be 1 1/2 inches of open space in the center to accommodate the filling.) Place the cake roll on a wire rack, and allow to cool to room temperature.

5. To make the filling, place the pudding mix and milk in a small bowl, and whip with a wire whisk for 2 minutes, or until well-mixed and thickened. Gently fold in the whipped topping, and set aside.

6. Gently unroll the cooled cake just enough to allow the filling to be spread over the top. Spread the filling to within 1/2 inch of each edge. Roll the cake up, and transfer to a serving platter. Cover and chill for several hours or overnight.

7. Just before serving, trim 1/2 inch off each end of the chilled cake, and discard. To make the glaze, place all of the glaze ingredients in a small bowl, and stir to mix well. If using a microwave oven, microwave on high power for about 30 seconds, or until hot and runny. If using a stovetop, place the glaze in a small pot and cook over medium heat, stirring constantly, for about 30 seconds, or until hot and runny.

8. Drizzle the hot glaze over the cake. Allow the cake to sit for at least 15 minutes before slicing into 3/4-inch-thick slices and serving.

NUTRITIONAL FACTS (PER SERVING)
Calories: 198 Carbohydrates: 46 g Cholesterol: 0 mg
Fat: 0.7 g Fiber: 1.3 g Protein: 3.5 g Sodium: 247 mg

You Save: Calories: 100 Fat: 11 g

Fudqe Marble Cake

1. Place the oat bran and buttermilk in a small bowl, and whisk to mix well. Set aside for at least 10 minutes.

2. Place the flour and baking soda in a medium-sized bowl, and stir to mix well. Set aside.

3. Place the margarine or butter in a large bowl, and beat with an electric mixer until smooth. Beat in the sugar ½ cup at a time. Then beat in the egg substitute and vanilla extract.

4. Add the flour mixture and the oat bran mixture to the margarine mixture, and stir with a wooden spoon to mix well. Set aside.

5. To make the fudge marble, place 1 cup of the batter in a small bowl. Add the cocoa and chocolate syrup, and stir to mix well.

6. Coat a 12-cup bundt pan with nonstick cooking spray, and spoon three-fourths of the white batter into the pan. Top the white batter with all of the chocolate batter, and finish off with the remaining white batter.

7. Bake at 350°F for about 43 minutes, or just until a wooden toothpick inserted in the center of the cake comes out clean. Be careful not to overbake. Allow the cake to cool in the pan for 40 minutes. Then invert onto a serving platter, and let the cake cool to room temperature.

8. To make the glaze, place all of the glaze ingredients in a small bowl, and stir to mix well. Drizzle the glaze over the cooled cake. Allow the cake to sit for at least 15 minutes before slicing and serving.

Yield: *18 servings*

⅔ cup oat bran

1 cup plus 2 tablespoons nonfat or low-fat buttermilk

2⅓ cups unbleached flour

1 teaspoon baking soda

1 stick (¼ pound) reduced-fat margarine or light butter, softened to room temperature

1½ cups sugar

¼ cup plus 2 tablespoons fat-free egg substitute

2½ teaspoons vanilla extract

FUDGE MARBLE

¼ cup Dutch processed cocoa powder

¼ cup chocolate syrup

GLAZE

½ cup powdered sugar

1 tablespoon Dutch processed cocoa powder

1 tablespoon skim milk

½ teaspoon vanilla extract

NUTRITIONAL FACTS (PER SERVING)
Calories: 182 Carbohydrates: 38 g Cholesterol: 0 mg
Fat: 3 g Fiber: 1.4 g Protein: 3.5 g Sodium: 141 mg

You Save: Calories: 98 Fat: 10 g

Chocolate Flavor With a Fraction of the Fat

For rich chocolate flavor with a minimum of fat, substitute cocoa powder for high-fat baking chocolate. Simply use 3 tablespoons of cocoa powder plus 1 tablespoon of water or another liquid to replace each ounce of baking chocolate in cakes, brownies, puddings, and other goodies. You'll save 111 calories and 13.5 grams of fat for each ounce of baking chocolate that you replace!

For the deepest, darkest, richest cocoa flavor, use Dutch processed cocoa in your chocolate treats. Dutching, a process that neutralizes the natural acidity in cocoa, results in a darker, sweeter, more mellow-flavored cocoa. Look for a brand like Hershey's Dutch Processed European Style cocoa. Like regular cocoa, this product has only half a gram of fat per tablespoon—although some Dutch processed cocoa does contain more fat. Dutched cocoa can be substituted for regular cocoa in any recipe, and since it has a smoother, sweeter flavor, you may find that you can reduce the sugar in your recipe by up to 25 percent.

In the interest of keeping sugar to a minimum, you'll find that some of the recipes in this book call specifically for Dutch processed cocoa. In these recipes, the smoother, sweeter flavor of Dutch cocoa best complements the recipe. When a recipe simply calls for "cocoa powder," use either regular or Dutch processed cocoa, depending on your preference.

CHERRY TUNNEL CAKE

For variety, substitute blueberry or lemon pie filling for the cherry pie filling.

1. Place the flours, baking soda, baking powder, and lemon rind in a medium-sized bowl, and stir to mix well. Set aside.

2. Place the margarine or butter in a large bowl, and beat with an electric mixer until smooth. Beat in the sugar ½ cup at a time. Then beat in the egg substitute and vanilla extract.

3. Add the flour mixture and the buttermilk to the margarine mixture, and stir with a wooden spoon just enough to mix well.

4. Coat a 12-cup bundt pan with nonstick cooking spray, and spread the batter evenly in the pan. Spoon the filling in a ring over the center of the batter. (The filling will sink into the batter as the cake bakes.)

5. Bake at 350°F for about 45 minutes, or just until a wooden toothpick inserted on either side of the filling comes out clean. Cool the cake in the pan for 45 minutes. Then invert the cake onto a serving platter and set aside while you prepare the glaze.

6. To make the glaze, place the powdered sugar and lemon rind in a small bowl, and stir to mix well. Stir in the vanilla extract and just enough of the milk to make a thick but pourable glaze. Drizzle the glaze over the cake. Let the cake cool completely before slicing and serving.

Yield: *20 servings*

2⅓ cups unbleached flour

⅔ cup oat flour

1 teaspoon baking soda

1 teaspoon baking powder

½ teaspoon dried grated lemon rind, or 1½ teaspoons fresh

1 stick (¼ pound) reduced-fat margarine or light butter, softened to room temperature

1½ cups sugar

¼ cup plus 2 tablespoons fat-free egg substitute

2 teaspoons vanilla extract

1 cup nonfat or low-fat buttermilk

FILLING

1½ cups light (reduced-sugar) cherry pie filling

GLAZE

½ cup powdered sugar

⅛ teaspoon dried grated lemon rind, or ½ teaspoon fresh

½ teaspoon vanilla extract

2½ teaspoons skim milk

NUTRITIONAL FACTS (PER SERVING)

Calories: 176 Carbohydrates: 34 g Cholesterol: 0 mg
Fat: 2.6 g Fiber: 0.9 g Protein: 2.9 g Sodium: 140 mg

You Save: Calories: 91 Fat: 9.4 g

Getting the Fat Out of Your Favorite Cake Recipes

Everyone knows that cakes are loaded with sugar, but fat is often the bigger problem in these sweet treats. In fact, most traditional cakes get more calories from fat than they do from sugar. Consider a cake that contains one cup of oil and two cups of sugar. The oil provides almost 2,000 calories, while the sugar provides just under 1,600 calories. Fortunately, most cakes can be made with less fat, and some can be made with no fat at all, trimming a significant number of calories in the process.

Before you begin trimming the fat from your own recipes, realize that some cakes are better candidates for fat reduction than others. Naturally dense cakes—carrot cakes, fudgy chocolate cakes, and many coffee cakes, for instance—can be made with little or no fat. Packaged cake mixes can also be easily prepared with no added fats. Cakes that are meant to have a very light and tender texture, however, are more difficult to modify—although you can usually eliminate up to half of the fat from even these recipes.

Which fat substitutes perform best in cakes? Applesauce and other fruit purées (page 9), Prune Purée (page 131), and even mashed cooked pumpkin are all excellent fat substitutes in cakes. Nonfat or low-fat buttermilk and yogurt will also work well. Use the following tricks of the trade to insure success when eliminating the fat from your favorite cake recipes.

☐ *Replace the desired amount of butter, margarine, or other solid shortening with half as much fat substitute.* For instance, if you are omitting ½ cup of butter from a recipe, replace it with ¼ cup of fruit purée, Prune Purée, nonfat buttermilk, mashed cooked pumpkin, or other fat substitute. (If the recipe calls for oil, substitute three-fourths as much fat substitute.) Mix up the batter. If it seems too dry, add more fat substitute. For extra flavor and tenderness, try substituting fruit purée or nonfat buttermilk for the recipe's liquid, as well.

☐ *Eliminate only half the fat in a recipe at first.* The next time you make the recipe, try replacing even more fat. Continue reducing the fat until you find the lowest amount that will give you the desired results. Realize that as you remove more and more fat from a recipe, the following tips—for using low-gluten flours and reducing the amount of eggs, for instance—will become even more important.

☐ *Use low-gluten flours.* One of the main functions of fat in cakes is to prevent the development of gluten, a protein in wheat flour that causes a tough, coarse texture in baked goods. While fat substitutes like applesauce and fruit purées also help prevent gluten from forming, they do not perform this function nearly as well as fat does. However, if you use a low-gluten flour like whole wheat pastry flour or oat flour in your low- and no-fat cakes, you can achieve maximum tenderness with minimum fat. For best results, substitute whole wheat pastry flour or oat flour for a third to a half of the refined white flour in your recipe. Or substitute oat bran for a quarter of the flour in the recipe. (For the smoothest texture, soak the oat bran in the recipe's liquid for at least 10 minutes before adding it to the batter.) Read more about whole wheat pastry flour and other low-gluten options on pages 11 to 13.

☐ *Minimize mixing.* Stirring batter excessively develops gluten and toughens the texture of baked goods. Stir only enough to mix well.

☐ *Avoid overbaking.* Reduced-fat baked goods tend to bake more quickly than do those made with fat, and if left in the oven too long, they can become dry. To prevent this, reduce the oven temperature by 25°F, and check the product for doneness a few minutes before the end of the usual baking time.

❑ *Reduce the amount of eggs.* You may have noticed that most of the fat-free cakes in this chapter contain a relatively small amount of eggs, and that some contain no eggs at all. Why? Fat adds tenderness to baked goods. Eggs, on the other hand, toughen the structure of baked goods as their proteins coagulate during baking and bind the batter together. For this reason, low- and no-fat cakes that contain too many eggs can have a tough texture. For maximum tenderness, substitute 1 egg white for each whole egg in your recipe. In some cases, you can alternatively substitute 2 tablespoons of your chosen fat substitute for each whole egg.

❑ *Increase the leavening, if necessary.* Fat lubricates batters and helps cakes rise better. When fats are creamed with sugar, they also incorporate air into the batter, which further aids rising. For these reasons, when you eliminate the fat from your cake recipe, your cake might not rise as well. If this happens, try adding a little extra baking soda to your recipe, starting with ¼ teaspoon. Avoid using more than 1 teaspoon of baking soda per cup of acidic liquid—such as fruit purée or buttermilk—as this may cause the product to take on a bitter, soapy taste. If a recipe contains little or no acidic liquids, try adding some extra baking powder for lightness, starting with ¾ to 1 teaspoon. For even greater lightness, whip the recipe's egg whites to soft peaks, and gently fold them into the prepared batter.

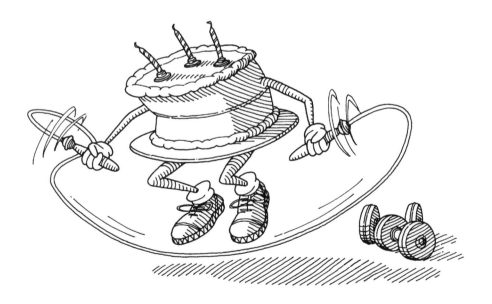

4

Pleasing Pies, Tarts, and Pastries

Flaky and delicious, pies, tarts, and pastries are always a welcome treat. And whether made with a filling of juicy fruit or one of creamy custard, these goodies can easily be prepared with little or no added fat, and, in many cases, with less sugar than usual. In fact, if you compare the recipes in this chapter with those in traditional cookbooks, you will see that most have 90 percent less fat and 25 to 50 percent less sugar than traditional versions.

How do you trim the fat from pies, tarts, and pastries? The best place to start is with the crust, as most traditional crusts are loaded with butter, margarine, or other fats. Even worse, homemade pie crusts can be an ordeal to prepare from scratch. Not these. As you will see, low-fat crumb crusts prepared with graham crackers or other wholesome ingredients are a snap to make. Even a rolled pie crust can be made with a minimum of fuss, and with less than half the fat of a traditional crust.

As for pie fillings, there are plenty of ways to reduce both fat and sugar. The custard, pudding, and cream pies in this chapter make use of a variety of nonfat dairy products, from nonfat yogurt to fat-free sweetened condensed milk. Many traditional fruit fillings are already low in fat, but most contain an over-abundance of sugar. In contrast, the fruit pies in this chapter get much of their sweetness from fresh fruit, dried fruit, and juices. This natural sweetness is then enhanced by spices like cinnamon and nutmeg.

So take out your pie and tart pans, and get ready to enjoy a galaxy of homemade goodies. Lusciously sweet and meltingly tender, these are desserts that you will find yourself making time and time again.

PIE CRUSTS AND TART SHELLS

Lite Graham Cracker Pie Crust

Yield: *One 9-inch pie crust*

8 large (2$\frac{1}{2}$-x-5-inch) reduced-fat plain or chocolate graham crackers

2 tablespoons sugar

1 tablespoon plus 1 teaspoon tub-style nonfat margarine, or 2 tablespoons reduced-fat margarine (do not melt)

1 tablespoon fat-free egg substitute

3 tablespoons honey crunch wheat germ

Fill this crust only with precooked or no-cook fillings, such as puddings.

1. Break the crackers into pieces, and place in the bowl of a food processor. Process into fine crumbs. Measure the crumbs. There should be 1 cup. (Adjust the amount if necessary.)

2. Return the crumbs to the food processor, add the sugar, and process for a few seconds to mix well. Add the margarine and egg substitute, and process for about 20 seconds, or until the mixture is moist (but not wet) and crumbly, and holds together when pinched. If the mixture seems too dry, mix in more margarine, $\frac{1}{2}$ teaspoon at a time, until the proper consistency is reached. Add the wheat germ, and process for a few seconds to mix well.

3. Coat a 9-inch pie pan with nonstick cooking spray, and use the back of a spoon to press the mixture against the bottom and sides of the pan, forming an even crust. (Periodically dip the spoon in sugar, if necessary, to prevent sticking.) Then use your fingers to finish pressing the crust firmly against the bottom and sides of the pan.

4. Bake at 350°F for 9 minutes, or until the edges feel firm and dry. Cool to room temperature before filling.

NUTRITIONAL FACTS (PER $\frac{1}{8}$ CRUST)
Calories: 79 Carbohydrates: 16 g Cholesterol: 0 mg
Fat: 1 g Fiber: 0.4 g Protein: 1.8 g Sodium: 110 mg

You Save: Calories: 55 Fat: 6.7 g

Coconut Crunch Pie Crust

Like Lite Graham Cracker Pie Crust (page 70), this crust should be filled only with precooked or no-cook fillings.

1. Place the cereal in the bowl of a food processor, and process into fine crumbs. Measure the crumbs. There should be 1 cup. (Adjust the amount if necessary.)

2. Return the crumbs to the food processor, add the sugar, and process for a few seconds to mix well. Add the egg substitute, and process for about 20 seconds, or until the mixture is moist and crumbly. Add the coconut, and process for a few seconds, or just until well mixed.

3. Coat a 9-inch pie pan with nonstick cooking spray, and use the back of a spoon to press the mixture against the bottom and sides of the pan, forming an even crust. (Periodically dip the spoon in sugar, if necessary, to prevent sticking.)

4. Bake at 350°F for 10 minutes, or until the edges feel firm and dry. Cool to room temperature before filling.

Yield: *One 9-inch pie crust*

2 cups oat flake-and-almond breakfast cereal, such as Quaker Toasted Oatmeal or Oatmeal Crisp With Almonds

1 tablespoon sugar

1 tablespoon fat-free egg substitute

¼ cup shredded sweetened coconut

NUTRITIONAL FACTS (PER ⅛ CRUST)
Calories: 69 Carbohydrates: 12.7 g Cholesterol: 0 mg
Fat: 1.6 g Fiber: 0.9 g Protein: 1.5 g Sodium: 56 mg

You Save: Calories: 66 Fat: 8.8 g

Making Crumb Crusts in a Snap

If you find yourself making crumb crusts often, there is an easy way to speed the preparation of each individual crust. Just whip up a large batch of graham cracker or cereal crumbs whenever you have the time, and store the crumbs in covered containers at room temperature for up to several months. You will then have a ready supply on hand to expedite the making of Lite Graham Cracker Pie Crust, Coconut Crunch Pie Crust, and many other recipes.

CRUNCHY NUTTY PIE CRUST

Yield: *One 9-inch pie crust*

1 cup barley nugget cereal

¼ cup honey crunch wheat germ or finely chopped pecans or almonds

2 tablespoons light brown sugar

3 tablespoons fat-free egg substitute

You can fill this crust with either precooked fillings or fillings that require baking.

1. Place the cereal, wheat germ or nuts, and brown sugar in a small bowl, and stir to mix well. Stir in the egg substitute.

2. Coat a 9-inch pie pan with nonstick cooking spray, and use the back of a spoon to pat the mixture against the bottom and sides of the pan, forming an even crust.

3. Bake at 350°F for about 12 minutes, or until the edges feel firm and dry. Cool the crust to room temperature and fill with a precooked filling, or fill and bake as directed in the recipe. (Note that this crust should be prebaked even when making pies that require additional baking, such as pumpkin and sweet potato pies. When further baking is required, cut 3-inch wide strips of aluminum foil, and fold them over the edges of the pie pan to prevent overbrowning.)

NUTRITIONAL FACTS (PER ⅛ CRUST)

Calories: 73 Carbohydrates: 15.6 g Cholesterol: 0 mg
Fat: 0.3 g Fiber: 1.5 g Protein: 2.9 g Sodium: 105 mg

You Save: Calories: 47 Fat: 7.7 g

Flaky Oat Pie Crust

This pie crust has less than half the fat of a traditional pie crust, with a tender flaky texture. Fill it with precooked fillings or with fillings that require baking.

1. Place the oats or oat bran, flour, baking powder, and salt in a medium-sized bowl, and stir to mix. Add the oil and just enough of the milk to form a stiff dough, stirring just until the mixture holds together and forms a ball.

2. Coat two 12-x-12-inch pieces of waxed paper with nonstick cooking spray. Lay the dough on 1 of the sheets of waxed paper, and pat it into a 7-inch circle. Place the other sheet of waxed paper over the circle of dough, and, using a rolling pin, roll the dough into an 11-inch circle.

3. Coat a 9-inch deep dish pie pan with nonstick cooking spray. Peel the top sheet of waxed paper from the pie crust, and invert the crust over the pie pan. Carefully peel the waxed paper from the crust, and press the crust into the pie pan. Pinch the edges of the crust or press with the tines of a fork to make a decorative edge. (As an alternative to steps 2 and 3, you can also pat the crust into the pan. Pinch off pieces of dough and press them in a thin layer against the sides of the pan. Then fill in the bottom with the remaining dough.)

4. For a prebaked crust, prick the crust with a fork at 1-inch intervals, and bake at 400°F for about 12 minutes, or until lightly browned. Allow the crust to cool to room temperature before filling. When a prebaked crust is not desired, simply fill and bake the crust as directed in the recipe.

Yield: *One 9-inch pie crust*

1/2 cup quick-cooking oats or oat bran

2/3 cup unbleached flour

1/2 teaspoon baking powder

1/8 teaspoon salt

2–3 tablespoons vegetable oil (try unrefined corn oil or walnut oil for extra flavor)

3 tablespoons plus 1 teaspoon skim milk

NUTRITIONAL FACTS (PER 1/8 CRUST)

Calories: 90 Carbohydrates: 11.5 g Cholesterol: 0 mg
Fat: 3.6 g Fiber: 1 g Protein: 2 g Sodium: 76 mg

You Save: Calories: 52 Fat: 6 g

Meringue Tart Shells

Yield: *8 shells*

3 egg whites, brought to room temperature

$1/4$ teaspoon cream of tartar

Pinch salt

$3/4$ cup sugar

$3/4$ teaspoon vanilla extract

These light-as-air shells have always been fat-free, and make an elegant base for fresh fruits, puddings, and a variety of other fillings.

1. Place the egg whites, cream of tartar, and salt in a medium-sized bowl, and beat with an electric mixer until soft peaks form when the beaters are raised.

2. Gradually add the sugar, a tablespoon at a time, while beating continuously, until all of the sugar has been incorporated, the mixture is glossy, and stiff peaks form when the beaters are raised. (The total beating time will be about 7 minutes.) Beat in the vanilla extract.

3. Place a sheet of waxed paper over the bottom of a large baking sheet, and drop the meringue onto the sheet in 8 mounds, spaced about 4 inches apart. Using the back of a spoon, spread each mound into a $3^{1}/2$-inch circle, creating a center that is about $1/2$ inch thick and building up the sides to about $1^{1}/4$ inches in height.

4. Bake at 250°F for 1 hour, or until the shells are creamy white and firm to the touch. Turn the oven off, and allow the shells to cool in the oven for 1 hour with the door closed. Fill as desired. (Note that the shells may be prepared the day before you plan to use them, and stored in an airtight container until ready to fill.)

NUTRITIONAL FACTS (PER SHELL)
Calories: 79 Carbohydrates: 18.8 g Cholesterol: 0 mg
Fat: 0 g Fiber: 0 g Protein: 1.3 g Sodium: 34 mg

You Save: Calories: 0 Fat: 0 g

Variation

To make Almond Meringue Tart Shells, reduce the vanilla extract to $1/2$ teaspoon, and add $1/2$ teaspoon of almond extract along with the vanilla. Gently fold $1/4$ cup of finely ground toasted almonds into the finished meringue. Then shape and bake as directed in the recipe.

NUTRITIONAL FACTS (PER SHELL)
Calories: 102 Carbohydrates: 19.6 g Cholesterol: 0 mg
Fat: 2.1 g Fiber: 0 g Protein: 2.1 g Sodium: 34 mg

You Save: Calories: 48 Fat: 4.3 g

Making Foolproof Meringue

Light as air with a delightfully crisp texture, meringue can form the base for many a show-stopping dessert. As if that wasn't reason enough to enjoy this ethereal confection, meringue has always been fat-free. As versatile as it is delicious, meringue can either top a pie or form its crust. It can also be made into small tart shells, cookies, and many other treats.

Unless you know a few tricks of the trade, making meringue can be a frustrating experience. But once you learn the secrets of making foolproof meringue, you'll want to make it often. Here are some important tips for baking up the lightest, fluffiest meringue possible.

☐ When separating the egg whites, be sure not to let any of the yolk get mixed in. Egg yolks contain fat, which interferes with the ability of the whites to whip. If even a little yolk is mixed in with the whites, they will not whip properly. If you accidentally do get some yolk mixed in with the whites, simply scoop it out with a piece of egg shell.

☐ Allow the egg whites to come to room temperature before whipping.

☐ Make sure the mixing bowl and beaters are spotless. If there is any residue of fat or oil on either, the whites will not whip properly.

☐ Use a glass or metal bowl for best results when whipping egg whites. Egg whites whipped in plastic bowls may not reach their full volume.

☐ Beat the egg whites with cream of tartar and salt to soft peaks before you begin to add the sugar. Then add the sugar gradually, a tablespoon at a time, to achieve maximum lightness.

☐ For best results, make meringue on a clear, dry day. Meringue can pick up excess humidity from the air and become sticky.

Flaky Phyllo Tart Shells

Yield: 6 shells

4 teaspoons sugar

$1/4$ teaspoon dried grated lemon rind, or $3/4$ teaspoon fresh (optional)

4 sheets (each about 14 x 18 inches) phyllo pastry (about $3^1/4$ ounces)

Butter-flavored cooking spray

Light and flaky, these shells make the perfect base for fillings of fresh fruit, pudding, or a scoop of your favorite ice cream.

1. Place the sugar and lemon rind in a small dish. Stir to mix well and set aside.

2. Spread the phyllo dough out on a clean dry surface. Cover the dough with plastic wrap to prevent it from drying out as you work. (Remove the sheets as you need them, being sure to re-cover the remaining dough.)

3. Remove 1 sheet of phyllo dough, and lay it on a clean dry surface. Spray the sheet lightly with the cooking spray, and sprinkle with 1 teaspoon of the sugar mixture. Top with another phyllo sheet, spray with the cooking spray, and sprinkle with another teaspoon of the sugar mixture. Repeat with the 2 remaining sheets.

4. Cut the stack of phyllo sheets lengthwise into two 18-inch-long strips. Then cut each strip crosswise to make 3 pieces, each measuring approximately 6 x 7 inches. You should now have 6 stacks of phyllo squares, each 4 layers thick.

5. Coat six jumbo muffin cups or six 6-ounce custard cups with non-stick cooking spray. Gently press 1 stack of phyllo squares into each cup, pleating as necessary to make it fit. Press the corners back slightly.

6. Bake at 350°F for about 8 minutes, or until golden brown. Remove the crusts from the oven and allow to cool for 5 minutes. Transfer the crusts to wire racks to cool completely. Then fill as desired. (Note that the shells may be prepared the day before you plan to use them, and stored in an airtight container until ready to fill.)

NUTRITIONAL FACTS (PER SERVING)
Calories: 56 Carbohydrates: 10.8 g Cholesterol: 0 mg
Fat: 0.9 g Fiber: 0 g Protein: 1.1 g Sodium: 74 mg

You Save: Calories: 68 Fat: 7.7 g

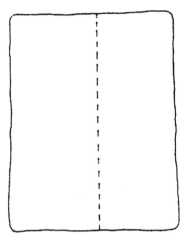

a. Cut the phyllo sheets into
2 long strips.

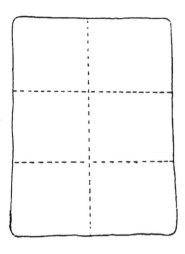

b. Cut each strip crosswise
to make 3 squares.

Making Flaky Phyllo Tart Shells.

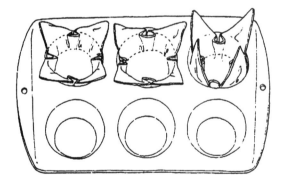

c. Press 1 stack of squares into
each muffin cup.

PIES, TARTS, AND PASTRIES

CREAMY LEMON PIE

Yield: *8 servings*

1 prebaked Lite Graham
Cracker Pie Crust (page 70)
made with plain graham
crackers

FILLING

1/2 cup boiling water

1 package (4-serving size)
regular or sugar-free
lemon gelatin

1 3/4 cups regular or sugar-free
nonfat or low-fat lemon
yogurt

1 1/2 cups nonfat or light
whipped topping

1. To make the filling, place the boiling water in a large bowl. Sprinkle the gelatin over the water, and whisk for 3 minutes, or until the gelatin is completely dissolved. Set the mixture aside for about 20 minutes, or until it has cooled to room temperature.

2. When the gelatin has cooled, whisk in the yogurt. Chill for 10 minutes. Stir the mixture; it should be the consistency of pudding. If necessary, chill for a few minutes longer.

3. When the gelatin mixture has reached the proper consistency, stir it well. Then gently fold in the whipped topping. Spoon the mixture into the prepared pie shell, swirling the top with a spoon, and chill for at least 3 hours, or until set, before cutting into wedges and serving.

NUTRITIONAL FACTS (PER SERVING)

Calories: 183 Carbohydrates: 38.8 g Cholesterol: 1 mg
Fat: 1.4 g Fiber: 0.4 g Protein: 4.5 g Sodium: 170 mg

You Save: Calories: 181 Fat: 24.3 g

KEY LIME CHEESE PIE

1. Place the condensed milk and cream cheese in a medium-sized bowl, and beat with an electric mixer until smooth. Add the lime juice, and beat until well mixed.

2. Pour the filling into the crust. Cover and chill for at least 8 hours, or until set, before cutting into wedges and serving.

NUTRITIONAL FACTS (PER SERVING)

Calories: 247 Carbohydrates: 49 g Cholesterol: 4 mg
Fat: 1.1 g Fiber: 0.4 g Protein: 9.5 g Sodium: 300 mg

You Save: Calories: 142   Fat: 20.6 g

Yield: *8 servings*

1 prebaked Lite Graham
  Cracker Pie Crust (page 70)
  made with plain graham
  crackers or Coconut Crunch
  Pie Crust (page 71)

FILLING

1 can (14 ounces) fat-free
  sweetened condensed milk

1 block (8 ounces) nonfat cream
  cheese, softened to room
  temperature

1/2 cup key lime juice

Razzleberry Pie

Yield: *8 servings*

1 prebaked Crunchy Nutty Pie Crust (page 72) or Coconut Crunch Pie Crust (page 71)

FILLING

3 cups fresh strawberry halves

2 cups fresh raspberries

GLAZE

1/4 cup sugar

2 tablespoons cornstarch

1 1/4 cups water

1 package (4-serving size) regular or sugar-free raspberry gelatin

TOPPING

1 cup nonfat or light whipped topping (optional)

1. To make the glaze, place the sugar and cornstarch in a 1-quart pot, and stir to mix well. Add the water, and stir until the cornstarch is dissolved. Place the pot over medium heat, and cook, stirring constantly, for several minutes, or until the mixture comes to a boil and thickens slightly.

2. Remove the pot from the heat, and whisk in the gelatin. Continue to whisk for a minute or 2, or until the gelatin is completely dissolved. Set the glaze aside, stirring occasionally, for about 45 minutes, or until it has cooled to room temperature.

3. Place the glaze in the refrigerator. Stirring every few minutes, chill for about 10 minutes, or until the mixture has thickened slightly. It should be a little thicker than raw egg whites and a little thinner than pudding. Be careful not to chill the glaze too long, or it will congeal.

4. Place the berries in a large bowl, and toss to mix well. Pour the glaze over the berries, and toss gently to mix well. Spread the berry mixture evenly in the crust.

5. Cover and chill for at least 4 hours, or until set, before cutting into wedges and serving. Top each serving with 2 tablespoons of whipped topping, if desired.

NUTRITIONAL FACTS (PER SERVING)

Calories: 176 Carbohydrates: 41 g Cholesterol: 0 mg
Fat: 0.6 g Fiber: 4.1 g Protein: 4.2 g Sodium: 145 mg

You Save: Calories: 148 Fat: 10.4 g

LITE AND LUSCIOUS KEY LIME PIE

1. To make the filling, place the egg substitute in a blender and sprinkle the gelatin over the egg substitute. Set aside for 2 minutes to allow the gelatin to soften.

2. Place ¼ cup of the lime juice in a small bowl. If using a microwave oven, microwave on high for about 1 minute, or until it comes to a boil. If using a stovetop, place the juice in a small pot, and cook over medium heat for about 1 minute, or until it comes to a boil.

3. Add the boiling hot lime juice to the blender, place the lid on, and blend for about 1 minute, or until the ingredients are well mixed and the gelatin is completely dissolved. Add the remaining ¼ cup of lime juice, and blend for about 30 seconds, or until well mixed. Add the condensed milk, and blend for about 1 minute, or until well mixed. Immediately pour the filling into the crust.

4. Cover and chill for at least 6 hours, or until set, before cutting into wedges and serving. Top each serving with 2 tablespoons of whipped topping, if desired.

NUTRITIONAL FACTS (PER SERVING)
Calories: 226 Carbohydrates: 47 g Cholesterol: 2 mg
Fat: 1 g Fiber: 0.4 g Protein: 6.4 g Sodium: 128 mg

You Save: Calories: 101 Fat: 14.9 g

Yield: *8 servings*

1 prebaked Lite Graham Cracker Pie Crust (page 70) made with plain graham crackers, or Coconut Crunch Pie Crust (page 71)

FILLING

¼ cup fat-free egg substitute

1⅛ teaspoons unflavored gelatin

½ cup key lime juice, divided

1 can (14 ounces) fat-free sweetened condensed milk

TOPPING

1 cup nonfat or light whipped topping (optional)

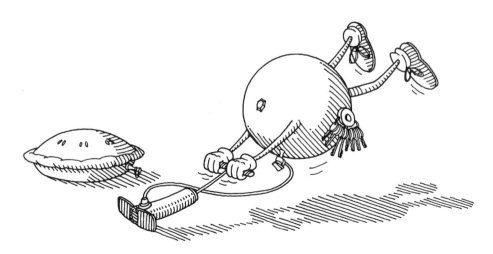

PEACH STREUSEL PIE

Yield: *8 servings*

1 unbaked Flaky Oat Pie Crust
(page 73)

FILLING

6 cups peeled sliced peaches
(about 6 medium-large)

1/4 cup plus 2 tablespoons light
brown sugar

1 tablespoon plus 2 teaspoons
cornstarch

1/2 teaspoon ground cinnamon

1/4 teaspoon ground nutmeg

TOPPING

1/4 cup plus 2 tablespoons
barley nugget cereal or
chopped toasted pecans
(page 167)

1/3 cup light brown sugar

1/4 cup plus 1 tablespoon
whole wheat pastry flour

1/2 teaspoon ground cinnamon

1 tablespoon plus 2 teaspoons
frozen white grape juice
concentrate, thawed

For variety, substitute sliced pears for the peaches.

1. To make the filling, place all of the filling ingredients in a large bowl, and toss to mix well.

2. Spread the mixture evenly in the pie shell. Cover the pie loosely with aluminum foil and bake at 400°F for 25 minutes, or until the fruit starts to soften and release its juices.

3. While the pie is baking, make the topping by placing the cereal or pecans, brown sugar, flour, and cinnamon in a small bowl. Stir to mix well. Add the juice concentrate, and stir until the mixture is moist and crumbly. Add a little more juice concentrate if the mixture seems too dry.

4. Remove the pie from the oven, and sprinkle the topping over the pie. Reduce the temperature to 375°F, and bake uncovered for 25 to 30 additional minutes, or until the topping is nicely browned and the filling is bubbly around the edges.

5. Allow the pie to cool at room temperature for at least 1 hour before cutting into wedges and serving. Serve warm or at room temperature, refrigerating any leftovers.

NUTRITIONAL FACTS (PER SERVING)

Calories: 243 Carbohydrates: 50 g Cholesterol: 0 mg
Fat: 3.9 g Fiber: 4.3 g Protein: 4.3 g Sodium: 136 mg

You Save: Calories: 193 Fat: 21.8 g

HARVEST PEAR PIE

For variety, substitute apples for the pears.

Yield: *8 servings*

1. Place the brown sugar, cornstarch, cinnamon, and nutmeg in a small bowl. Stir to mix well and set aside.

2. Place the pear slices in a large bowl. Add the sugar mixture, and toss to coat the pears with the mixture.

3. Arrange a layer of pear slices in a spiral pattern over the bottom of the prepared crust. Continue building layers in this manner until all of the slices are used.

4. Place the honey and juice concentrate in a small bowl, and stir to mix well. Drizzle the mixture over the top of the pie.

5. Spray a square of aluminum foil with nonstick cooking spray, and cover the pie loosely with the foil, placing it sprayed side down. Bake at 400°F for 15 minutes. Reduce the heat to 375°F, and bake for 40 additional minutes, or until the filling is bubbly around the edges. Remove the foil, and bake for 5 minutes more.

6. Allow the pie to cool to room temperature before cutting into wedges and serving.

1 unbaked Flaky Oat Pie Crust (page 73)

FILLING

1/4 cup light brown sugar

2 tablespoons plus 1 teaspoon cornstarch

1/2 teaspoon ground cinnamon

1/4 teaspoon ground nutmeg

6 cups sliced peeled pears (about 6 medium-large)

1/4 cup honey

1 tablespoon frozen orange juice concentrate, thawed

NUTRITIONAL FACTS (PER SERVING)
Calories: 223 Carbohydrates: 46 g Cholesterol: 0 mg
Fat: 3.9 g Fiber: 3.9 g Protein: 2.6 g Sodium: 79 mg

You Save: Calories: 82 Fat: 10.1 g

Sour Cream Apple Pie

Yield: *8 servings*

1 unbaked Flaky Oat Pie Crust
(page 73)

FILLING

1 cup nonfat sour cream

$^1/_2$ cup sugar

2 tablespoons unbleached flour

1 teaspoon vanilla extract

$^1/_4$ cup fat-free egg substitute

4 cups sliced peeled apples
(about 6 medium)

$^1/_4$ cup golden raisins (optional)

TOPPING

$^1/_4$ cup barley nugget cereal or
chopped walnuts

3 tablespoons whole wheat
pastry flour

3 tablespoons light brown sugar

$^1/_2$ teaspoon ground cinnamon

1 tablespoon frozen apple juice
concentrate, thawed

1. To make the filling, place the sour cream, sugar, flour, vanilla extract, and egg substitute in a large bowl, and stir to mix well. Add the apples and, if desired, the raisins, and toss to mix well.

2. Spread the mixture evenly in the pie shell. Spray a square of aluminum foil with nonstick cooking spray, and cover the pie loosely with the foil, placing it sprayed side down. Bake at 400°F for 25 minutes, or until the filling begins to set around the edges.

3. While the pie is baking, make the topping by placing the cereal or walnuts, flour, brown sugar, and cinnamon in a small bowl, and stirring to mix well. Add the juice concentrate, and stir until the mixture is moist and crumbly.

4. Remove the pie from the oven, remove and discard the foil, and sprinkle the pie with the topping. Reduce the oven temperature to 375°F, and bake uncovered for 25 to 30 additional minutes, or until the topping is nicely browned and the filling just starts to bubble around the edges.

5. Allow the pie to cool for at least 1 hour before cutting into wedges and serving. Serve warm or at room temperature, refrigerating any leftovers.

NUTRITIONAL FACTS (PER SERVING)
Calories: 249 Carbohydrates: 48 g Cholesterol: 0 mg
Fat: 3.9 g Fiber: 2.7 g Protein: 5.7 g Sodium: 126 mg

You Save: Calories: 221 Fat: 22.6 g

Pie Apples That Please

Dozens of varieties of apples are available in grocery stores. Many of the crisp, sweet varieties that we love to eat out of hand, however, can become mushy when cooked. For best results when making pies, crisps, and tarts, use a firm-textured variety such as Crispin, Fuji, Golden Delicious, Granny Smith, Jonathan, Newton Pippin, Rome, or Winesap. The sweetest of these varieties—Crispin, Fuji, Golden Delicious, and Rome—will require the least amount of added sugar.

Top Left: Peach Streusel Pie (page 82)
Top Right: Strawberry Angel Tarts (page 88)
Bottom: Apricot Custard Tart (page 85)

Top Right: Delightful Peach Trifle (page 113)
Center Left and Bottom Right: Tiramisu Treats (page 106)
Center Right and Bottom Left: Crème Caramel (page 115)

Apricot Custard Tart

1. To make the filling, pour the milk into a medium-sized bowl. Add the pudding mix, and beat with a wire whisk or electric mixer for 2 minutes, or until the mixture starts to thicken. Immediately pour the pudding into the cooled shell. Chill for at least 10 minutes, or until the pudding starts to set.

2. Drain the apricot halves well, reserving the juice and 1 of the halves. Arrange the remaining apricot halves, cut side down, on top of the pudding.

3. Place ½ cup of the reserved apricot juice, the reserved apricot half, the sugar, and the cornstarch in a blender, and blend until smooth. Pour the mixture into a small saucepan, place over medium heat, and cook, stirring constantly, until the mixture is thickened and bubbly. Allow to cool for 5 minutes. Then stir the mixture and drizzle it over the tart, covering the apricots.

4. Cover and chill for several hours, or until set, before cutting into wedges and serving.

Yield: *8 servings*

1 prebaked Lite Graham Cracker Pie Crust (page 70) made with plain graham crackers, and pressed over the bottom and 1 inch up the sides of a 9-inch tart or springform pan

FILLING

1¾ cups skim or 1% low-fat milk

1 package (4-serving size) instant fat-free vanilla pudding mix

TOPPING

1 can (1 pound) apricot halves in juice, undrained

2 tablespoons sugar

1 tablespoon corn-starch

NUTRITIONAL FACTS (PER SERVING)

Calories: 180 Carbohydrates: 40 g Cholesterol: 1 mg
Fat: 1.1 g Fiber: 0.9 g Protein: 3.9 g Sodium: 308 mg

You Save: Calories: 106 Fat: 10 g

Pear Phyllo Pie

Yield: *8 servings*

For variety, substitute peaches for the pears.

CRUST

2 tablespoons sugar

1/2 teaspoon ground cinnamon

1/4 teaspoon ground nutmeg

6 sheets (about 14 x 18 inches) phyllo pastry (about 5 ounces)

Butter-flavored cooking spray

FILLING

1/3 cup sugar

2 tablespoons cornstarch

1/4 teaspoon ground cinnamon

1/4 teaspoon ground nutmeg

6 cups sliced peeled pears (about 6 medium)

1/4 cup dark raisins or dried cranberries

1. To make the filling, place the sugar, cornstarch, cinnamon, and nutmeg in a small bowl. Stir to mix well, and set aside.

2. Place the pears in a large bowl. Sprinkle the sugar mixture over the pears, and toss to mix well. Toss in the raisins or cranberries, and set aside.

3. To make the crust, place the sugar, cinnamon, and nutmeg in a small dish, and stir to mix well. Set aside.

4. Spread the phyllo dough out on a clean dry surface. Cover the dough with plastic wrap to prevent it from drying out as you work. (Remove the sheets as you need them, being sure to re-cover the remaining dough.)

5. Remove 1 sheet of phyllo dough, and lay it on a clean dry surface. Spray the dough lightly with the cooking spray, and sprinkle with 1 teaspoon of the sugar mixture. Top with another phyllo sheet, spray with cooking spray, and sprinkle with 1 teaspoon of the sugar mixture.

6. Coat a 9-inch pie pan with nonstick cooking spray, and gently press the double-stacked phyllo sheets into the pan, allowing the ends to extend over the edges. Rotate the pie pan slightly, and repeat the procedure with 2 more sheets. Rotate the pan again, and repeat with the 2 remaining sheets.

7. Spread the filling evenly in the crust, and fold the phyllo in to cover the filling. Spray the top lightly with nonstick cooking spray, and sprinkle the remaining sugar mixture over the top. Using a sharp knife, score through the top crust to make 8 wedges. (This will prevent the top from flaking excessively when the pie is cut into serving pieces.)

8. Bake at 350°F for 45 minutes, or until the top is golden brown. Allow the pie to cool for 30 minutes to 1 hour before cutting into wedges and serving. Serve warm.

NUTRITIONAL FACTS (PER SERVING)
Calories: 183 Carbohydrates: 43 g Cholesterol: 0 mg
Fat: 1.4 g Fiber: 3.3 g Protein: 1.6 g Sodium: 69 mg

You Save: Calories: 103 Fat: 11.5 g

Making Pear Phyllo Pie.

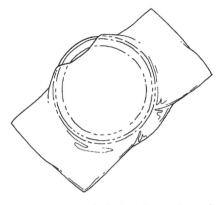

a. Press 1 set of plyllo sheets into the pan.

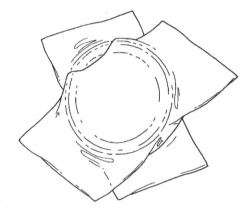

b. Rotate the pan, and press in another set of sheets.

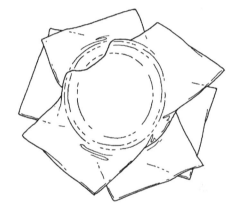

c. Rotate the pan, and press in the remaining sheets.

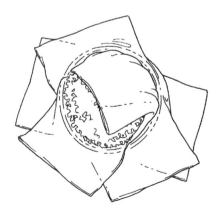

d. Fold the pastry over the filling.

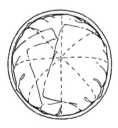

e. Score the pastry to make 8 wedges.

Strawberry Angel Tarts

Yield: *8 tarts*

8 Meringue Tart Shells, plain or almond (page 74)

2 cups nonfat or light whipped topping

3 cups sliced fresh strawberries

1/2 cup seedless strawberry jam

1. Place one tart shell on each of 8 serving plates. Fill the center of each tart shell with 1/4 cup of the whipped topping; then place 1/4 cup plus 2 tablespoons of the strawberries over the whipped topping, allowing a few of the berry slices to tumble down the sides.

2. Place the jam in a small pot. Cook over medium heat, stirring constantly, for about 1 minute, or until runny. Drizzle 1 tablespoon of the jam over the fruit, and serve immediately.

NUTRITIONAL FACTS (PER TART)

Calories: 176 Carbohydrates: 42 g Cholesterol: 0 mg
Fat: 0.8 g Fiber: 1.2 g Protein: 1.8 g Sodium: 52 mg

You Save: Calories: 81 Fat: 10 g

Variation

To make Raspberry Angel Tarts, substitute fresh raspberries for the strawberries, and chocolate syrup for the strawberry jam. (Do not heat the chocolate syrup; just drizzle it over the berries straight from the bottle.)

NUTRITIONAL FACTS (PER TART)

Calories: 172 Carbohydrates: 41 g Cholesterol: 0 mg
Fat: 1 g Fiber: 2.2 g Protein: 2.1 g Sodium: 62 mg

You Save: Calories: 81 Fat: 10 g

LEMON-RASPBERRY TARTS

1. To make the custard, place the sugar, cornstarch, and milk powder in a 1 1/2-quart pot, and stir to mix well. Slowly add the milk, stirring constantly with a wire whisk to mix well. Place the pot over medium heat, and cook, stirring constantly, for about 5 minutes, or until the mixture is thickened and bubbly.

2. Reduce the heat to medium-low. Place the egg substitute in a small bowl. Remove 1/4 cup of the hot milk mixture from the pot, and stir it into the egg substitute. Slowly whisk the egg mixture back into the pudding.

3. Add the lemon rind to the custard mixture, and cook and stir for a couple of minutes, or until the mixture thickens slightly and begins to boil. Remove the pot from the heat, and whisk in the lemon juice. Transfer the custard to a covered container, and chill for at least 4 hours, or until well-chilled and set.

4. When ready to assemble the tarts, place one tart shell on each of 6 serving plates. Stir the custard with a wire whisk until smooth. Then fill the center of each tart shell with 1/3 cup of the custard. Place 1/3 cup of the berries over the pudding.

5. Place the jam in a small pot. Cook over medium heat, stirring constantly, for about 1 minute, or until runny. Drizzle 2 teaspoons of the jam over the berries on each tart, and serve immediately.

Yield: *6 tarts*

6 Flaky Phyllo Tart Shells (page 76)

2 cups fresh raspberries

1/4 cup seedless raspberry jam

LEMON CUSTARD

1/2 cup plus 2 tablespoons sugar

1/4 cup cornstarch

3 tablespoons instant nonfat dry milk powder

1 1/2 cups skim or 1% low-fat milk

1/4 cup fat-free egg substitute

1 1/2 teaspoons freshly grated lemon rind, or 1/2 teaspoon dried

1/4 cup plus 3 tablespoons lemon juice

NUTRITIONAL FACTS (PER TART)
Calories: 248 Carbohydrates: 54 g Cholesterol: 1 mg
Fat: 1.3 g Fiber: 2.1 g Protein: 5.4 g Sodium: 136 mg

You Save: Calories: 153 Fat: 16.8 g

Mini Cherry Strudels

Yield: *24 pastries*

CRUSTS

12 sheets (about 14 x 18 inches) phyllo pastry (about 10 ounces)

Butter-flavored cooking spray

2 tablespoons powdered sugar (optional)

FILLING

1/4 cup plus 2 tablespoons sugar

2 tablespoons plus 1 1/2 teaspoons cornstarch

2 tablespoons white grape juice or orange juice

1 bag (1 pound) frozen pitted cherries, unthawed

GLAZE

1 tablespoon plus 1 teaspoon fat-free egg substitute

1 tablespoon plus 1 teaspoon sugar

1. To make the filling, place the sugar and cornstarch in a 1 1/2-quart pot, and stir to mix well. Stir in first the juice, and then the cherries. Place the pot over medium heat, and cook, stirring constantly, for about 5 minutes, or until the cherries are thawed and the mixture is thickened and bubbly. Remove the pot from the heat, and set aside to cool to room temperature.

2. To make the glaze, place the egg substitute and sugar in a small bowl. Stir to mix well, and set aside.

3. Spread the phyllo dough out on a clean, dry surface, with the short end facing you. Cut the phyllo lengthwise down the center to make 2 stacks, each measuring about 18 x 7 inches. Lay one stack on top of the other to make one 18-x-7-inch stack of 24 phyllo sheets. Cover the dough with plastic wrap to prevent it from drying out as you work. (Remove strips as you need them, being sure to re-cover the remaining dough.)

4. Remove 1 strip of the phyllo dough, and lay it flat on a clean dry surface. Spray the strip lightly with cooking spray. Fold the bottom up to form a double layer of phyllo measuring approximately 9 x 7 inches.

5. Spread 1 level tablespoon of filling over the bottom of the phyllo sheet, leaving a 2-inch margin on each side. Fold the left and right edges inward to enclose the filling. Then roll the pastry up from the bottom, jelly-roll style. Repeat steps 4 and 5 with the remaining filling and phyllo sheets to make 24 strudels. (At this point, the strudels may be frozen for future use. See the Time-Saving Tip on page 92.)

6. Coat a large baking sheet with nonstick cooking spray, and arrange the strudels on the sheets. Brush the top of each strudel with some of the glaze.

7. Bake at 375°F for 12 to 15 minutes, or until golden brown. Allow to cool for at least 15 minutes before serving warm. Sift the powdered sugar over the strudels just before serving, if desired.

NUTRITIONAL FACTS (PER PASTRY)
Calories: 65 Carbohydrates: 13 g Cholesterol: 0 mg
Fat: 0.9 g Fiber: 0.5 g Protein: 1.1 g Sodium: 59 mg

You Save: Calories: 31 Fat: 4.6 g

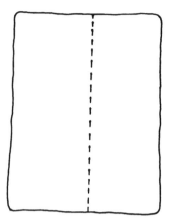

a. Cut the phyllo sheets into 2 long strips.

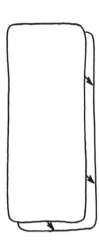

b. Lay 1 stack of strips on top of the other.

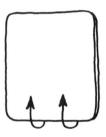

c. Fold the bottom of each strip up to double the strip.

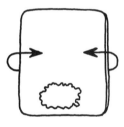

d. Spread the filling over the bottom of each strip. Fold the left and right edges inward.

Making Mini Cherry Strudels.

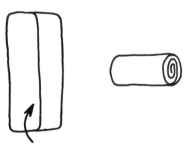

e. Roll the pastry up jelly-roll style.

Time-Saving Tip

To save time on the day you bake Mini Cherry Strudels (page 90) or Apricot-Apple Turnovers (page 94), prepare the pastries ahead of time to the point of baking, and arrange them in single layers in airtight containers, separating the layers with sheets of waxed paper. Then place the pastries in the freezer until needed. When ready to bake, arrange the frozen pastries on a coated sheet and allow them to sit at room temperature for 45 minutes before baking.

GREEK CUSTARD TARTS

Yield: *6 tarts*

6 Flaky Phyllo Tart Shells (page 76)

CUSTARD

2 1/4 cups skim or 1% low-fat milk

1/3 cup quick-cooking Cream of Wheat cereal or farina

1/3 cup sugar

1/2 cup fat-free egg substitute

3 tablespoons finely chopped dried apricots

1/2 teaspoon vanilla extract

1/8 teaspoon ground nutmeg

SYRUP

3 tablespoons orange juice

3/4 teaspoon cornstarch

3 tablespoons honey

1. To make the filling, place the milk in a 2-quart pot. Place the pot over medium heat, and cook, stirring constantly, until the milk begins to boil. Whisk in the cereal and the sugar, reduce the heat to medium-low, and cook, still stirring, for 3 to 4 additional minutes, or until the mixture thickens slightly.

2. Place the egg substitute in a small bowl. Remove 1/2 cup of the hot milk mixture from the pot, and stir it into the egg substitute. Slowly whisk the egg mixture back into the pot. Cook and stir for a couple of minutes, or until the mixture thickens slightly and begins to boil.

3. Remove the pot from the heat, and stir in the apricots, vanilla extract, and nutmeg. Allow the custard to cool at room temperature for 15 minutes.

4. To make the syrup, place the orange juice and cornstarch in a small pot, and stir to dissolve the cornstarch. Add the honey, and stir to mix well. Place over medium heat, and cook, stirring constantly, until the mixture thickens slightly and begins to boil. Remove the pot from the heat, and set aside.

5. To assemble the tarts, stir the custard, and place 1/2 cup of the warm mixture in each crust. Drizzle 1 tablespoon of the hot syrup over the custard and the edges of the pastry, and serve immediately.

NUTRITIONAL FACTS (PER TART)
Calories: 223 Carbohydrates: 46 g Cholesterol: 2 mg
Fat: 1.2 g Fiber: 1.5 g Protein: 7.4 g Sodium: 156 mg

You Save: Calories: 179 Fat: 16.8 g

Pumpkin Cheese Pie

1. To make the filling, place ¼ cup of the orange juice in a blender. Sprinkle the gelatin over the top, and set aside for 2 minutes to soften the gelatin.

2. Place the remaining ¼ cup of juice in a small pot, and bring to a boil over medium heat. Add the boiling hot juice to the blender, place the lid on, and blend at low speed for about 2 minutes, or until the gelatin is completely dissolved. Allow the mixture to sit for about 20 minutes, or until it cools to room temperature.

3. Add the cream cheese, pumpkin, brown sugar, pumpkin pie spice, and vanilla extract to the blender, and blend until smooth. Pour the mixture into a large bowl, cover, and chill for at least 4 hours, or until firm.

4. When the gelatin mixture has become firm, beat it with an electric mixer until it is the consistency of pudding. Gently fold in the whipped topping.

5. Spread the mixture in the cooled crust, swirling the top with a knife. Cover and chill for at least 4 hours, or until set, before cutting into wedges and serving.

NUTRITIONAL FACTS (PER SERVING)
Calories: 179 Carbohydrates: 36 g Cholesterol: 2 mg
Fat: 1.3 g Fiber: 1.2 g Protein: 6.3 g Sodium: 233 mg

You Save: Calories: 161 Fat: 19.3 g

Yield: *8 servings*

1 prebaked Lite Graham Cracker Pie Crust (page 70) made with plain graham crackers

FILLING

½ cup orange juice, divided

1 envelope (¼ ounce) unflavored gelatin

1 block (8 ounces) nonfat cream cheese, softened to room temperature

1 cup mashed cooked or canned pumpkin

⅔ cup light brown sugar

1½ teaspoons pumpkin pie spice

1 teaspoon vanilla extract

1 cup nonfat or light whipped topping

Apricot-Apple Turnovers

Yield: *20 pastries*

CRUSTS

10 sheets (about 14 x 18 inches) phyllo pastry (about 8 ounces)

Butter-flavored cooking spray

2 tablespoons powdered sugar (optional)

FILLING

3 cups chopped peeled apples (about 4 medium)

$1/2$ cup apricot preserves

2 tablespoons water, divided

1 tablespoon cornstarch

GLAZE

1 tablespoon plus 1 teaspoon fat-free egg substitute

1 tablespoon plus 1 teaspoon sugar

1. To make the filling, place the apples, apricot preserves, and 1 tablespoon of the water in a 2-quart pot. Stir to mix well, cover, and cook over medium-low heat, stirring occasionally, for about 5 minutes, or until the apples are tender.

2. Place the cornstarch and remaining tablespoon of water in a small bowl, and stir to dissolve the cornstarch. Add the cornstarch mixture to the simmering apple mixture, and cook, stirring constantly, for about 1 minute, or until the mixture is thick and bubbly. Remove the pot from the heat, and set aside to cool to room temperature.

3. To make the glaze, place the egg substitute and sugar in a small bowl. Stir to mix well, and set aside.

4. Spread the phyllo dough out on a clean, dry surface, with the short end facing you. Cut the phyllo lengthwise into 4 long strips, each measuring about $3^1/2$ x 18 inches. Cover the dough with plastic wrap to prevent it from drying out as you work. (Remove strips as you need them, being sure to re-cover the remaining dough.)

5. Remove 2 strips of phyllo dough and stack 1 on top of the other. Spray the top strip lightly with the cooking spray. Spread 1 level tablespoon of the filling over the bottom right-hand corner of the double phyllo strip. Fold the filled corner up and over to the left, so that the corner meets the left side of the strip. Continue folding in this manner until you form a triangle of dough. Repeat with the remaining filling and dough to make 20 pastries. (At this point, the turnovers may be frozen for future use. See the Time-Saving Tip on page 92.)

6. Coat a large baking sheet with nonstick cooking spray, and arrange the pastries seam side down on the sheet. Brush the top of each pastry with some of the glaze.

7. Bake at 375°F for 12 to 15 minutes, or until golden brown. Allow to cool for at least 15 minutes before serving warm. Sift the powdered sugar over the strudels just before serving, if desired.

NUTRITIONAL FACTS (PER PASTRY)
Calories: 59 Carbohydrates: 12.3 g Cholesterol: 0 mg
Fat: 0.8 g Fiber: 0.4 g Protein: 0.8 g Sodium: 50 mg

You Save: Calories: 36 Fat: 4.8 g

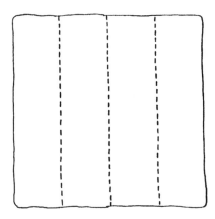

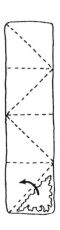

a. Cut the phyllo sheets into 4 strips.

b. Fold the filled corner up and over.

c. Continue folding to form a triangle

Making Apricot-Apple Turnovers.

Praline Pumpkin Pie

Yield: *8 servings*

1 prebaked Crunchy Nutty Pie Crust (page 72) or unbaked Flaky Oat Pie Crust (page 73)

FILLING

1³/₄ cups mashed cooked or canned pumpkin (about one 15-ounce can)

1 cup evaporated skimmed milk

¹/₂ cup fat-free egg substitute

³/₄ cup light brown sugar

2¹/₂ teaspoons pumpkin pie spice*

1¹/₂ teaspoons vanilla extract

TOPPING

3 tablespoons light brown sugar

3 tablespoons honey crunch wheat germ or finely chopped toasted pecans (page 167)

*If you don't have any pumpkin pie spice on hand, you can use 1¹/₂ teaspoons ground cinnamon, ¹/₂ teaspoon ground nutmeg, and ¹/₂ teaspoon ground ginger.

1. To make the topping, place the brown sugar and the wheat germ or pecans in a small bowl, and stir to mix well. Set aside.

2. To make the filling, place all of the filling ingredients in a blender, and process until smooth.

3. Pour the filling into the crust, and bake at 400°F for 15 minutes. Sprinkle the topping over the top of the pie. Reduce the oven temperature to 350°F, and bake for about 45 additional minutes, or until a sharp knife inserted in the center of the pie comes out clean. (Note that if you use the Crunchy Nutty Pie Crust, you will need to shield the edges of the crust during baking with aluminum foil, as directed on page 72.)

4. Allow the pie to cool to room temperature before cutting into wedges and serving. Or refrigerate and serve chilled.

NUTRITIONAL FACTS (PER SERVING)

Calories: 197 Carbohydrates: 41 g Cholesterol: 1 mg
Fat: 0.8 g Fiber: 3.1 g Protein: 7.9 g Sodium: 176 mg

You Save: Calories: 138 Fat: 14.9 g

5

Creamy Puddings, Mousses, and Trifles

Rich, creamy, and inviting, puddings are among the most popular of comfort foods. Puddings are versatile, too. Hearty noodle puddings and baked custards make healthful snacks, or can provide a sweet conclusion to a home-style family dinner. Elegant mousses and trifles fill the bill when you want a dessert for that special-occasion dinner.

Unfortunately, most puddings and mousses are loaded with an unhealthy amount of fat. In traditional recipes, whole milk, cream, and egg yolks top the list of ingredients. Consider, for instance, a traditionally prepared dish of chocolate mousse. Believe it or not, just one moderate serving can contain up to 25 grams of fat!

The good news is that puddings are among the easiest of desserts to prepare with little or no fat. But can you skim the fat without sacrificing flavor? Absolutely! Fat-saving products like evaporated skimmed milk, nonfat sour cream, and nonfat whipped toppings add creamy richness with no fat, and with a lot less calories than their traditional counterparts. More fat and calories are saved by using fat-free egg substitutes instead of whole eggs to thicken puddings and custards.

Besides being ultra-low in fat, many of the desserts found in the following pages contain only moderate amounts of sugar. Fruits and juices, as well as sweet flavorings like cinnamon, add natural sweetness to many of these recipes, reducing the need for added sugar.

This chapter offers a pleasing assortment of deceptively rich-tasting desserts, ranging from down-home Sour Cream and Apple Bread Pudding to elegant Chocolate-Hazelnut Mousse. But the proof is in the pudding. So whip up a creamy dish of comfort, and enjoy a treat that is so sweetly satisfying, even you will find it hard to believe that it's also guilt-free!

Sour Cream and Apple Bread Pudding

Yield: *8 servings*

5 cups ¹/₂-inch cubes firm multigrain or French bread (about 6 ounces)

1³/₄ cups skim or 1% low-fat milk

¹/₂ cup nonfat sour cream

¹/₂ cup plus 2 tablespoons fat-free egg substitute

¹/₄ cup plus 2 tablespoons sugar

1¹/₂ teaspoons vanilla extract

³/₄ cup diced peeled apples (about 1 medium)

¹/₄ cup golden or dark raisins

TOPPING

1 tablespoon plus 1¹/₂ teaspoons sugar

¹/₈ teaspoon ground cinnamon

For variety, substitute diced peaches for the apples.

1. Place the bread cubes in a large bowl and set aside.

2. Place the milk, sour cream, egg substitute, sugar, and vanilla extract in a large bowl, and whisk until smooth. Pour the milk mixture over the bread cubes, and set aside for 10 minutes.

3. Stir the apples and raisins into the bread mixture. Coat a 2-quart casserole dish with nonstick cooking spray, and pour the mixture into the dish.

4. To make the topping, place the sugar and cinnamon in a small bowl, and stir to mix well. Sprinkle the topping over the pudding.

5. Bake at 350°F for about 1 hour, or until a sharp knife inserted in the center of the dish comes out clean. Allow to cool at room temperature for 45 minutes before serving. Serve warm or at room temperature, refrigerating any leftovers.

NUTRITIONAL FACTS (PER ³/₄-CUP SERVING)

Calories: 161 Carbohydrates: 32 g Cholesterol: 1 mg
Fat: 0.9 g Fiber: 1.8 g Protein: 6.7 g Sodium: 180 mg

You Save: Calories: 69 Fat: 10 g

Rum-Raisin Bread Pudding

1. Place the raisins and rum in a small bowl, and stir to mix well. Set aside for at least 15 minutes.

2. Place the bread cubes in a large bowl and set aside.

3. Place the evaporated milk, skim milk, egg substitute, brown sugar, and vanilla extract in a large bowl, and whisk until smooth. Pour the milk mixture over the bread cubes, and set aside for 10 minutes.

4. Stir the raisin mixture into the bread mixture. Coat a 1½-quart casserole dish with nonstick cooking spray, and pour the mixture into the dish. Sprinkle the sugar over the pudding.

5. Bake at 350°F for about 1 hour, or until a sharp knife inserted in the center of the dish comes out clean. Allow to cool at room temperature for 45 minutes before serving. Serve warm or at room temperature, refrigerating any leftovers.

Yield: *6 servings*

¼ cup dark raisins

2 tablespoons light rum

4 cups ½-inch cubes firm multigrain or oatmeal bread (about 5 ounces)

1 can (12 ounces) evaporated skimmed milk

½ cup skim or 1% low-fat milk

¼ cup plus 2 tablespoons fat-free egg substitute

¼ cup plus 2 tablespoons light brown sugar

1 teaspoon vanilla extract

1 tablespoon sugar

NUTRITIONAL FACTS (PER ¾-CUP SERVING)
Calories: 184 Carbohydrates: 33 g Cholesterol: 2 mg
Fat: 0.4 g Fiber: 1.1 g Protein: 8.4 g Sodium: 227 mg

You Save: Calories: 65 Fat: 10.6 g

CREAMY TApioca PuddiNG

Yield: *5 servings*

3 cups skim or 1% low-fat milk

1/3 cup instant nonfat dry milk powder

1/4 cup plus 2 tablespoons small pearl tapioca

1/4 cup plus 2 tablespoons sugar

1/3 cup fat-free egg substitute

1 teaspoon vanilla extract

1. Place the milk, milk powder, tapioca, and sugar in a 2-quart pot, and stir to mix well. Place the pot over medium heat, and cook, stirring frequently, until the mixture comes to a boil. Reduce the heat to low, and simmer, stirring frequently, for 5 minutes, or until the tapioca begins to swell and becomes translucent.

2. Place the egg substitute in a small bowl, and stir in 1/2 cup of the hot tapioca mixture. Slowly stir the mixture back into the pot. Cook and stir over low heat for another couple of minutes, or until the mixture begins to boil and thickens slightly.

3. Remove the pot from the heat, and stir in the vanilla extract. Allow the pudding to cool at room temperature for 15 minutes.

4. Divide the pudding among five 8-ounce serving dishes, cover, and chill for several hours, or until thick and creamy. (The mixture will thicken as it cools.) Serve chilled.

NUTRITIONAL FACTS (PER 2/3-CUP SERVING)

Calories: 176 Carbohydrates: 44 g Cholesterol: 3 mg
Fat: 0.3 g Fiber: 0.1 g Protein: 11.3 g Sodium: 175 mg

You Save: Calories: 55 Fat: 7.5 g

Variation

To make Tapioca Pudding Parfaits, prepare the pudding as directed through Step 3. Then pour the warm pudding into a medium-sized bowl, cover, and chill for several hours or until thick and creamy. To assemble the parfaits, place 2 tablespoons of light cherry, blueberry, chopped apple, or chopped peach pie filling in the bottom of each of six 8-ounce parfait or wine glasses. Top the pie filling with 1/4 cup of the pudding; then repeat the layers. Cover each parfait with plastic wrap, and chill for at least 2 hours before serving.

NUTRITIONAL FACTS (PER 3/4-CUP SERVING)

Calories: 199 Carbohydrates: 42 g Cholesterol: 3 mg
Fat: 0.7 g Fiber: 0.5 g Protein: 8 g Sodium: 123 mg

You Save: Calories: 67 Fat: 6 g

Pineapple Tapioca Pudding

1. Place the milk, milk powder, tapioca, and sugar in a 2-quart pot, and stir to mix well. Place the pot over medium heat, and cook, stirring frequently, until the mixture comes to a boil. Reduce the heat to low, and simmer, stirring frequently, for 5 minutes, or until the tapioca begins to swell and becomes translucent.

2. Place the egg substitute in a small bowl, and stir in 1/2 cup plus 2 tablespoons of the hot tapioca mixture. Slowly stir the mixture back into the pot. Cook and stir over low heat for another couple of minutes, or until the mixture begins to boil and thickens slightly.

3. Remove the pot from the heat, and stir in the pineapple with its juice and the vanilla extract. Allow the pudding to cool at room temperature for 15 minutes.

4. Divide the pudding among five 8-ounce serving dishes, cover, and chill for several hours, or until thick and creamy. (The mixture will thicken as it cools.) Serve chilled.

Yield: *5 servings*

2 1/2 cups skim or 1% low-fat milk

1/3 cup instant nonfat dry milk powder

1/4 cup plus 2 tablespoons small pearl tapioca

1/4 cup plus 2 tablespoons sugar

1/2 cup plus 2 tablespoons fat-free egg substitute

1 can (8 ounces) crushed pineapple in juice, undrained

1 teaspoon vanilla extract

NUTRITIONAL FACTS (PER 3/4-CUP SERVING)

Calories: 197 Carbohydrates: 41 g Cholesterol: 3 mg
Fat: 0.3 g Fiber: 0.4 g Protein: 9 g Sodium: 138 mg

You Save: Calories: 63 Fat: 6.9 g

Variation

To make Ambrosia Tapioca Pudding, prepare the pudding as directed through Step 3. Then pour the warm pudding into a medium-sized bowl, cover, and chill for several hours or until thick and creamy. Add 1 can (10 ounces) well-drained mandarin oranges, 1 cup miniature marshmallows, and 1/4 cup shredded sweetened coconut, and stir to mix well. Cover and chill for at least 2 hours. Divide the pudding among seven 8-ounce dessert dishes, and serve immediately.

NUTRITIONAL FACTS (PER 3/4-CUP SERVING)

Calories: 192 Carbohydrates: 39 g Cholesterol: 2 mg
Fat: 1.4 g Fiber: 0.6 g Protein: 6.8 g Sodium: 112 mg

You Save: Calories: 51 Fat: 6.6 g

Cherry Chiffon Pudding

Yield: *4 servings*

1 cup canned light (reduced-sugar) cherry pie filling

1 can (8 ounces) crushed pineapple in juice, well drained

3/4 cup regular or sugar-free nonfat or low-fat vanilla yogurt, or 3/4 cup yogurt cheese made from nonfat or low-fat vanilla yogurt (page 23)*

1/2 cup miniature marshmallows

1/4 cup chopped toasted pecans (page 167) (optional)

1 cup nonfat or light whipped topping

*Using yogurt cheese instead of yogurt will result in a thicker, creamier pudding.

1. Place the pie filling, pineapple, and yogurt or yogurt cheese in a large bowl, and stir to mix well. Fold in the marshmallows and, if desired, the pecans. Gently fold in the whipped topping.

2. Divide the pudding among four 8-ounce wine glasses or dessert dishes. Cover the puddings, and chill for at least 2 hours before serving.

NUTRITIONAL FACTS (PER 3/4-CUP SERVING)

Calories: 192 Carbohydrates: 43 g Cholesterol: 1 mg
Fat: 0.9 g Fiber: 0.8 g Protein: 3.1 g Sodium: 52 mg

You Save: Calories: 149 Fat: 15.3 g

Strawberries n' Cream

For variety, substitute raspberry gelatin and frozen raspberries for the strawberry gelatin and frozen strawberries.

Yield: *6 servings*

1. Drain the strawberries, reserving the juice. Set both the strawberries and the juice aside.

2. Pour the boiling water into a blender, and sprinkle the gelatin over the top. Cover with the lid, and carefully blend at low speed for about 30 seconds, or until the gelatin is completely dissolved. Allow the mixture to sit in the blender for about 20 minutes, or until it reaches room temperature.

3. When the gelatin mixture has cooled to room temperature, add the sour cream and the reserved juice from the strawberries, and blend for about 30 seconds, or until well mixed. Pour the mixture into a large bowl, and chill for 15 minutes. Stir the mixture; it should be the consistency of pudding. If it is too thin, return it to the refrigerator for a few minutes.

4. When the gelatin mixture has reached the proper consistency, stir it with a wire whisk until smooth. Gently fold in first the strawberries, and then the whipped topping.

5. Divide the mixture among six 8-ounce wine glasses, cover, and chill for at least 3 hours, or until set, before serving.

1 package (10 ounces) frozen sweetened sliced strawberries, undrained

1/2 cup boiling water

1 package (4-serving size) regular or sugar-free strawberry gelatin

1/2 cup nonfat sour cream

2 cups nonfat or light whipped topping

NUTRITIONAL FACTS (PER 3/4-CUP SERVING)

Calories: 159 Carbohydrates: 36 g Cholesterol: 0 mg
Fat: 0.9 g Fiber: 0.9 g Protein: 2.5 g Sodium: 67 mg

You Save: Calories: 117 Fat: 17.9 g

PEACH BAVARIAN

Yield: *6 servings*

1 can (1 pound) sliced peaches in juice, undrained

1 package (4-serving size) peach gelatin mix

1 cup regular or sugar-free nonfat peach yogurt

2 cups nonfat or light whipped topping

For variety, substitute canned apricots and apricot gelatin for the canned peaches and peach gelatin.

1. Drain the peaches, reserving the juice. Dice the peaches and set aside.

2. Place ¾ cup of the reserved juice in a small pot. (If there is not enough juice, add water to bring the volume to ¾ cup.) Bring the mixture to a boil over high heat.

3. Pour the boiling juice into a large bowl. Sprinkle the gelatin over the top, and stir for about 3 minutes, or until the gelatin is completely dissolved. Set the mixture aside for about 20 minutes, or until it reaches room temperature.

4. When the gelatin mixture has cooled to room temperature, whisk in the yogurt. Chill for 15 minutes. Stir the mixture; it should be the consistency of pudding. If it is too thin, return it to the refrigerator for a few minutes.

5. When the gelatin mixture has reached the proper consistency, stir it with a wire whisk until smooth. Gently fold in first the diced peaches, and then the whipped topping.

6. Divide the mixture among six 8-ounce wine glasses, cover, and chill for at least 3 hours, or until set, before serving.

NUTRITIONAL FACTS (PER ¾-CUP SERVING)
Calories: 161 Carbohydrates: 36.7 g Cholesterol: 0 mg
Fat: 0.9 g Fiber: 1.3 g Protein: 3.3 g Sodium: 77 mg

You Save: Calories: 160 Fat: 21.8 g

Banana Pudding Parfaits

For variety, substitute chocolate pudding and chocolate wafers for the vanilla pudding and vanilla wafers.

1. Use the skim milk to prepare the pudding according to package directions. Cover the mixture and chill for at least 2 hours for cook-and-serve pudding or 30 minutes for instant pudding, or until chilled and thickened.

2. To assemble the parfaits, spoon 1 tablespoon of pudding into the bottom of each of four 8-ounce wine or parfait glasses. Top the pudding with 2½ tablespoons of sliced bananas, 2 crumbled vanilla wafers, and a scant ¼ cup of pudding. Repeat the banana, wafer, and pudding layers.

3. Serve immediately, topping each serving with a rounded tablespoon of whipped topping, if desired. Or cover each glass with plastic wrap and chill for up to 2 hours before serving.

Yield: *4 servings*

- 2 cups skim or 1% low-fat milk

- 1 package (4-serving size) fat-free cook-and-serve or instant vanilla pudding mix, regular or sugar-free

- 1¼ cups sliced bananas (about 1¼ large)

- 16 reduced-fat vanilla wafers

- ½ cup nonfat or light whipped topping (optional)

NUTRITIONAL FACTS (PER 1-CUP SERVING)
Calories: 237 Carbohydrates: 51 g Cholesterol: 2 mg
Fat: 2.1 g Fiber: 1.1 g Protein: 5.6 g Sodium: 229 mg

You Save: Calories: 46 Fat: 6 g

TIRAMISU TREATS

Yield: *4 servings*

8 unsplit ladyfingers

BERRY MIXTURE

1 cup fresh or frozen (thawed) sliced strawberries or raspberries

1 tablespoon sugar

LIQUEUR MIXTURE

1/4 cup coffee liqueur

1 1/2 teaspoons cocoa powder

PUDDING MIXTURE

2 cups skim or 1% low-fat milk

1 package (4-serving size) fat-free cook-and-serve or instant vanilla pudding mix, regular or sugar-free

TOPPINGS (OPTIONAL)

1/2 cup nonfat or light whipped topping

1/2 teaspoon cocoa powder

Creamy pudding replaces high-fat mascarpone cheese in this slimmed-down recipe.

1. To make the berry mixture, place the berries and sugar in a small bowl, and mash with a fork. Set aside.

2. To make the liqueur mixture, place the liqueur and cocoa in a small bowl, and stir to mix. Set aside.

3. To make the pudding mixture, use the skim or low-fat milk to prepare the pudding according to package directions. Cover and chill for at least 2 hours for cook-and-serve pudding or for at least 30 minutes for instant pudding, or until chilled and thickened.

4. To assemble the desserts, place 1 tablespoon of the berry mixture in the bottom of each of four 8-ounce parfait or wine glasses. Crumble one ladyfinger over the berries in each glass. Drizzle 1 1/2 teaspoons of liqueur over each ladyfinger, and top with 1/4 cup of the pudding. Repeat the berry, ladyfinger, liqueur, and pudding layers.

5. Cover each glass with plastic wrap, and chill for at least 3 hours. If desired, top each serving with a rounded tablespoon of whipped topping and a sprinkling of cocoa powder just before serving.

NUTRITIONAL FACTS (PER 7/8-CUP SERVING)

Calories: 260 Carbohydrates: 51 g Cholesterol: 27 mg
Fat: 1.2 g Fiber: 1.1 g Protein: 5.8 g Sodium: 265 mg

You Save: Calories: 253 Fat: 34.3 g

Black Forest Pudding

1. Use the skim milk to prepare the pudding according to package directions. Cover the mixture and chill for at least 2 hours for cook-and-serve pudding or for at least 30 minutes for instant pudding, or until chilled and thickened.

2. Arrange 4 of the cake slices in a single layer over the bottom of a 2-quart glass bowl, and drizzle 1 tablespoon of liqueur over the cake slices. Spread half of the pudding over the cake, and follow with a layer of half the pie filling. Repeat the cake, liqueur, pudding, and pie filling layers.

3. To make the topping, place the whipped topping in a medium-sized bowl, and gently fold in the yogurt. Spread the mixture over the top of the pie filling.

4. Cover the dish, and chill for at least 3 hours. If desired, sprinkle the almonds over the top just before serving.

NUTRITIONAL FACTS (PER ¾-CUP SERVING)
Calories: 222 Carbohydrates: 48 g Cholesterol: 1 mg
Fat: 1 g Fiber: 0.8 g Protein: 4.8 g Sodium: 224 mg

You Save: Calories: 277 Fat: 23.1 g

Yield: *9 servings*

2 cups skim or 1% low-fat milk

1 package (4-serving size) fat-free cook-and-serve or instant chocolate pudding mix, regular or sugar-free

8 slices (½-inch each) fat-free chocolate loaf cake

2 tablespoons amaretto or hazelnut liqueur

1 can (20 ounces) light (reduced-sugar) cherry pie filling

TOPPING

1½ cups nonfat or light whipped topping

¾ cup regular or sugar-free nonfat or low-fat vanilla yogurt

3 tablespoons sliced toasted almonds (page 167) (optional)

Apple Cheesecake Parfaits

Yield: *4 servings*

3/4 cup nonfat cream cheese, softened to room temperature

2 tablespoons sugar

2 tablespoons skim or 1% low-fat milk

3/4 cup yogurt cheese made from vanilla yogurt (page 23)

1 1/4 cups canned light (reduced-sugar) apple pie filling

1/4 cup crushed reduced-fat graham crackers, low-fat vanilla wafers, or low-fat gingersnaps

For variety, substitute light cherry pie filling for the light apple pie filling.

1. Place the cream cheese and sugar in a medium-sized bowl, and beat with an electric mixer until smooth. Add the milk, and beat until smooth. Add the yogurt cheese, and beat just until well mixed.

2. To assemble the parfaits, spoon 2 1/2 tablespoons of the pie filling into the bottom of each of each of four 8-ounce wine or parfait glasses. Top with 2 1/2 tablespoons of the cheese mixture. Repeat the pie filling and cheese layers.

3. Cover each glass with plastic wrap, and chill for at least 3 hours. Top each parfait with a tablespoon of the graham cracker or cookie crumbs just before serving.

NUTRITIONAL FACTS (PER 2/3-CUP SERVING)

Calories: 191 Carbohydrates: 34 g Cholesterol: 4 mg
Fat: 0.8 g Fiber: 0.6 g Protein: 11.9 g Sodium: 227 mg

You Save: Calories: 227 Fat: 25.2 g

Apple-Raisin Risotto

1. Place the rice and milk in a heavy 2½-quart pot, and place over medium heat. Cook, stirring frequently, until the milk comes to a boil. Reduce the heat to low, cover, and simmer, stirring occasionally, for 15 minutes.

2. Add the apple to the rice mixture. Cover and simmer, stirring occasionally, for 10 additional minutes, or until the most of the milk has been absorbed and the rice is tender.

3. Add the raisins to the rice mixture. Cover and simmer for about 2 minutes, or until the raisins begin to soften.

4. Place the evaporated milk, egg substitute, sugar, cinnamon, and vanilla extract in a small bowl, and stir to mix well. Slowly stir the evaporated milk mixture into the rice mixture. Cook, stirring constantly, for 3 to 5 minutes, or until the mixture is thick and creamy.

5. Remove the pot from the heat, and allow to cool at room temperature for 10 minutes. Stir the pudding, and divide among six 8-ounce dessert dishes. Serve warm, refrigerating any leftovers.

Yield: *6 servings*

½ cup plus 2 tablespoons uncooked arborio rice*

3 cups skim or 1% low-fat milk

1 cup chopped peeled Granny Smith or Rome apple (about 1 large)

¼ cup dark raisins

¼ cup plus 2 tablespoons evaporated skimmed milk

¼ cup plus 2 tablespoons fat-free egg substitute

¼ cup plus 2 tablespoons sugar

¼ teaspoon ground cinnamon

1 teaspoon vanilla extract

*Arborio rice, a short grain rice that is best for making risotto, is available in most supermarkets and specialty stores.

NUTRITIONAL FACTS (PER ¾-CUP SERVING)
Calories: 187 Carbohydrates: 39 g Cholesterol: 2 mg
Fat: 0.4 g Fiber: 0.7 g Protein: 8 g Sodium: 107 mg

You Save: Calories: 95 Fat: 13.9 g

Trimming the Fat From Your Favorite Pudding Recipes

It's a shame that most pudding recipes are so high in fat because, when properly prepared, pudding makes a great low-fat snack or dessert. Happily, it's easy to do a slimming makeover of virtually any pudding recipe. Just use the following table to replace the high-fat ingredients in your own treasured pudding recipes with low-fat and no-fat ingredients. You'll find that any pudding—from hearty bread puddings and light-as-air mousses to custard-filled trifles—can be made ultra-light without sacrificing the creamy richness you love.

Fat-Saving Substitutions in Puddings

Instead of	Use	You Save	Special Considerations
1 cup whole milk	1 cup skim milk	65 calories 8 g fat	For extra richness, add 2 table-spoons of instant nonfat dry milk powder to each cup of skim or low-fat milk.
	1 cup 1% low-fat milk	50 calories 6 g fat	
1 cup cream	1 cup evaporated skimmed milk	622 calories 88 g fat	This ingredient may be used in cooked puddings and custards.
	1 cup skim milk mixed with 1/3 cup instant nonfat dry milk powder	622 calories 88 g fat	This ingredient may be used in cooked puddings and custards.
	2/3 cup nonfat ricotta cheese blended with 1/3 cup skim milk until smooth	674 calories 88 g fat	This ingredient may be used only in uncooked puddings and mousses.
1 cup regular cream cheese	1 cup nonfat cream cheese	600 calories 80 g fat	For best results, use a firm block-style nonfat cream cheese.
	1 cup reduced-fat (Neufchâtel) cream cheese	240 calories 26 g fat	
1 cup sour cream	1 cup nonfat sour cream	252 calories 48 g fat	Some brands of sour cream will separate when heated. Choose a brand like Land O Lakes or Breakstone's, both of which are heat-stable, if the sour cream will be used in a cooked pudding.

Instead of	Use	You Save	Special Considerations
1 cup sour cream	1 cup nonfat yogurt	355 calories 48 g fat	All yogurts will separate if heated. To prevent this, stir 2 tablespoons of flour or 1 tablespoon of cornstarch into each cup of yogurt before adding it to a pudding that will be cooked.
1 cup whipped cream	1 cup light whipped topping	250 calories 36 g fat	
	1 cup fat-free whipped topping	290 calories 42 g fat	
1 cup butter or margarine	½ cup Butter Buds liquid	1,500 calories 176 g fat	
	¾ cup reduced-fat margarine or light butter	800–1,200 calories 88–112 g fat	
1 large egg	3 tablespoons fat-free egg substitute	60 calories 5 g fat	
1 egg yolk	1 tablespoon fat-free egg substitute	40 calories 5 g fat	
1 ounce baking chocolate	3 tablespoons cocoa powder plus 1 tablespoon water or another liquid	111 calories 13.5 g fat	

CHOCOLATE-HAZELNUT MOUSSE

Yield: *4 servings*

³⁄₄ cup plus 2 tablespoons skim
or 1% low-fat milk, divided

1 envelope (¼ ounce)
unflavored gelatin

1 cup nonfat ricotta cheese

¼ cup plus 2 tablespoons light
brown sugar

2 tablespoons Dutch processed
cocoa powder

2 tablespoons Frangelico
(hazelnut) liqueur

1 teaspoon vanilla extract

1 cup nonfat or light whipped
topping

TOPPINGS (OPTIONAL)

¼ cup plus 2 tablespoons nonfat or light whipped topping

2 teaspoons Frangelico
(hazelnut) liqueur

1 tablespoon plus 1 teaspoon
chopped toasted hazelnuts
(page 167)

For variety, substitute amaretto or coffee liqueur for the hazelnut liqueur.

1. Place ¼ cup plus 2 tablespoons of the milk in a blender, and sprinkle the gelatin over the top. Set aside for 2 minutes to allow the gelatin to soften.

2. Place the remaining ½ cup of milk in a small pot, and cook over medium heat, stirring frequently, until the milk comes to a boil.

3. Add the boiling hot milk to the blender, place the lid on, and blend at low speed for about 2 minutes, or until the gelatin is completely dissolved. Set the mixture aside for about 20 minutes, or until it cools to room temperature.

4. Add the ricotta, brown sugar, cocoa, liqueur, and vanilla extract to the blender, and blend until smooth. Pour the mixture into a large bowl, cover, and chill for at least 6 hours, or until the mixture is completely set and very firm. (You can complete this step the day before you prepare the mousse and let it chill overnight, if you wish.)

5. When the gelatin mixture has set, beat it with an electric mixer until it is the consistency of pudding. Gently fold in the whipped topping.

6. Divide the mixture among four 8-ounce wine glasses or dessert dishes. Cover each glass with plastic wrap, and chill for at least 3 hours. Top each serving with a rounded tablespoon of whipped topping, a splash of liqueur, and a sprinkling of nuts just before serving, if desired.

NUTRITIONAL FACTS (PER ¾-CUP SERVING)
Calories: 199 Carbohydrates: 32 g Cholesterol: 5 mg
Fat: 0.9 g Fiber: 0.8 g Protein: 13.7 g Sodium: 108 mg

You Save: Calories: 221 Fat: 26.5 g

Delightful Peach Trifle

1. Use the skim milk to prepare the pudding according to package directions. Cover the mixture and chill for at least 2 hours for cook-and-serve pudding or for at least 30 minutes for instant pudding, or until chilled and thickened.

2. To make the peach mixture, place the peaches, sugar, and liqueur in a medium-sized bowl, and stir to mix well. Set aside for 15 minutes to allow the juices to develop.

3. To make the cake mixture, arrange the cake slices on a flat surface, and spread each slice with 1 teaspoon of the jam.

4. To assemble the trifle, arrange half of the cake slices, jam side up, in a single layer over the bottom of a 2-quart glass bowl. Spread half of the peach mixture over the cake slices, and cover the peaches with half of the pudding. Repeat the cake, peach, and pudding layers.

5. To make the topping, place the whipped topping in a medium-sized bowl, and gently fold in the yogurt. Spread the mixture over the top of the pudding.

6. Cover and chill for at least 3 hours. If desired, sprinkle the almonds over the top just before serving.

Yield: *9 servings*

PUDDING MIXTURE

2 cups skim or 1% low-fat milk

1 package (4-serving size) fat-free cook-and-serve or instant vanilla pudding mix, regular or sugar-free

PEACH MIXTURE

2 cups diced peeled fresh peaches

1 tablespoon sugar

2 tablespoons amaretto liqueur

CAKE MIXTURE

8 slices ($^1\!/_2$-inch each) fat-free vanilla loaf cake or fat-free pound cake

2 tablespoons plus 2 teaspoons raspberry jam

TOPPING

1$^1\!/_2$ cups nonfat or light whipped topping

$^3\!/_4$ cup regular or sugar-free nonfat or low-fat vanilla yogurt

3 tablespoons sliced toasted almonds (page 167) (optional)

NUTRITIONAL FACTS (PER ¾-CUP SERVING)

Calories: 205 Carbohydrates: 45 g Cholesterol: 2 mg
Fat: 0.8 g Fiber: 1 g Protein: 4.3 g Sodium: 206 mg

You Save: Calories: 123 Fat: 16.4 g

Baked Brown Rice Pudding

Yield: *6 servings*

²/₃ cup uncooked brown rice

1 cup water

2¹/₂ cups skim or 1% low-fat milk, divided

¹/₂ teaspoon dried grated orange rind, or 1¹/₂ teaspoons fresh

¹/₂ cup plus 2 tablespoons fat-free egg substitute

¹/₄ cup plus 2 tablespoons sugar

¹/₄ cup instant nonfat dry milk powder

1¹/₂ teaspoons vanilla extract

¹/₄ cup golden or dark raisins or dried cherries

Ground nutmeg (garnish)

1. Place the rice, water, 1 cup of the milk, and the orange rind in a 2¹/₂-quart pot, and bring to a boil over medium-high heat. Reduce the heat to low, cover, and simmer for 45 minutes, or until the rice is tender and most of the liquid has been absorbed.

2. Place the remaining 1¹/₂ cups of milk and all of the egg substitute, sugar, milk powder, and vanilla extract in a medium-sized bowl. Stir to mix well.

3. Add the milk mixture and the raisins or dried cherries to the rice, and cook over medium heat, stirring constantly, for about 5 minutes, or until the mixture thickens slightly.

4. Coat a 1¹/₂-quart casserole dish with nonstick cooking spray. Pour the pudding into the dish, and sprinkle with the nutmeg. Set the casserole dish in a large roasting pan, and add hot tap water to the pan until it reaches halfway up the sides of the dish.

5. Bake uncovered at 325°F for 50 minutes, or until a sharp knife inserted midway between the center of the dish and the rim comes out clean.

6. Allow the pudding to cool at room temperature for at least 1 hour. Serve warm, or refrigerate for several hours and serve chilled. Refrigerate any leftovers.

NUTRITIONAL FACTS (PER ³/₄-CUP SERVING)

Calories: 204 Carbohydrates: 41 g Cholesterol: 2 mg
Fat: 0.8 g Fiber: 1.1 g Protein: 8.9 g Sodium: 114 mg

You Save: Calories: 178 Fat: 21.9 g

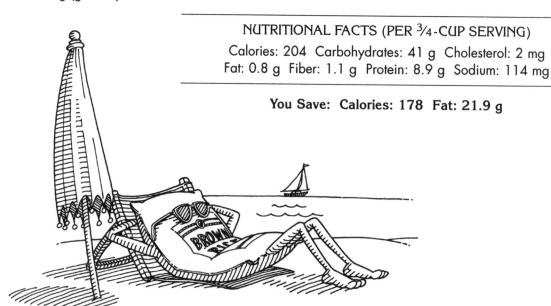

CRÈME CARAMEL

1. To make the caramel sauce, place ⅓ cup of the sugar in a heavy 1-quart saucepan. Cook over medium-high heat without stirring for about 1 minute, shaking the saucepan occasionally, until the sugar begins to liquefy around the edges. Reduce the heat to medium, and cook, stirring constantly, for another minute or 2, or until the sugar has completely liquefied and has turned a golden caramel color. Be careful not to cook the sugar too long, as it will continue to cook and darken after you remove it from the heat.

2. Immediately pour about 1 tablespoon of the caramel mixture into the bottom of each of four 6-ounce custard cups. (Be aware that the caramel mixture will be very hot!) Swirl each cup to coat the bottom and about ½-inch up the sides with the caramel mixture. Set the cups aside for 10 minutes to allow the caramel mixture to harden.

3. To make the custard, place the egg substitute, the remaining ⅓ cup of sugar, and the vanilla extract in a small bowl, and stir to dissolve the sugar. Set aside.

4. Place the evaporated milk in a 1-quart pot, and cook over medium heat, stirring frequently, just until the milk begins to boil. Remove the pot from the heat, and slowly whisk in the egg substitute mixture. Pour the custard into the caramel-lined cups.

5. Place the custards in a 9-x-9-inch baking pan, and add hot tap water to the pan until it reaches halfway up the sides of the custard cups. Bake at 325°F for about 50 minutes, or until a sharp knife inserted slightly off center in the custards comes out clean.

6. Remove the custards from the pan, and allow to cool to room temperature. Cover with plastic wrap, and chill for at least 24 hours before serving. (During this time, the hardened caramel sauce will become liquid.)

7. To serve, carefully run a sharp knife around the edge of the custards, taking care not to cut into the pudding itself. Invert the cups onto individual serving plates, allowing the sauce to flow over and around the custards. Serve immediately.

Yield: *4 servings*

⅔ cup sugar, divided

¼ cup plus 2 tablespoons fat-free egg substitute

1½ teaspoons vanilla extract

1 can (12 ounces) evaporated skimmed milk

NUTRITIONAL FACTS (PER SERVING)
Calories: 205 Carbohydrates: 43 g Cholesterol: 3 mg
Fat: 0.2 g Fiber: 0 g Protein: 8.7 g Sodium: 135 mg

You Save: Calories: 152 Fat: 19.8 g

Polenta Pudding

Yield: *8 servings*

1/4 cup plus 2 tablespoons whole grain cornmeal

2 1/2 cups skim or 1% low-fat milk

1 cup evaporated skimmed milk

1/4 cup plus 2 tablespoons honey

1 cup fat-free egg substitute

2 teaspoons vanilla extract

1/3 cup golden raisins or chopped dried apricots

Ground nutmeg (garnish)

1. Place the cornmeal in a 2 1/2-quart pot, and slowly stir in the milk and the evaporated milk. Cook over medium heat, stirring constantly, for 10 to 12 minutes, or until the mixture comes to a boil. Reduce the heat to low, and continue cooking for 2 additional minutes, or until slightly thickened. Slowly stir in the honey.

2. Place the egg substitute in a small bowl, and stir in 1 cup of the hot cornmeal mixture. Slowly stir the egg mixture into the pudding, and continue cooking and stirring for 2 minutes, or until slightly thickened. Remove the pot from the heat, and stir in the vanilla extract and the raisins or apricots.

3. Coat a 2-quart round casserole dish with nonstick cooking spray. Pour the pudding mixture into the dish, and sprinkle with the nutmeg. Place the dish in a pan filled with 1 inch of hot water.

4. Bake uncovered at 350°F for 1 hour, or until set. When done, a sharp knife inserted midway between the center of the pudding and the rim of the dish will come out clean.

5. Allow the pudding to cool at room temperature for at least 30 minutes. Serve warm, or refrigerate for several hours and serve chilled. Refrigerate any leftovers.

NUTRITIONAL FACTS (PER 2/3-CUP SERVING)
Calories: 156 Carbohydrates: 30 g Cholesterol: 2 mg
Fat: 0.5 g Fiber: 0.8 g Protein: 9 g Sodium: 150 mg

You Save: Calories: 89 Fat: 10.1 g

Spiced Pumpkin Flan

Yield: *6 servings*

1. To make the caramel sauce, place the $1/2$ cup of sugar in a heavy 1-quart saucepan. Cook over medium-high heat without stirring for about 1 minute, shaking the saucepan occasionally, until the sugar begins to liquefy around the edges. Reduce the heat to medium, and cook, stirring constantly, for another minute or 2, or until the sugar has completely liquefied and has turned a golden caramel color. Be careful not to cook the sugar too long, as it will continue to cook and darken after you remove it from the heat.

2. Immediately pour about 1 tablespoon of the caramel mixture into the bottom of each of four 6-ounce custard cups. (Be aware that the caramel mixture will be very hot!) Swirl each cup to coat the bottom and about $1/2$ inch up the sides with the caramel mixture. Set the cups aside for 10 minutes to allow the caramel mixture to harden.

3. To make the custard, place all of the remaining ingredients in a blender, and process until smooth. Pour the custard mixture into the caramel-lined cups.

4. Place the custards in a 9-x-13-inch baking pan, and add hot tap water to the pan until it reaches halfway up the sides of the custard cups. Bake at 350°F for about 45 minutes, or until a sharp knife inserted slightly off center in the custards comes out clean.

5. Remove the custards from the pan, and allow to cool to room temperature. Cover with plastic wrap, and chill for at least 24 hours before serving. (During this time, the hardened caramel sauce will become liquid.)

6. To serve, carefully run a sharp knife around the edge of the custards, taking care not to cut into the pudding itself. Invert the cups onto individual serving plates, allowing the sauce to flow over and around custards. Serve immediately.

$1/2$ cup sugar

1 can (12 ounces) evaporated skimmed milk

$1/2$ cup mashed cooked or canned pumpkin

$1/2$ cup plus 1 tablespoon fat-free egg substitute

$1/4$ cup orange juice

$1/2$ cup light brown sugar

2 teaspoons vanilla extract

1 teaspoon pumpkin pie spice

NUTRITIONAL FACTS (PER SERVING)
Calories: 177 Carbohydrates: 38 g Cholesterol: 2 mg
Fat: 0.2 g Fiber: 0.6 g Protein: 6.8 g Sodium: 109 mg

You Save: Calories: 61 Fat: 9.7 g

Peach Noodle Pudding

Yield: *8 servings*

4 ounces wide or extra-broad no-yolk egg noodles (about 3 cups)

1 block (8 ounces) nonfat cream cheese, softened to room temperature

1/2 cup sugar

1 cup nonfat cottage cheese

3/4 cup nonfat sour cream

3/4 cup fat-free egg substitute

2 1/2 teaspoons vanilla extract

1 1/2 cups diced peeled fresh or frozen (thawed) peaches (about 2 medium)

1/4 cup plus 2 tablespoons dark or golden raisins

TOPPING

2 tablespoons sugar

1/2 teaspoon ground cinnamon

Butter-flavored cooking spray

For variety, substitute diced apples for the peaches.

1. Cook the noodles according to package directions until tender. Drain well, and return the noodles to the pot.

2. While the noodles are cooking, place the cream cheese and sugar in a medium-sized bowl, and stir until smooth. Add the cottage cheese, sour cream, egg substitute, and vanilla extract, and stir to mix well.

3. Pour the cheese mixture over the drained noodles, and toss to mix well. Add the peaches and raisins, and toss to mix well.

4. Coat an 8-x-8-inch (2-quart) casserole dish with nonstick cooking spray, and spread the noodle mixture evenly in the dish. Set aside.

5. To make the topping, place the sugar and cinnamon in a small bowl, and stir to mix well. Sprinkle the sugar mixture over the top of the noodle mixture. Then spray the top lightly with the cooking spray.

6. Bake at 350°F for about 1 hour, or until a sharp knife inserted in the pudding about 1 inch off center comes out clean. Allow the pudding to sit at room temperature for 1 hour before cutting into squares and serving. Serve warm or at room temperature, refrigerating any leftovers.

NUTRITIONAL FACTS (PER 3/4-CUP SERVING)

Calories: 203 Carbohydrates: 37 g Cholesterol: 4 mg
Fat: 0.3 g Fiber: 1.4 g Protein: 12.7 g Sodium: 237 mg

You Save: Calories: 105 Fat: 16.1 g

CREAMY CLAFOUTI

This baked fruit and custard dessert is a slimmed-down version of a French classic. When fresh fruit is not available, substitute 2 cups of frozen peaches or cherries (thawed and drained), or a 1-pound can of peaches or apricots (drained and chopped).

Yield: *6 servings*

2 cups peeled fresh peaches or apricots cut into ³/₄-inch chunks, or 2 cups fresh pitted dark sweet cherries (or any combination)

¹/₂ cup plus 2 tablespoons fat-free egg substitute

¹/₄ cup plus 2 tablespoons sugar

2 teaspoons vanilla extract

2 tablespoons cornstarch

¹/₄ cup instant nonfat dry milk powder

1¹/₄ cups skim or 1% low-fat milk

1 tablespoon powdered sugar

1. Coat a 9-inch deep dish pie pan with nonstick cooking spray, and spread the fruit over the bottom of the pan. Alternatively, coat six 6-ounce custard cups with cooking spray, and divide the fruit among the cups. Set aside.

2. Place the egg substitute, sugar, and vanilla extract in a medium-sized bowl, and stir to mix well. Set aside.

3. Place the cornstarch and milk powder in a 2-quart pot. Add ¹/₄ cup of the milk, and stir to dissolve the cornstarch and milk powder. Slowly stir in the remaining milk. Place the pot over medium heat and cook, stirring constantly, for about 5 minutes, or until the mixture is thickened and bubbly.

4. Remove the pot from the heat. Stir the egg substitute mixture, and add it to the hot milk mixture in a thin stream while whisking constantly. Pour the egg-milk mixture over the fruit, and bake at 375°F for about 25 minutes, or until the clafouti is puffed around the edges and just beginning to brown. If you are baking the custard in individual custard cups, arrange them on a baking sheet before placing in the oven, and bake for only about 23 minutes.

5. Allow the clafouti to sit at room temperature for at least 15 minutes. (It will fall a bit.) Sift the powdered sugar over the top, and serve warm, refrigerating any leftovers.

NUTRITIONAL FACTS (PER ²/₃-CUP SERVING)

Calories: 128 Carbohydrates: 26.8 g Cholesterol: 1 mg
Fat: 0.2 g Fiber: 1 g Protein: 5.6 g Sodium: 84 mg

You Save: Calories: 81 Fat: 8.3 g

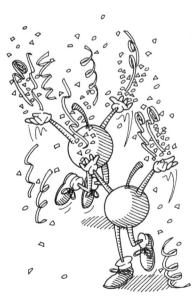

6

Colossal Cookies

Cookies are the perfect treat when you want a bite of something sweet. A crisp, crunchy biscotti is just the right accompaniment to a steaming cup of cappuccino. And a soft oatmeal cookie makes a satisfyingly chewy mid-morning snack.

Unfortunately, cookies also tend to contain higher proportions of fat, sugar, and refined flour than other sweet treats do. In response to consumer demand, manufacturers have flooded the market with low- and no-fat cookies. But while lower in fat, these treats often contain extra sugar to help maintain a pleasing texture. As a result, the calorie count remains high—and the nutrient count, low.

The good news is that when made properly, cookies can provide great taste and nutrition without an overabundance of fat, sugar, and calories. Unlike most cookie recipes, the recipes in this chapter feature wholesome ingredients like whole wheat flour and whole grain cereals. Just as important, these recipes keep fat to a minimum. The secret? Prune Purée, an easy-to-prepare fat substitute, is often used to replace the fat. Slightly sweet and mild in flavor, Prune Purée is one of the very best fat substitutes for cookies. Reduced-fat margarine and light butter also slash fat, while helping maintain the texture that you love.

Although it is impossible to make a good cookie without some sugar, the following recipes avoid adding the abundance of extra sugar found in many fat-free cookies. Instead, ingredients like whole grain flours and nonfat dry milk powder help provide texture, while dried fruits and flavorings like vanilla enhance sweetness.

So get out your cookie sheets and mixing bowl, and get ready to make some temptingly sweet, guilt-free treats. From Mocha Oatmeal Cookies to Cinnamon-Raisin Biscotti to Moist and Chewy Fudge Brownies, this chapter presents a variety of delightful cookies that will satisfy even the most discriminating of cookie monsters.

MAPLE-DATE DROPS

Yield: *40 cookies*

1 cup plus 2 tablespoons whole wheat pastry flour

$^3/_4$ cup sugar

1 teaspoon baking soda

$^1/_2$ teaspoon ground cinnamon

$^1/_4$ cup maple syrup

$^1/_4$ cup water

1 teaspoon vanilla extract

2 cups bran flake and raisin cereal

$^1/_2$ cup chopped dates or dark raisins

$^1/_4$ cup plus 2 tablespoons chopped toasted pecans or walnuts (page 167)

1. Place the flour, sugar, baking soda, and cinnamon in a large bowl, and stir to mix well. Add the maple syrup, water, and vanilla extract, and stir to mix well. Finally, add the cereal, dates or raisins, and nuts, and stir to mix well.

2. Coat a baking sheet with nonstick cooking spray. Drop rounded teaspoonfuls of dough onto the sheet, placing them 1$^1/_2$ inches apart. Slightly flatten each cookie with the tip of a spoon. (Note that the dough will be slightly crumbly, so that you may have to press it together slightly to make it hold its shape.)

3. Bake at 275°F for about 18 minutes, or until lightly browned. Cool the cookies on the pan for 2 minutes. Then transfer the cookies to wire racks, and cool completely. Serve immediately, or transfer to an airtight container and arrange in single layers separated by sheets of waxed paper.

NUTRITIONAL FACTS (PER COOKIE)

Calories: 53 Carbohydrates: 11.5 g Cholesterol: 0 mg
Fat: 0.9 g Fiber: 1 g Protein: 0.9 g Sodium: 50 mg

You Save: Calories: 21 Fat: 2.1 g

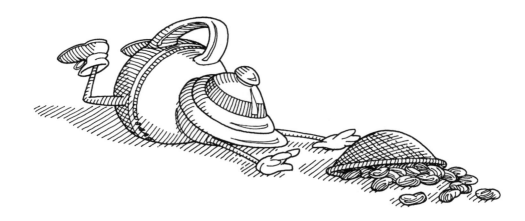

Apricot-Almond Drops

For variety, substitute dried cranberries or cherries for the apricots, and toasted pecans for the almonds.

Yield: *40 cookies*

1. Place the flour, sugar, and baking soda in a large bowl, and stir to mix well. Add the Prune Purée, maple syrup, water, and vanilla extract, and stir to mix well. The mixture will seem dry at first, but will become moist and hold together as you keep stirring. (Add a little more water, 1/2 teaspoon at a time, only if needed.) Finally, add the cereal, apricots, and almonds, and stir to mix well.

2. Coat a baking sheet with nonstick cooking spray. Drop rounded teaspoonfuls of dough onto the sheet, placing them 1 1/2 inches apart. Slightly flatten each cookie with the tip of a spoon. (Note that the dough will be slightly crumbly, so that you may have to press it together slightly to make it hold its shape.)

3. Bake at 350°F for about 9 minutes, or until lightly browned. Cool the cookies on the pan for 2 minutes. Then transfer the cookies to wire racks, and cool completely. Serve immediately, or transfer to an airtight container and arrange in single layers separated by sheets of waxed paper.

1 cup plus 2 tablespoons whole wheat pastry flour

3/4 cup sugar

1 teaspoon baking soda

3 tablespoons Prune Purée (page 131)

3 tablespoons maple syrup

1 tablespoon water

1 teaspoon vanilla extract

1 7/8 cups oat bran flakes* or wheat bran flakes

2/3 cup chopped dried apricots

1/4 cup plus 2 tablespoons chopped toasted almonds (page 167)

*Kellogg's Common Sense Oat Bran flakes are a good choice.

NUTRITIONAL FACTS (PER COOKIE)
Calories: 48 Carbohydrates: 10.5 g Cholesterol: 0 mg
Fat: 0.6 g Fiber: 1 g Protein: 1 g Sodium: 49 mg

You Save: Calories: 27 Fat: 2.4 g

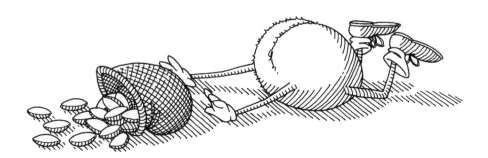

Trimming the Fat From Your Favorite Cookie Recipes

Of all treats, cookies are by far the most difficult to make without fat. Why? Most cookies rely on large amounts of fat as well as sugar for their texture. If you substitute products like applesauce or fruit purées for more than half the fat in these recipes, the excess liquid will most likely produce a cakey or rubbery texture.

Fortunately, there are ways to reduce the fat in cookie recipes and still maintain a pleasing texture. One fruit-based fat substitute—Prune Purée—works exceptionally well in cookies and many other baked goods, and is used in many of the recipes in this chapter. This ingredient, which can be easily made at home using the recipe on page 131, can actually replace all of the fat in many cookie recipes.

Contrary to popular belief, you can also use reduced-fat margarine and light butter in many of your favorite cookie recipes. These products make it possible to reduce fat by more than half, and still enjoy buttery-tasting treats that have a more traditional texture than you can obtain by using most fat substitutes. And as you will see by leafing through the recipes in this chapter, other ingredients, too, can help you give a slimming makeover to your treasured cookie recipes.

The following table and the tips that follow it will guide you in using a variety of fat substitutes with delicious results.

Using Fat Substitutes in Cookies

Fat Substitute	Tips for Using the Substitute
Applesauce, mashed banana, fruit purées, and mashed cooked pumpkin or sweet potatoes	☐ Replace up to half the butter, margarine, or other solid fat with half as much fat substitute. (Replace up to half of the oil with three-fourths as much fat substitute.) Mix up the dough. If it seems too dry, add a little more fat substitute. ☐ To trim more fat and cholesterol, replace each whole egg with 3 tablespoons of fat-free egg substitute if desired. ☐ Bake at 300°F to 325°F until golden brown. This will generally take about 12 to 15 minutes, depending on the size of the cookie.
Liquid sweeteners, such as honey, maple syrup, molasses, chocolate syrup, Fruit Source liquid, corn syrup, fruit juice concentrates, and fruit jams and spreads	☐ Replace part or all of the butter, margarine, or other solid fat with three-fourths as much fat substitute. (Replace part or all of the oil with an equal amount of fat substitute.) Mix up the dough. If it seems too dry, add a little more fat substitute. Note that totally fat-free cookies will be chewy in texture. If you want crisp cookies, replace no more than half the fat. (Maple syrup will produce the crispest results.) ☐ Replace each whole egg in the recipe with 2 tablespoons of water. ☐ To prevent the product from being overly sweet, reduce the sugar in the recipe by the amount of liquid sweetener being added. ☐ Bake at 275°F to 300°F for 15 to 20 minutes, or until lightly browned.

Fat Substitute	Tips for Using the Substitute
Prune Purée (page 131)	☐ Replace part or all of the butter, margarine, or other solid fat with half as much fat substitute. (Replace part or all of the oil with three-fourths as much fat substitute.) Mix up the dough. If it seems too dry, add a little more fat substitute. ☐ Replace each whole egg in the recipe with 2 tablespoons of Prune Purée or water. ☐ Bake at 350°F for about 9 minutes, or until lightly browned.
Reduced-fat margarine and light butter	☐ Be sure to choose a brand of butter or margarine that contains 5 to 6 grams of fat and 50 calories per tablespoon. Brands with less fat than this do not generally work well in baking. ☐ Avoid using reduced-fat margarine and light butter in cookie recipes that already contain liquid ingredients such as applesauce, pumpkin, or milk. Since these cookies already contain some water, a reduced-fat product will likely produce a cakey or rubbery texture. ☐ Replace all of the full-fat margarine, butter, or other solid fat with three-fourths as much reduced-fat margarine or light butter. ☐ Bake reduced-fat cookies at 300°F to 325°F until golden brown. This will generally take about 12 to 15 minutes, depending on the size of the cookie.

A few more general tips will help insure the best possible results when trimming the fat from your favorite cookie recipes.

☐ If your recipe is made with 100 percent white flour, substitute whole wheat pastry flour for at least half of the flour in the recipe. Or substitute oat flour, quick-cooking oats, or oat bran for at least a third of the flour. Since these products are lower in gluten than white flour, they will help maintain a pleasing texture.

☐ Try adding a few tablespoons of instant nonfat dry milk powder to the recipe. This will improve the texture, promote browning, and boost nutritional value.

☐ If you find that your low- and no-fat drop cookies do not spread enough during baking, try flattening them slightly with your fingertips or the tip of a spoon before putting them in the oven. Or add a little extra baking soda—about ¼ teaspoon—to the recipe.

☐ Realize that you may have to experiment a bit to perfect your recipe. For instance, if your cookies spread too much during baking, you may need to reduce the amount of liquid or slightly increase the amount of flour.

FAT-FREE MARSHMALLOW TREATS

Yield: *18 bars*

1 tablespoon nonfat margarine, or 1 tablespoon plus 1 1/2 teaspoons reduced-fat margarine

6 cups miniature marshmallows

6 cups crisp rice cereal, regular or cocoa-flavored

1. Coat a 4-quart pot with butter-flavored nonstick cooking spray. Add the margarine and marshmallows, cover, and cook over low heat without stirring for 3 minutes. Then remove the lid and continue to cook, stirring constantly, for 2 to 3 additional minutes, or until the mixture is melted and smooth.

2. Remove the pot from the heat, and stir in the cereal. Coat a 9-x-13-inch pan with nonstick cooking spray, and use the back of a wooden spoon to pat the mixture firmly into the pan. (Coat the spoon with cooking spray to help prevent sticking.)

3. Allow the mixture to cool to room temperature before cutting into squares. Serve immediately, or store in an airtight container in single layers separated by sheets of waxed paper.

NUTRITIONAL FACTS (PER BAR)

Calories: 86 Carbohydrates: 20.7 g Cholesterol: 0 mg
Fat: 0.1 g Fiber: 0.1 g Protein: 0.8 g Sodium: 81 mg

You Save: Calories: 30 Fat: 3.4 g

Variation

To make Peanut Butter Marshmallow Treats, add 1/4 cup plus 2 tablespoons reduced-fat or regular peanut butter to the pot along with the margarine and marshmallows.

NUTRITIONAL FACTS (PER BAR)

Calories: 116 Carbohydrates: 23 g Cholesterol: 0 mg
Fat: 1.9 g Fiber: 0.5 g Protein: 2.2 g Sodium: 106 mg

You Save: Calories: 31 Fat: 4.3 g

MOCHA OATMEAL COOKIES

1. Place the flour, oats, cocoa, and brown sugar in a large bowl, and stir to mix well. Using the back of a wooden spoon, press out any lumps in the brown sugar. Add the baking soda and cinnamon, and stir to mix well. Set aside.

2. Place the Prune Purée, coffee granules, and vanilla extract in a small bowl, and stir to dissolve the coffee granules. Add the Prune Purée mixture to the oat mixture, and stir to mix well. The mixture will seem dry at first, but will become moist and hold together as you keep stirring. (Add a little more Prune Purée, 1/2 teaspoon at a time, only if needed.)

3. Add the chocolate chips, fruit, and nuts to the dough, and stir to mix well. Coat a baking sheet with nonstick cooking spray. Drop rounded teaspoonfuls of dough onto the sheet, placing them 1 1/2 inches apart. Slightly flatten each cookie with the tip of a spoon.

4. Bake at 350°F for about 9 minutes, or until lightly browned. Cool the cookies on the pan for 2 minutes. Then transfer the cookies to wire racks, and cool completely. Serve immediately, or transfer to an airtight container and arrange in single layers separated by sheets of waxed paper.

Yield: *42 cookies*

3/4 cup plus 1 tablespoon whole wheat pastry flour

1 cup quick-cooking oats

3 tablespoons Dutch processed cocoa powder

3/4 cup plus 2 tablespoons light or dark brown sugar

3/4 teaspoon baking soda

1/4 teaspoon ground cinnamon

1/4 cup plus 3 tablespoons Prune Purée (page 131)

1/2 teaspoon instant coffee granules

1 teaspoon vanilla extract

1/3 cup semi-sweet chocolate chips

1/3 cup dark raisins, chopped dried apricots, or dried cherries

1/3 cup chopped toasted almonds, pecans, or walnuts (page 167)

NUTRITIONAL FACTS (PER COOKIE)

Calories: 45 Carbohydrates: 8.6 g Cholesterol: 0 mg
Fat: 1.2 g Fiber: 0.9 g Protein: 1 g Sodium: 24 mg

You Save: Calories: 24 Fat: 2.8 g

Chocolate Jumbles

Yield: *42 cookies*

1 cup whole wheat pastry flour

2 tablespoons Dutch processed
cocoa powder

3/4 cup sugar

1 teaspoon baking soda

3 tablespoons Prune Purée
(page 131)

3 tablespoons chocolate syrup

1 tablespoon water

1 teaspoon vanilla extract

2 cups oat bran flakes* or
wheat bran flakes

2/3 cup semi-sweet, milk
chocolate, or white
chocolate chips

1/3 cup chopped toasted
almonds, pecans, hazelnuts,
or macadamia nuts (page
167)

*Kellogg's Common Sense Oat Bran
flakes are a good choice.

1. Place the flour, cocoa powder, sugar, and baking soda in a large bowl, and stir to mix well. Add the Prune Purée, chocolate syrup, water, and vanilla extract, and stir to mix well. The mixture will seem dry at first, but will become moist and hold together as you keep stirring. (Add a little more Prune Purée, 1/2 teaspoon at a time, only if needed.) Finally, add the cereal, chocolate chips, and nuts, and stir to mix well.

2. Coat a baking sheet with nonstick cooking spray. Drop rounded teaspoonfuls of dough onto the sheet, placing them 1 1/2 inches apart. Slightly flatten each cookie with the tip of a spoon. (Note that the dough will be slightly crumbly, so that you may have to press it together slightly to make it hold its shape.)

3. Bake at 350°F for about 9 minutes, or until lightly browned. Cool the cookies on the pan for 2 minutes. Then transfer the cookies to wire racks, and cool completely. Serve immediately, or transfer to an airtight container and arrange in single layers separated by sheets of waxed paper.

NUTRITIONAL FACTS (PER COOKIE)

Calories: 52 Carbohydrates: 10.1 g Cholesterol: 0 mg
Fat: 1.5 g Fiber: 1 g Protein: 1 g Sodium: 49 mg

You Save: Calories: 19 Fat: 2.5 g

Variation

To make Peanutty Chocolate Jumbles, substitute peanut butter chips for the chocolate chips, and use chopped roasted unsalted peanuts for the nuts.

NUTRITIONAL FACTS (PER COOKIE)

Calories: 52 Carbohydrates: 10.1 g Cholesterol: 0 mg
Fat: 1.5 g Fiber: 1 g Protein: 1 g Sodium: 49 mg

You Save: Calories: 19 Fat: 2.5 g

Maple Oatmeal Cookies

1. Place the flour, oats, sugar, baking soda, cinnamon, and nutmeg in a large bowl, and stir to mix well. Add the maple syrup, water, and vanilla extract, and stir to mix well. Finally, add the raisins and walnuts, and stir to mix well.

2. Coat a baking sheet with nonstick cooking spray. Drop rounded teaspoonfuls of dough onto the sheet, placing them 1 1/2 inches apart. Slightly flatten each cookie with a tip of a spoon.

3. Bake at 275°F for about 18 minutes, or until lightly browned. Cool the cookies on the pan for 2 minutes. Then transfer the cookies to wire racks, and cool completely. Serve immediately, or transfer to an airtight container and arrange in single layers separated by sheets of waxed paper.

Yield: *36 cookies*

1 cup whole wheat pastry flour

1 cup quick-cooking oats

2/3 cup sugar

3/4 teaspoon baking soda

1/2 teaspoon ground cinnamon

1/2 teaspoon ground nutmeg

1/4 cup maple syrup

1/4 cup water

1 teaspoon vanilla extract

1/2 cup dark raisins

1/3 cup chopped walnuts

NUTRITIONAL FACTS (PER COOKIE)

Calories: 52 Carbohydrates: 10.8 g Cholesterol: 0 mg
Fat: 0.9 g Fiber: 0.8 g Protein: 1.1 g Sodium: 27 mg

You Save: Calories: 22 Fat: 2.1 g

Chewy Chocolate Chip Cookies

Yield: *42 cookies*

1 1/3 cups whole wheat pastry flour

1/4 cup instant nonfat dry milk powder

1/2 cup plus 2 tablespoons sugar

1/4 cup dark brown sugar

3/4 teaspoon baking soda

1/4 cup plus 2 tablespoons Prune Purée (page 131)

1 teaspoon vanilla extract

2/3 cup semi-sweet chocolate chips

1/3 cup chopped toasted walnuts or pecans (page 167)

1. Place the flour, milk powder, and sugars in a large bowl, and stir to mix well. Using the back of a wooden spoon, press out any lumps in the brown sugar.

2. Add the baking soda to the flour mixture, and stir to mix well. Add the Prune Purée and vanilla extract, and stir to mix well. The mixture will seem dry at first, but will become moist and hold together as you keep stirring. (Add a little water, 1/2 teaspoon at a time, only if needed.) Finally, add the chocolate chips and nuts, and stir to mix well.

3. Coat a baking sheet with nonstick cooking spray. Drop rounded teaspoonfuls of dough onto the sheet, placing them 1 1/2 inches apart. Slightly flatten each cookie with a tip of a spoon.

4. Bake at 350°F for about 9 minutes, or until lightly browned. Cool the cookies on the pan for 2 minutes. Then transfer the cookies to wire racks, and cool completely. Serve immediately, or transfer to an airtight container and arrange in single layers separated by sheets of waxed paper.

NUTRITIONAL FACTS (PER COOKIE)

Calories: 49 Carbohydrates: 9.2 g Cholesterol: 0 mg
Fat: 1.4 g Fiber: 0.8 g Protein: 1 g Sodium: 26 mg

You Save: Calories: 20 Fat: 2.6 g

Making Prune Purée

The dessert and baked goods recipes in this book use a variety of fat substitutes. Most of them—mashed bananas, applesauce, and nonfat buttermilk, for instance—are readily available in the grocery store. One excellent fat substitute, however, can also be made at home. High in fiber and nutrients, Prune Purée can be used in a variety of baked goods, including cakes and quick breads. And, as you'll see by glancing through the recipes in this chapter, Prune Purée is an especially good substitute in cookies.

To make this simple product, follow the recipe provided below. Then keep Prune Purée on hand for use in your fat-free and low-fat baked goods. If you like, make a double batch and store some in the freezer. Prune Purée can be kept frozen for up to several months.

Several prune-based fat substitutes are also available in grocery stores and health foods stores. WonderSlim, which is similar to Prune Purée, can be used interchangeably in all recipes that call for this ingredient. Sunsweet Lighter Bake, a combination of prunes, apples, and other ingredients, can be used interchangeably in many recipes with Prune Purée. However, since Lighter Bake is thicker than Prune Purée, it does not substitute well in the cookie recipes in this book.

To use Prune Purée in your own recipes, replace the butter, margarine, or other solid fat in the recipes with half as much Prune Purée. Replace any oil in the recipe with three-fourths as much Prune Purée. (For information on using this product specifically in cookies and brownies, see the insets on pages 125 and 142.)

PRUNE PURÉE

Yield: 1¼ *cups*

3 ounces (about ½ cup unpacked) pitted prunes

1 cup water

2 teaspoons lecithin granules*

1. Place all of the ingredients in a blender, and blend at high speed for about 2 minutes, or until the mixture is smooth.

2. Use immediately, place in an airtight container and store in the refrigerator for up to 3 weeks, or store in the freezer for several months.

NUTRITIONAL FACTS (PER ½ CUP)

Calories: 102 Carbohydrates: 27 g Cholesterol: 0 mg
Fat: 1.8 g Fiber: 3.7 g Protein: 1 g Sodium: 2 mg

You Save: Calories: 1,825 Fat: 216 g

*Lecithin, a by-product of soybean oil refining, is sold in health foods stores as a food supplement. Because lecithin improves the texture of baked goods, commercial bakers often add small amounts of this product to fat-free and low-fat cakes, cookies, breads, and muffins.

Chewy Chocolate-Chocolate Chip Cookies

Yield: *42 cookies*

1 cup plus 2 tablespoons whole wheat pastry flour

3 tablespoons plus 1 teaspoon Dutch processed cocoa powder

1/4 cup instant nonfat dry milk powder

1/2 cup plus 2 tablespoons sugar

1/4 cup dark brown sugar

3/4 teaspoon baking soda

1/4 cup plus 2 tablespoons Prune Purée (page 131)

1 teaspoon vanilla extract

2/3 cup semi-sweet, milk chocolate, or white chocolate chips

1/3 cup chopped toasted almonds, macadamia nuts, hazelnuts, or pecans (page 167)

1. Place the flour, cocoa, milk powder, and sugars in a large bowl, and stir to mix well. Using the back of a wooden spoon, press out any lumps in the brown sugar.

2. Add the baking soda to the flour mixture, and stir to mix well. Add the Prune Purée and vanilla extract, and stir to mix well. The mixture will seem dry at first, but will become moist and hold together as you keep stirring. (Add a little water, 1/2 teaspoon at a time, only if needed.) Finally, add the chocolate chips and nuts, and stir to mix well.

3. Coat a baking sheet with nonstick cooking spray. Drop rounded teaspoonfuls of dough onto the sheet, placing them 1 1/2 inches apart. Slightly flatten each cookie with the tip of a spoon.

4. Bake at 350°F for about 9 minutes, or until lightly browned. Cool the cookies on the pan for 2 minutes. Then transfer the cookies to wire racks, and cool completely. Serve immediately, or transfer to an airtight container and arrange in single layers separated by sheets of waxed paper.

NUTRITIONAL FACTS (PER COOKIE)

Calories: 48 Carbohydrates: 9 g Cholesterol: 0 mg
Fat: 1.5 g Fiber: 0.8 g Protein: 1 g Sodium: 26 mg

You Save: Calories: 21 Fat: 2.5 g

Top Left: Maple Oatmeal Cookies (page 129)
Bottom Left: Citrus Sugar Cookies (page 134)
Bottom Right: Cream Cheese Marble Brownies (page 143)

Top: Cool Chocolate-Raspberry Torte
(page 156)

Bottom Left: Strawberry Angel Parfaits
(page 154)

Bottom Right: Simple Apricot Sorbet
(page 152)

Orange Oatmeal Cookies

1. Place the flour, oats, and brown sugar in a large bowl, and stir to mix well. Using the back of a wooden spoon, press out any lumps in the brown sugar.

2. Add the baking soda and orange rind to the flour mixture, and stir to mix well. Add the Prune Purée, juice concentrate, and vanilla extract, and stir to mix well. The mixture will seem dry at first, but will become moist and hold together as you keep stirring. (Add a little more Prune Purée, ½ teaspoon at a time, only if needed.) Finally, add the raisins or dried cranberries and the nuts, and stir to mix well.

3. Coat a baking sheet with nonstick cooking spray. Drop rounded teaspoonfuls of dough onto the sheet, placing them 1½ inches apart. Slightly flatten each cookie with the tip of a spoon.

4. Bake at 350°F for about 9 minutes, or until lightly browned. Cool the cookies on the pan for 2 minutes. Then transfer the cookies to wire racks, and cool completely. Serve immediately, or transfer to an airtight container and arrange in single layers separated by sheets of waxed paper.

Yield: *42 cookies*

1 cup whole wheat pastry flour

1 cup quick-cooking oats

3/4 cup plus 2 tablespoons light brown sugar

3/4 teaspoon baking soda

1/2 teaspoon dried grated orange rind, or 1 1/2 teaspoons fresh

1/4 cup plus 2 tablespoons Prune Purée (page 131)

1 tablespoon frozen orange juice concentrate, thawed

1 teaspoon vanilla extract

2/3 cup dark raisins or dried cranberries

1/3 cup chopped toasted pecans or walnuts (page 167)

NUTRITIONAL FACTS (PER COOKIE)

Calories: 44 Carbohydrates: 9 g Cholesterol: 0 mg
Fat: 0.8 g Fiber: 0.8 g Protein: 0.9 g Sodium: 24 mg

You Save: Calories: 24 Fat: 1.9 g

Keeping Fat-Free Cookies Soft and Moist

Fat-free cookies have the best texture within a few hours of coming out of the oven. Then, as they stand, they tend to take on a chewier and sometimes tough texture. If this happens, simply place some 1/4-inch-thick unpeeled apple wedges in with the cookies. Place one wedge with each layer of cookies, making sure the apple wedge is not touching any of the cookies. (The layers should be separated by sheets of waxed paper.) Cover and let stand for several hours or overnight. The moisture from the apples will seep into the cookies and help soften them.

As an alternative, tear slices of bread into 1 1/2- to 2-inch pieces, and place with the cookies. The bread will become stale as its moisture is released and absorbed by the cookies. When the cookies reach the desired degree of softness, remove the apple wedges or bread pieces to prevent further softening.

Citrus Sugar Cookies

Yield: *36 cookies*

1/4 cup plus 1 tablespoon reduced-fat margarine or light butter, softened to room temperature

1/2 cup plus 2 tablespoons sugar

3 tablespoons frozen orange juice concentrate, thawed

1 teaspoon vanilla extract

1 cup plus 2 tablespoons unbleached flour

3/4 cup oat bran

1/4 cup instant nonfat dry milk powder

3/4 teaspoon baking soda

1 teaspoon dried grated lemon rind, or 1 tablespoon fresh

COATING

1 tablespoon plus 1 1/2 teaspoons sugar

1. Place the margarine or butter, sugar, juice concentrate, and vanilla extract in a large bowl, and beat with an electric mixer until smooth. Set aside.

2. Place the flour, oat bran, milk powder, baking soda, and lemon rind in a medium-sized bowl, and stir to mix well. Add the flour mixture to the margarine mixture, and beat to mix well. (Add 1 to 2 teaspoons of additional orange juice concentrate if the mixture seems too dry.)

3. Place the sugar coating in a small shallow dish, and set aside.

4. Coat a baking sheet with nonstick cooking spray. Using your hands, shape the dough into 1-inch balls. (If the dough is too sticky to handle, place it in the freezer for a few minutes.) Roll the balls in the sugar coating; then arrange on the baking sheet, spacing them 1 1/2 inches apart. Using the bottom of a glass, flatten each ball to 1/4-inch thickness.

5. Bake at 300°F for about 14 minutes. To check for doneness, lift a cookie from the sheet with a spatula. The bottom should be lightly browned. Cool the cookies on the pan for 2 minutes. Then transfer the cookies to wire racks, and cool completely. Serve immediately, or transfer to an airtight container.

NUTRITIONAL FACTS (PER COOKIE)
Calories: 45 Carbohydrates: 8.8 g Cholesterol: 0 mg
Fat: 0.9 g Fiber: 0.4 g Protein: 0.9 g Sodium: 39 mg

You Save: Calories: 31 Fat: 2.8 g

Molasses Spice Cookies

1. Place the margarine, brown sugar, molasses, applesauce, and vanilla extract in a large bowl, and beat with an electric mixer until smooth. Set aside.

2. Place the flour, milk powder, baking soda, ginger, and cinnamon in a medium-sized bowl, and stir to mix well. Add the flour mixture to the margarine mixture, and beat to mix well. (Add a couple of teaspoons of additional applesauce if the mixture seems too dry.)

3. Place the sugar coating in a small shallow dish, and set aside.

4. Coat a baking sheet with nonstick cooking spray. Using your hands, shape the dough into 1-inch balls. (If the dough is too sticky to handle, place it in the freezer for a few minutes.) Roll the balls in the sugar coating; then arrange on the baking sheet, spacing them 1 1/2 inches apart. Using the bottom of a glass, flatten each ball to 1/4-inch thickness.

5. Bake at 300°F for about 14 minutes. To check for doneness, lift a cookie from the sheet with a spatula. The bottom should be lightly browned. Cool the cookies on the pan for 2 minutes. Then transfer the cookies to wire racks, and cool completely. Serve immediately, or transfer to an airtight container.

Yield: *40 cookies*

1/4 cup plus 2 tablespoons reduced-fat margarine or light butter, softened to room temperature

2/3 cup light brown sugar

1/4 cup molasses

1 tablespoon unsweetened applesauce

1 teaspoon vanilla extract

2 cups whole wheat pastry flour

2 tablespoons instant nonfat dry milk powder

3/4 teaspoon baking soda

1 1/4 teaspoons ground ginger

1 1/4 teaspoons ground cinnamon

COATING

2 tablespoons sugar

NUTRITIONAL FACTS (PER COOKIE)
Calories: 47 Carbohydrates: 8.9 g Cholesterol: 0 mg
Fat: 0.9 g Fiber: 0.8 g Protein: 0.9 g Sodium: 38 mg

You Save: Calories: 21 Fat: 2.4 g

Maple Snickerdoodles

Yield: *40 cookies*

1/4 cup plus 2 tablespoons
  reduced-fat margarine or
  light butter, softened to room
  temperature

3/4 cup sugar

3 tablespoons maple syrup

1 tablespoon lemon juice

1 1/2 teaspoons vanilla extract

1 1/4 cups unbleached flour

3/4 cup plus 2 tablespoons
  oat bran

1/4 cup instant nonfat dry milk
  powder

3/4 teaspoon baking soda

COATING

1 tablespoon plus 1 1/2
  teaspoons sugar

1 1/2 teaspoons ground
  cinnamon

1. Place the margarine, sugar, maple syrup, lemon juice, and vanilla extract in a large bowl, and beat with an electric mixer until smooth. Set aside.

2. Place the flour, oat bran, milk powder, and baking soda in a medium-sized bowl, and stir to mix well. Add the flour mixture to the margarine mixture, and beat to mix well.

3. To make the coating, place the sugar and cinnamon in a small shallow dish, and stir to mix well. Set aside.

4. Coat a baking sheet with nonstick cooking spray. Using your hands, shape the dough into 1-inch balls. (If the dough is too sticky to handle, place it in the freezer for a few minutes.) Roll the balls in the sugar coating; then arrange on the baking sheet, spacing them 1 1/2 inches apart. Using the bottom of a glass, flatten each ball to 1/4-inch thickness.

5. Bake at 300°F for about 14 minutes. To check for doneness, lift a cookie from the sheet with a spatula. The bottom should be lightly browned. Cool the cookies on the pan for 2 minutes. Then transfer the cookies to wire racks, and cool completely. Serve immediately, or transfer to an airtight container.

NUTRITIONAL FACTS (PER COOKIE)
Calories: 48   Carbohydrates: 9.4 g   Cholesterol: 0 mg
Fat: 0.9 g   Fiber: 0.4 g   Protein: 0.9 g   Sodium: 37 mg

You Save: Calories: 26 Fat: 2.8 g

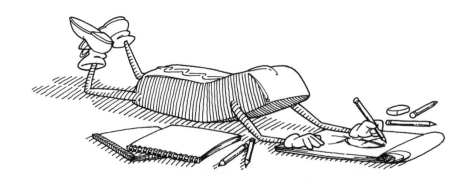

Cinnamon-Raisin Biscotti

1. Place the flours, brown sugar, and cinnamon in a large bowl, and stir to mix well. Using the back of a wooden spoon, press out any lumps in the brown sugar. Add the baking powder, and stir to mix well.

2. Using a pastry cutter or 2 knives, cut the margarine or butter into the flour mixture until it resembles coarse meal. Stir in the raisins and the wheat germ or walnuts.

3. Add the egg substitute and vanilla extract to the dough, and stir just until the dry ingredients are moistened and the dough holds together. Add a little more egg substitute if the mixture seems too dry.

4. Spray your hands with nonstick cooking spray, and divide the dough into 2 pieces. Shape each piece into a 9-x-2½-inch log. Coat a large baking sheet with nonstick cooking spray, and place the logs on the sheet, spacing them 4 inches apart to allow for spreading. Bake at 325°F for 25 to 30 minutes, or until lightly browned and firm to the touch.

5. Using a spatula, carefully transfer the logs to a wire rack, and allow to cool at room temperature for 10 minutes. Then place the logs on a cutting board, and use a serrated knife to slice them diagonally into ½-inch-thick slices.

6. Arrange the slices in a single layer on an ungreased baking sheet, cut side down. Bake for 6 minutes at 325°F. Turn the slices and bake for 6 additional minutes, or until dry and crisp.

7. Transfer the biscotti to wire racks, and cool completely. Serve immediately, or transfer to an airtight container.

Yield: *28 biscotti*

1 cup whole wheat pastry flour

1 cup unbleached flour

3/4 cup plus 2 tablespoons light brown sugar

1 teaspoon ground cinnamon

2½ teaspoons baking powder

1/4 cup (1/8 pound) chilled reduced-fat margarine or light butter, cut into pieces

1/2 cup dark raisins

1/3 cup honey crunch wheat germ or chopped toasted walnuts (page 167)

1/4 cup plus 1 tablespoon fat-free egg substitute

1½ teaspoons vanilla extract

NUTRITIONAL FACTS (PER BISCOTTI)

Calories: 69 Carbohydrates: 13.7 g Cholesterol: 0 mg
Fat: 0.9 g Fiber: 0.7 g Protein: 1.7 g Sodium: 61 mg

You Save: Calories: 46 Fat: 3.6 g

Triple Chocolate Biscotti

Yield: *28 biscotti*

1²/3 cups whole wheat pastry flour

1/3 cup Dutch processed cocoa powder

3/4 cup sugar

2 teaspoons baking powder

1/4 teaspoon baking soda

1/4 cup plus 1 tablespoon fat-free egg substitute

1/4 cup chocolate syrup

2 teaspoons vanilla extract

1/2 cup semi-sweet, milk chocolate, or white chocolate chips

1/2 cup chopped toasted pecans, hazelnuts, walnuts, or almonds (page 167) (optional)

1. Place the flour, cocoa, sugar, baking powder, and baking soda in a large bowl, and stir to mix well. Set aside.

2. Place the egg substitute, chocolate syrup, and vanilla extract in a small bowl, and stir to mix well. Add the egg mixture, chocolate chips, and, if desired, the nuts to the flour mixture, and stir just until the dry ingredients are moistened and the dough holds together. Add a little more egg substitute if the mixture seems too dry.

3. Spray your hands with nonstick cooking spray, and divide the dough into 2 pieces. Shape each piece into a 9-x-2¹/2-inch log. Coat a large baking sheet with nonstick cooking spray, and place the logs on the sheet, spacing them 4 inches apart to allow for spreading. Bake at 325°F for 25 to 30 minutes, or until lightly browned and firm to the touch.

4. Using a spatula, carefully transfer the logs to a wire rack, and allow to cool at room temperature for 10 minutes. Then place the logs on a cutting board, and use a serrated knife to slice them diagonally into ¹/2-inch-thick slices.

5. Arrange the slices in a single layer on an ungreased baking sheet, cut side down. Bake for 6 minutes at 325°F. Turn the slices and bake for 6 additional minutes, or until dry and crisp.

6. Transfer the biscotti to wire racks, and cool completely. Serve immediately, or transfer to an airtight container.

NUTRITIONAL FACTS (PER BISCOTTI)
Calories: 74 Carbohydrates: 15.8 g Cholesterol: 0 mg
Fat: 1.5 g Fiber: 1.4 g Protein: 2 g Sodium: 54 mg

You Save: Calories: 41 Fat: 3.5 g

Mocha Meringues

1. Place the vanilla extract and coffee granules in a small bowl, and stir to mix well. Set aside.

2. Place the egg whites in the bowl of an electric mixer, and beat on high speed until foamy. Add the cream of tartar and salt, and continue beating until soft peaks form. Still beating, slowly add the sugar, 1 tablespoon at a time. Beat the mixture just until stiff peaks form when the beaters are raised. Then beat in first the cocoa, and then the vanilla-coffee mixture.

3. Remove the beaters from the meringue mixture. Fold in the chocolate chips and, if desired, the nuts.

4. Line a large baking sheet with aluminum foil. (Do not grease the sheet or coat it with cooking spray.) Drop heaping teaspoonfuls of the mixture onto the baking sheet, spacing them 1 inch apart.

5. Bake at 250°F for 45 minutes, or until firm to the touch. Turn the oven off, and allow the meringues to cool in the oven for 2 hours with the door closed. Remove the pans from the oven, and peel the meringues from the foil. Serve immediately, or transfer to an airtight container.

Yield: *24 cookies*

1 teaspoon vanilla extract

1/2 teaspoon instant coffee granules

2 large egg whites, warmed to room temperature

1/4 teaspoon cream of tartar

1/8 teaspoon salt

1/4 cup plus 2 tablespoons sugar

1 tablespoon cocoa powder (use regular, not Dutch processed)

1/2 cup semi-sweet or white chocolate chips

1/3 cup chopped toasted pecans or hazelnuts (page 167) (optional)

NUTRITIONAL FACTS (PER COOKIE)

Calories: 30 Carbohydrates: 5.4 g Cholesterol: 0 mg
Fat: 1 g Fiber: 0.2 g Protein: 0.4 g Sodium: 16 mg

You Save: Calories: 20 Fat: 2.2 g

TOASTED COCONUT MERINGUES

Yield: *24 cookies*

¹/₂ cup plus 2 tablespoons shredded sweetened coconut

2 large egg whites, warmed to room temperature

¹/₈ teaspoon cream of tartar

¹/₈ teaspoon salt

¹/₄ cup plus 2 tablespoons sugar

¹/₂ teaspoon coconut-flavored extract

¹/₂ teaspoon vanilla extract

1. Spread the coconut in a thin layer on a small baking sheet, and bake at 350°F, stirring occasionally, for about 5 minutes, or until the coconut turns light golden brown. Remove from the oven and set aside to cool to room temperature.

2. Place the egg whites in the bowl of an electric mixer, and beat on high speed until foamy. Add the cream of tartar and salt, and continue beating until soft peaks form. Still beating, slowly add the sugar, 1 tablespoon at a time. Beat the mixture just until stiff peaks form when the beaters are raised. Beat in the extracts.

3. Remove the beaters from the meringue mixture, and fold in the coconut.

4. Line a large baking sheet with aluminum foil. (Do not grease the sheet or coat it with cooking spray.) Drop heaping teaspoonfuls of the mixture onto the baking sheet, spacing them 1 inch apart.

5. Bake at 250°F for 45 minutes, or until firm to the touch. Turn the oven off, and allow the meringues to cool in the oven for 2 hours with the door closed. Remove the pans from the oven, and peel the meringues from the foil. Serve immediately, or transfer to an airtight container.

NUTRITIONAL FACTS (PER COOKIE)
Calories: 25   Carbohydrates: 4.3 g   Cholesterol: 0 mg
Fat: 0.7 g   Fiber: 0.1 g   Protein: 0.4 g   Sodium: 22 mg

You Save: Calories: 20   Fat: 2.2 g

Moist and Chewy Fudge Brownies

1. Place the flour, cocoa, sugar, milk powder, and baking soda in a medium-sized bowl, and stir to mix well. Add the egg substitute, chocolate syrup, water or coffee, and vanilla extract, and stir to mix well. Set the batter aside for 15 minutes.

2. If desired, stir the nuts into the batter. Coat the bottom only of an 8-x-8-inch pan with nonstick cooking spray, and spread the mixture evenly in the pan. Bake at 325°F for about 23 minutes, or just until the edges are firm and the center is almost set. Be careful not to over-bake.

3. Allow the brownies to cool to room temperature before cutting into squares and serving. For easier cutting, rinse the knife off periodically.

Yield: *16 brownies*

2/3 cup oat flour

1/4 cup Dutch processed cocoa powder

3/4 cup sugar

2 tablespoons instant nonfat dry milk powder

1 pinch baking soda

1/4 cup plus 2 tablespoons fat-free egg substitute

1/4 cup chocolate syrup

1 tablespoon water or strong black coffee, cooled to room temperature

1 teaspoon vanilla extract

1/3 cup chopped toasted walnuts, pecans, hazelnuts, macadamia nuts, or almonds (page 167) (optional)

NUTRITIONAL FACTS (PER BROWNIE)
Calories: 72 Carbohydrates: 16.4 g Cholesterol: 0 mg
Fat: 0.5 g Fiber: 1 g Protein: 1.9 g Sodium: 22 mg

You Save: Calories: 65 Fat: 7.8 g

Trimming the Fat From Your Favorite Brownie Recipes

Whether made from scratch or a mix, moist and chewy brownies are among the easiest of recipes to prepare without fat. The following table and the tips that follow it will guide you in using a variety of products to trim the fat from your favorite brownie recipes.

Using Fat Substitutes in Brownies

Fat Substitute	Tips for Using the Substitute
Applesauce, mashed banana, fruit purées, mashed cooked pumpkin or sweet potatoes, and Prune Purée (page 131)	☐ Replace part or all of the butter, margarine, or other solid fat with half as much fat substitute. (Replace part or all of the oil with three-fourths as much fat substitute.) Mix up the batter. If it seems too dry, add a little more fat substitute. ☐ To trim more fat and cholesterol, replace each whole egg with 3 tablespoons of fat-free egg substitute, if desired. ☐ Bake at 325°F just until the edges are firm and the center is almost set. Be careful not to overbake.
Liquid sweeteners, such as chocolate syrup, corn syrup, honey, molasses, and fruit jams and spreads	☐ Replace part or all of the butter, margarine, or other solid fat with three-fourths as much fat substitute. (Replace part or all of the oil with an equal amount of fat substitute.) Mix up the batter. If it seems too dry, add a little more fat substitute. Note that liquid sweeteners add a delightfully chewy texture to brownies. ☐ To prevent the product from being overly sweet, reduce the sugar in the recipe by the amount of liquid sweetener being added. ☐ To trim more fat and cholesterol, replace each whole egg with 3 tablespoons of fat-free egg substitute, if desired. ☐ Bake at 325°F just until the edges are firm and the center is almost set. Be careful not to overbake.
Reduced-fat margarine and light butter	☐ Be sure to choose a brand of butter or margarine that contains 5 to 6 grams of fat and 50 calories per tablespoon. Brands with less fat than this do not generally work well in baking. ☐ Replace the full-fat margarine, butter, or other solid fat with three-fourths as much reduced-fat margarine or light butter. ☐ Bake at 325°F just until the edges are firm and the center is almost set. Be careful not to overbake.

A few more general tips will help insure the best possible results when trimming the fat from your favorite brownie recipes.

☐ If your recipe is made with 100 percent white flour, try substituting oat flour for the white flour in the recipe, or substitute oat bran or quick-cooking oats for half of the flour. These products will hold in moisture and help produce a pleasantly chewy texture.

☐ Try adding a few tablespoons of instant nonfat dry milk powder to the recipe. This will improve the texture and boost nutritional value.

CREAM CHEESE MARBLE BROWNIES

1. Prepare the brownie mix as directed on the package. Coat the bottom only of a 9-x-13-inch pan with nonstick cooking spray, and spread the mixture evenly in the pan. Set aside.

2. Place the cream cheese and sugar in a medium-sized bowl, and beat with an electric mixer until smooth. Add the flour, and beat to mix well. Add the egg substitute and vanilla extract, and beat to mix well.

3. Pour the cheese mixture over the brownie batter in an "S" pattern. Then draw a knife through the batter to create a marbled effect.

4. Bake at 325°F for 30 to 33 minutes, or just until the edges are firm and the center is almost set. Be careful not to overbake.

5. Allow the brownies to cool to room temperature before cutting into squares and serving. For easier cutting, rinse the knife off periodically.

Yield: 24 brownies

1 package (about 1 pound, 5 ounces) low-fat fudge brownie mix, such as Betty Crocker Sweet Rewards*

1 block (8 ounces) nonfat cream cheese, softened to room temperature

1/3 cup sugar

1 tablespoon unbleached flour

3 tablespoons fat-free egg substitute

1 teaspoon vanilla extract

* Alternatively, use a regular brownie mix, replacing the fat with a fat substitute, as directed on page 142.

NUTRITIONAL FACTS (PER BROWNIE)
Calories: 119 Carbohydrates: 23 g Cholesterol: 0 mg
Fat: 1.5 g Fiber: 0.7 g Protein: 3.1 g Sodium: 132 mg

You Save: Calories: 64 Fat: 10.2 g

7

Refreshing Frozen Desserts

Cool and refreshing, frozen desserts are everyone's favorite treat on a sizzling summer day. But don't limit these icy confections to the summer months. Elegant and surprisingly simple to make, frozen desserts are perfect for year-round entertaining. And since they must be prepared in advance, these toothsome temptations are a real boon to the busy cook.

The star ingredients in this chapter's frozen delights make these treats as healthful as they are delicious. Ripe fruits and juices provide a bounty of nutrients, as well as great flavor and natural sweetness. And nonfat dairy products—including nonfat yogurt, buttermilk, and more—add creamy richness and a calcium boost without the usual fat.

No time to make frozen desserts from scratch? Don't fear. These days, your local supermarket stocks just as many no- and low-fat brands of ice cream as it does full-fat brands. How great are your savings when you switch to these products? One cup of premium ice cream can contain up to 600 calories and 40 grams of fat—the equivalent of a half-stick of butter. The same size serving of nonfat or low-fat ice cream contains only 180 to 240 calories and from 0 to 6 grams of fat.

As for sugar, many of these desserts contain considerably less than most traditional recipes do. In many cases, fruits and fruit juices provide natural sweetness, which is then enhanced with moderate amounts of sugar and sweet flavorings like vanilla extract. This means that even sorbets, granitas, and sherbets, which have always been low in fat or fat-free, can be made lower in calories and higher in nutrients.

So whether you are looking for a simple ice cream sandwich to take the heat out of a sultry afternoon or a tropical fruit sorbet to impress even the most discriminating guest, you need look no further. These temptingly sweet treats will prove, once and for all, that even easy-to-make, good-for-you desserts can be satisfying and delicious.

Tangy Peach Sherbet

Yield: *6 servings*

4 cups diced peeled peaches
(about 5 1/2 medium)

1/2 cup plus 2 tablespoons
sugar

1 1/4 teaspoons unflavored
gelatin

1/8 teaspoon ground nutmeg

1 1/4 cups nonfat or low-fat
buttermilk

1 1/4 teaspoons vanilla extract

For variety, substitute fresh sliced strawberries or nectarines for the peaches.

1. Place the peaches and sugar in a 2-quart pot, stir to mix well, and place over medium heat. Cover and cook, stirring occasionally, for about 5 minutes, or until the peaches are soft and the liquid is syrupy.

2. Place the peach mixture in a blender, and sprinkle the gelatin and nutmeg over the top. Leaving the lid slightly ajar to allow steam to escape, carefully process at low speed for about 1 minute, or until the mixture is smooth and the gelatin is completely dissolved. Return the mixture to the pot, and allow to cool to room temperature.

3. When mixture has cooled, whisk in the buttermilk and vanilla extract.

4. Pour the mixture into a 1 1/2-quart ice cream maker, and proceed as directed by the manufacturer. (If you don't own an ice cream maker, see the inset on page 150 for directions on making the sherbet in your freezer.) Scoop into individual dessert dishes, and serve immediately.

NUTRITIONAL FACTS (PER 7/8-CUP SERVING)
Calories: 150 Carbohydrates: 36 g Cholesterol: 2 mg
Fat: 0.5 g Fiber: 2 g Protein: 2.5 g Sodium: 54 mg

You Save: Calories: 80 Fat: 3 g

Fresh Mango Sorbet

1. Place the juice and sugar in a small pot, and bring to a boil over high heat. Reduce the heat to low, cover, and simmer for 3 minutes, stirring occasionally.

2. Remove the pot from the heat, and sprinkle the gelatin over the juice mixture. Whisk for about 2 minutes, or until the gelatin is completely dissolved. Set aside for about 30 minutes to cool to room temperature.

3. Place the mangoes and the cooled juice mixture in a blender, and process until smooth.

4. Pour the mixture into a 1½-quart ice cream maker, and proceed as directed by the manufacturer. (If you don't own an ice cream maker, see the inset on page 150 for directions on making the sorbet in your freezer.) Scoop into individual dessert dishes, and serve immediately.

Yield: *6 servings*

1½ cups pineapple juice

½ cup sugar

¾ teaspoon unflavored gelatin

3 cups diced peeled fresh mangoes (about 2 large)

NUTRITIONAL FACTS (PER ¾-CUP SERVING)
Calories: 150   Carbohydrates: 38 g   Cholesterol: 0 mg
Fat: 0.2 g   Fiber: 2.4 g   Protein: 0.7 g   Sodium: 2 mg

You Save: Calories: 66 Fat: 0 g

Strawberry-Cheesecake Sherbet

Yield: *5 servings*

5 cups sliced fresh strawberries

1/2 cup plus 2 tablespoons sugar

1 block (8 ounces) nonfat cream cheese

1 1/2 teaspoons vanilla extract

For variety, substitute fresh peaches for the strawberries.

1. Place the strawberries and sugar in a 2 1/2-quart pot, stir to mix well, and place over medium heat. Cover the pot, and cook, stirring occasionally, for about 5 minutes, or until the strawberries are soft and the liquid is syrupy. Remove the pot from the heat, and allow to cool to room temperature.

2. Place the cooled strawberry mixture in a blender or food processor. Add the cream cheese and vanilla extract, and process until smooth.

3. Pour the mixture into a 1 1/2-quart ice cream maker, and proceed as directed by the manufacturer. (If you don't own an ice cream maker, see the inset on page 150 for directions on making the sherbet in your freezer.) Scoop into individual dessert dishes, and serve immediately.

NUTRITIONAL FACTS (PER 7/8-CUP SERVING)

Calories: 187 Carbohydrates: 39 g Cholesterol: 3 mg
Fat: 0.6 g Fiber: 2.5 g Protein: 8 g Sodium: 221 mg

You Save: Calories: 112 Fat: 16 g

VERY STRAWBERRY ICE CREAM

For variety, substitute other fruits, such as peaches, nectarines, pineapples, bananas, or apricots, for the strawberries.

1. Place all of the ingredients in a food processor, and process until smooth.

2. Pour the mixture into a 2-quart ice cream maker, and proceed as directed by the manufacturer. (If you don't own an ice cream maker, see the inset on page 150 for directions on making the dessert in your freezer.) Scoop into individual dessert dishes, and serve immediately.

Yield: 8 servings

6 cups sliced fresh strawberries

1 can (12 ounces) fat-free sweetened condensed milk

1 cup nonfat sour cream

2 teaspoons vanilla extract

NUTRITIONAL FACTS (PER 7/8-CUP SERVING)

Calories: 182 Carbohydrates: 39 g Cholesterol: 2 mg
Fat: 0.4 g Fiber: 1.6 g Protein: 5.6 g Sodium: 67 mg

You Save: Calories: 45 Fat: 10.1 g

TROPICAL BREEZE FREEZE

1. Place the pineapple with its juice and the yogurt, condensed milk, and vanilla extract in a blender or food processor, and process until smooth.

2. Pour the mixture into a 1½-quart ice cream maker, and proceed as directed by the manufacturer. (If you don't own an ice cream maker, see the inset on page 150 for directions on making the sherbet in your freezer.) Scoop into individual dessert dishes, and serve immediately.

Yield: 5 servings

3 cans (8 ounces each) crushed pineapple in juice, undrained

1 cup nonfat vanilla or coconut yogurt

½ cup fat-free sweetened condensed milk

¾ teaspoon vanilla extract

NUTRITIONAL FACTS (PER 7/8-CUP SERVING)

Calories: 179 Carbohydrates: 40 g Cholesterol: 3 mg
Fat: 0.2 g Fiber: 0.8 g Protein: 5.1 g Sodium: 60 mg

You Save: Calories: 118 Fat: 15.8 g

Fruitful Frozen Yogurt

Yield: *9 servings*

3 1/2 cups coarsely chopped
  fresh fruit (try strawberries,
  peaches, apricots,
  pineapples, bananas,
  or blueberries)

3 cups plain nonfat yogurt

1 can (14 ounces) fat-free
  sweetened condensed milk

2 teaspoons vanilla extract

1. Place all of the ingredients in a food processor, and process until smooth.

2. Pour the mixture into a 2-quart ice cream maker, and proceed as directed by the manufacturer. (If you don't own an ice cream maker, see the inset below for directions on making the dessert in your freezer.) Scoop into individual dessert dishes, and serve immediately.

NUTRITIONAL FACTS (PER 7/8-CUP SERVING)
Calories: 188 Carbohydrates: 37.4 g Cholesterol: 4 mg
Fat: 0.5 g Fiber: 0.9 g Protein: 9 g Sodium: 109 mg

You Save: Calories: 33 Fat: 6.2 g

Making Ice Cream, Sherbet, Sorbet, and Frozen Yogurt in Your Freezer

An ice cream maker will produce the smoothest, creamiest fat-free ice creams, sherbets, and sorbets imaginable. Inexpensive machines that do not require any ice, salt, or electricity are now widely available. The simplest machines have an inner canister that you store in the freezer until you are ready to make your frozen confection. You then pour your mixture into the canister, place the canister in the machine, and turn the handle every few minutes. Machines like these, as well as fancier models, are convenient to have on hand if you plan on making your own frozen desserts on a regular basis. However, if you don't have an ice cream maker, you can still enjoy frozen treats by using the following steps to prepare them in your freezer.

1. Prepare the ice cream, sorbet, or sherbet mixture as directed in the recipe, but instead of transferring the mixture to an ice cream maker, pour it into an 8-inch square pan. Cover the pan with aluminum foil, and place in the freezer for several hours, or until the outer 2-inch edge of the mixture is frozen. If you prefer, you can prepare the mixture a few days ahead of time. Then remove it from the freezer, and allow it to sit at room temperature for about 20 minutes, or until thawed enough to break into chunks, before proceeding with Step 2.

2. Break the mixture into chunks, and place in the bowl of a food processor or electric mixer. Process for several minutes, or until light, creamy, and smooth. (Note that, depending on the capacity of your food processor, you may have to process the mixture in 2 batches.)

3. Return the mixture to the pan, cover, and return to the freezer. Freeze for at least 2 hours, or until firm.

4. About 20 minutes before serving, remove the dessert from the freezer and allow it to soften slightly at room temperature. Scoop into individual dessert dishes, and serve immediately.

PRESTO PEACH ICE CREAM

1. Place the sour cream, sugar, and vanilla extract in a small bowl, and stir to mix well. Set aside.

2. Dice the frozen peaches into ³⁄₄-inch chunks. Place the peaches in the bowl of a food processor, and process for a couple of minutes, or until finely ground.

3. Add the sour cream mixture to the food processor, and process for a couple of minutes, or until the mixture is light, creamy, and smooth. Serve immediately. Freeze leftovers in a covered container, and let sit at room temperature for about 10 minutes, or until slightly softened, before serving.

Yield: *4 servings*

¹⁄₂ cup nonfat sour cream

¹⁄₃ cup sugar

1 teaspoon vanilla extract

1 bag (1 pound) frozen sliced peaches, unthawed

NUTRITIONAL FACTS (PER ³⁄₄-CUP SERVING)

Calories: 143 Carbohydrates: 34 g Cholesterol: 0 mg
Fat: 0.1 g Fiber: 2 g Protein: 2.6 g Sodium: 22 mg

You Save: Calories: 82 Fat: 11.9 g

Simple Apricot Sorbet

Yield: *4 servings*

1 can (1 pound) apricot halves
    in juice, undrained

1/4 cup plus 1 tablespoon
    frozen white grape juice
    concentrate, unthawed

1. Place the apricots with their juice and the juice concentrate in a blender, and process until smooth.

2. Pour the mixture into an 8-x-4-inch loaf pan. Cover the pan with aluminum foil, and place in the freezer for about 3 hours and 30 minutes, or until the outer 1-inch edge of the mixture is frozen.

3. Place the partially frozen mixture in the bowl of a food processor or electric mixer, breaking up the frozen outer edges. Process for about 2 minutes, or until light, creamy, and smooth.

4. Return the mixture to the pan, cover, and return the pan to the freezer. Freeze for at least 2 hours, or until firm.

5. About 10 minutes before serving, remove the dessert from the freezer and allow it to soften slightly at room temperature. Scoop into individual dessert dishes, and serve immediately.

NUTRITIONAL FACTS (PER 2/3-CUP SERVING)

Calories: 107 Carbohydrates: 27 g Cholesterol: 0 mg
Fat: 0 g Fiber: 1.3 g Protein: 0.7 g Sodium: 4 mg

You Save: Calories: 93 Fat: 0 g

VERY CRANBERRY GRANITA

1. Place 1 cup of the juice and all of the sugar in a 1-quart pot, and stir to mix. Bring the mixture to a boil over medium-high heat. Reduce the heat to low, cover, and simmer, stirring occasionally, for a minute or 2, or until the sugar is completely dissolved and the liquid is slightly syrupy. Remove the pot from the heat, and allow the mixture cool to room temperature.

2. Pour the cooled sugar mixture into an 8-inch square pan, and add the remaining juice and the juice concentrate. Stir to mix well.

3. Place the pan in the freezer for about 25 minutes, or until ice crystals begin to form around the sides of the pan. Using a spoon, stir the frozen crystals from around the edges and bottom of the pan back into the liquid portion. Repeat the scraping process every 20 minutes for about 2 hours, or until the mixture is icy and granular.

4. Spoon the granita into four 8-ounce wine glasses, and serve immediately.

Yield: *5 servings*

3 cups cranberry juice cocktail, divided

1/4 cup plus 1 tablespoon sugar

3 tablespoons frozen (thawed or unthawed) or liquid cranberry juice cocktail concentrate

NUTRITIONAL FACTS (PER 3/4-CUP SERVING)
Calories: 153 Carbohydrates: 39 g Cholesterol: 0 mg
Fat: 0.1 g Fiber: 0.2 g Protein: 0 g Sodium: 4 mg

You Save: Calories: 45 Fat: 0 g

Strawberry Angel Parfaits

Yield: *5 servings*

10 ounces frozen sliced sweetened strawberries, thawed

5 slices ($^1/_2$-inch each) angel food cake

3$^1/_3$ cups nonfat or low-fat vanilla ice cream

1. Place 1 tablespoon of the strawberries in the bottom of each of five 10-ounce balloon wine glasses.

2. Crumble a half-slice of cake over the berries in each glass. Top the cake with $^1/_3$ cup of ice cream, and then spoon 2 tablespoons of strawberries over the ice cream.

3. Repeat the cake, ice cream, and strawberry layers, and serve immediately.

NUTRITIONAL FACTS (PER SERVING)
Calories: 248 Carbohydrates: 56.4 g Cholesterol: 2 mg
Fat: 0.3 g Fiber: 1.5 g Protein: 7.3 g Sodium: 214 mg

You Save: Calories: 117 Fat: 16 g

Tiramisu Sundaes

Yield: *4 servings*

$^1/_4$ cup plus 2 tablespoons coffee liqueur

1 tablespoon Dutch processed cocoa powder, divided

8 ladyfingers

2$^2/_3$ cups nonfat or low-fat vanilla, cappuccino, or cheesecake ice cream

$^1/_4$ cup plus 2 tablespoons nonfat or light whipped topping

1. Place the liqueur and 2$^1/_2$ teaspoons of the cocoa in a small bowl, and stir to dissolve the cocoa powder. Set aside.

2. Crumble 1 ladyfinger into the bottom of each of four 10-ounce balloon wine glasses. Drizzle 2 teaspoons of the liqueur mixture over the lady finger. Then top with $^1/_3$ cup of the ice cream. Repeat the ladyfinger, liqueur, and ice cream layers.

3. Drizzle $^1/_2$ teaspoon of the liqueur mixture over the top of each sundae. Then top each sundae with a rounded tablespoon of whipped topping and a sprinkling of cocoa. Serve immediately.

NUTRITIONAL FACTS (PER SERVING)
Calories: 268 Carbohydrates: 49 g Cholesterol: 27 mg
Fat: 1.2 g Fiber: 0.6 g Protein: 5.4 g Sodium: 181 mg

You Save: Calories: 160 Fat: 21.3 g

Light Ice Cream Sandwiches

For variety, try making these sandwiches with different ice cream flavors, such as vanilla, cherry vanilla, chocolate, raspberry ripple, cappuccino, and praline swirl.

Yield: *8 servings*

8 large (2^1/$_2$-x-5-inch) reduced-fat chocolate graham crackers

2 cups nonfat or low-fat ice cream, any flavor, slightly softened

1. Break each graham cracker in half so that you have 16 squares, each measuring 2^1/$_2$ x 2^1/$_2$ inches.

2. Spread ^{1}/$_4$ cup of the ice cream over 1 square, top with another square, and gently press the crackers together. Smooth the edges of the ice cream with a knife. Wrap the sandwich in plastic wrap, and place in the freezer. Repeat with the remaining ingredients to make 8 sandwiches.

3. Freeze the sandwiches for at least 1 hour before serving.

NUTRITIONAL FACTS (PER SERVING)

Calories: 105 Carbohydrates: 20.5 g Cholesterol: 1 mg
Fat: 1.5 g Fiber: 0.2 g Protein: 2.5 g Sodium: 117 mg

You Save: Calories: 40 Fat: 6.6 g

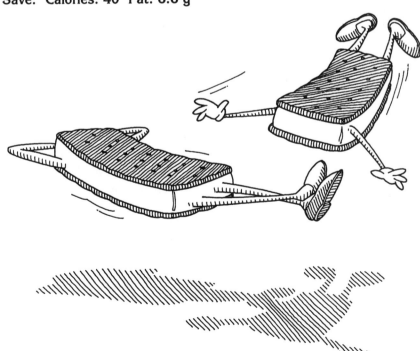

Cool Chocolate-Raspberry Torte

Yield: *12 servings*

CRUST

8 large (2½-x-5-inch) reduced-fat chocolate graham crackers

2 tablespoons sugar

1 tablespoon plus 1½ teaspoons tub-style nonfat margarine, or 2 tablespoons plus ½ teaspoon reduced-fat margarine or light butter, cut into pieces

3 tablespoons honey crunch wheat germ or finely chopped toasted walnuts or almonds (page 167)

For variety, substitute low-fat cappuccino, cookies and cream, mint chocolate chip, or peanut butter ice cream for the raspberry ice cream or sherbet.

1. To make the crust, break the crackers into pieces, and place in the bowl of a food processor. Process into fine crumbs. Measure the crumbs. There should be 1 cup. Adjust the amount if necessary.

2. Return the crumbs to the food processor, add the sugar, and process for a few seconds to mix well. Add the margarine, and process for about 20 seconds, or until the mixture is moist (but not wet) and crumbly, and holds together when pinched. If the mixture seems too dry, mix in more margarine, ½ teaspoon at a time, until the proper consistency is reached. Add the wheat germ or nuts, and process to mix well.

3. Coat a 9-inch springform pan with nonstick cooking spray, and use the back of a spoon to press the mixture against the bottom and sides of the pan, forming an even crust. (Periodically dip the spoon in sugar, if necessary, to prevent sticking.) Then use your fingers to finish pressing the crust firmly against the bottom and sides of the pan.

4. Bake at 350°F for 10 minutes, or until the edges feel firm and dry. Set aside to cool to room temperature before filling.

5. Allow the chocolate ice cream to sit at room temperature for about 10 minutes, or until slightly softened. Spread the ice cream

evenly in the crust. Cover the pan, and freeze for at least 1 hour. Then top with the raspberry ice cream or sherbet in the same manner. Freeze for at least 2 hours.

6. To make the optional fudge topping, place the sugar, cocoa, and cornstarch in a 1-quart pot, and stir to mix well. Slowly stir in the milk, and cook over medium heat, stirring constantly, for about 5 minutes, or until the mixture is thickened and bubbly.

7. Remove the pot from the heat, and stir in the vanilla extract. Transfer the topping to a covered container and refrigerate for at least 2 hours, or until well chilled.

8. Stir the chilled topping, and spread it over the top of the torte. Return the torte to the freezer, and freeze for at least 2 additional hours.

9. When ready to serve, remove the torte from the freezer, and allow to sit at room temperature for 5 minutes. Run a sharp knife between the edge of the torte and the rim of the pan, and remove the collar. Slice and serve immediately.

FILLING

4 cups nonfat or low-fat chocolate ice cream

4 cups nonfat or low-fat raspberry ripple ice cream or raspberry sherbet

FUDGE TOPPING (OPTIONAL)

1/2 cup sugar

1/4 cup Dutch processed cocoa powder

1 tablespoon plus 1 1/2 teaspoons cornstarch

3/4 cup skim milk

1 teaspoon vanilla extract

NUTRITIONAL FACTS (PER SERVING)

Calories: 175 Carbohydrates: 35 g Cholesterol: 3 mg
Fat: 1.4 g Fiber: 0.8 g Protein: 5.5 g Sodium: 154 mg

You Save: Calories: 192 Fat: 19.3 g

Time-Saving Tip

Instead of making the fudge sauce from scratch, substitute 1 cup of ready-made fat-free hot fudge topping.

Cool Peach Melba

Yield: *6 servings*

3/4 cup orange juice

3 medium peaches, peeled, halved, and pitted

3 cups nonfat or low-fat vanilla ice cream

SAUCE

1 tablespoon plus 1 teaspoon cornstarch

3 tablespoons sugar

1 1/4 cups fresh or frozen (unthawed) raspberries

1. Place the orange juice in the bottom of a microwave or conventional steamer, and arrange the peach halves in the steamer. Cover and cook at high power or over high heat for about 4 minutes, or until the peaches are tender but not mushy. Transfer the peaches and juice to a covered container, and chill for several hours or overnight.

2. Just before serving, make the sauce by placing the cornstarch and sugar in a 1-quart pot. Remove 1/2 cup of juice from the container of peaches, and add it to the sugar mixture, stirring until the cornstarch is dissolved.

3. Place the saucepan over medium heat, and cook, stirring constantly, for about 2 minutes, or until the mixture becomes thickened and bubbly. Add the raspberries, and bring to a second boil. Cook and stir just until the berries begin to break up. Remove the pot from the heat, and set aside.

4. To assemble the desserts, place a 1/2-cup scoop of ice cream in each of 6 dessert bowls. Top each scoop with a well-drained peach half, placing the hollow side down. Top with 3 tablespoons of the warm sauce, and serve immediately.

NUTRITIONAL FACTS (PER SERVING)

Calories: 161 Carbohydrates: 37 g Cholesterol: 2 mg
Fat: 0.5 g Fiber: 1.9 g Protein: 3.7 g Sodium: 55 mg

You Save: Calories: 96 Fat: 12 g

Mocha Meringue Tarts

1. Place each tart on an individual serving dish, and place a $1/2$-cup scoop of ice cream in the center of each tart.

2. Scatter $1/4$ cup of berries over and around the ice cream in each tart, and drizzle 1 tablespoon of the chocolate syrup over the top. Serve immediately.

Yield: *8 servings*

8 Meringue Tart Shells (page 74)

1 quart nonfat or low-fat mocha or cappuccino ice cream

2 cups fresh raspberries

$1/2$ cup chocolate syrup

NUTRITIONAL FACTS (PER SERVING)
Calories: 224 Carbohydrates: 51 g Cholesterol: 2 mg
Fat: 0.5 g Fiber: 1.6 g Protein: 4.9 g Sodium: 107 mg

You Save: Calories: 89 Fat: 12 g

Ice Cream With Cherry-Amaretto Sauce

1. Place the sugar and cornstarch in a 1-quart pot, and stir to mix well. Slowly add the orange juice while stirring to dissolve the cornstarch. Add the frozen cherries.

2. Place the pot over medium heat and cook, stirring constantly, for about 5 minutes, or until the mixture is thickened and bubbly. Add the amaretto, and stir for 30 additional seconds. Remove from the heat.

3. Place $3/4$ cup of ice cream in each of 4 serving bowls, and top each serving with $1/3$ cup of the warm cherry sauce. Serve immediately.

Yield: *4 servings*

2 tablespoons sugar

$2 1/4$ teaspoons cornstarch

$1/4$ cup plus 2 tablespoons orange juice

1 bag (12 ounces) frozen sweet pitted cherries, unthawed (about $2 1/4$ cups)

2 tablespoons amaretto liqueur

3 cups nonfat or low-fat vanilla, chocolate, or fudge ripple ice cream

NUTRITIONAL FACTS (PER SERVING)
Calories: 256 Carbohydrates: 54 g Cholesterol: 3 mg
Fat: 0.4 g Fiber: 1.9 g Protein: 5.3 g Sodium: 83 mg

You Save: Calories: 157 Fat: 17.7 g

FROZEN MOCHA PIE

Yield: *8 servings*

1/4 cup chocolate syrup

2 tablespoons coffee or amaretto liqueur

2 cups nonfat or light whipped topping

4 ounces ladyfingers (about 16 whole cookies)

4 cups nonfat or low-fat cappuccino ice cream, slightly softened

1 teaspoon cocoa powder

For variety, substitute raspberry ripple or chocolate ice cream for the cappuccino ice cream.

1. To make the syrup, place the chocolate syrup and liqueur in a small bowl, and stir to mix well. Set aside.

2. To make the topping, place the whipped topping in a medium-sized bowl, and gently fold in 1 tablespoon of the chocolate syrup mixture. Set aside.

3. To assemble the pie, first split each of the ladyfingers in half lengthwise. (Most ladyfingers come presplit.) Line the bottom and sides of a 9-inch deep dish pie pan with about two-thirds of the ladyfinger halves, arranging them split side-up. Drizzle half of the chocolate syrup mixture over the ladyfingers that line the bottom of the pan.

4. Spread the ice cream over the ladyfingers. Then top with the remaining ladyfingers, this time arranging them split side-down.

5. Drizzle the remaining chocolate syrup mixture over the ladyfingers layer. Then spread the whipped topping mixture over the syrup, swirling the topping.

6. Cover the pie loosely with aluminum foil, and freeze for several hours or overnight. When ready to serve, sprinkle the cocoa over the top of the pie. Cut the pie into wedges, place the wedges on individual serving plates, and allow to sit at room temperature for 5 minutes before serving.

NUTRITIONAL FACTS (PER SERVING)

Calories: 202 Carbohydrates: 42 g Cholesterol: 27 mg
Fat: 1.4 g Fiber: 0.4 g Protein: 4.4 g Sodium: 176 mg

You Save: Calories: 93 Fat: 12.6 g

Chocolate Ice Cream Cake

For variety, try making this cake with different ice cream flavors, such as cherry vanilla, raspberry ripple, cappuccino, banana, chocolate mint, pistachio, and others.

1. To make the cake, place the cake mix in a large bowl. Add the water or coffee, yogurt, and egg substitute, and beat with an electric mixer for about 2 minutes, or until well mixed.

2. Coat three 9-inch round cake pans with nonstick cooking spray, and divide the batter evenly among the pans. Bake at 350°F for about 23 minutes, or just until the tops spring back when lightly touched and a wooden toothpick inserted in the center of the cakes comes out clean. Be careful not to overbake. Allow the cakes to cool to room temperature.

3. When ready to assemble the cake, place the ice cream in a large bowl, and set aside for about 10 minutes, or until soft enough to spread.

4. Place one cake layer on a serving platter, with the bottom facing up. Spread half of the ice cream over the cake layer. Place another cake layer over the ice cream, bottom side up, and spread with the remaining ice cream. Top with the remaining cake layer, top side up. Cover with aluminum foil, and place in the freezer for at least 1 hour.

5. To make the frosting, place the cocoa powder and chocolate syrup in a medium-sized bowl and stir to mix well. Add $1/2$ cup of the whipped topping, and gently fold the mixture together. Fold in the remaining whipped topping.

6. Spread the frosting over the top and sides of the cake. Cover loosely with foil or a cake lid, and return to the freezer for at least 4 hours, or until firm. Remove the cake from the freezer and allow to sit at room temperature for about 10 minutes before slicing and serving.

Yield: *16 servings*

5 cups nonfat or low-fat vanilla or chocolate ice cream

CAKE

1 box (1 pound, 2.25 ounces) reduced-fat or regular chocolate cake mix

1 cup water or coffee, cooled to room temperature

$3/4$ cup plain nonfat yogurt

$1/2$ cup fat-free egg substitute

FROSTING

2 tablespoons Dutch processed cocoa powder

2 tablespoons chocolate syrup

3 cups nonfat or light whipped topping

NUTRITIONAL FACTS (PER SERVING)
Calories: 223 Carbohydrates: 45 g Cholesterol: 2 mg
Fat: 2.8 g Fiber: 0.9 g Protein: 5 g Sodium: 328 mg

You Save: Calories: 140 Fat: 19.4 g

8

Crisps, Cobblers, and Other Fabulous Fruit Desserts

When you want a dessert full of down-home goodness, think cobblers and crisps. With their juicy fruit fillings, cobblers and crisps are naturally sweet and delicious. And when made properly, these treats contain little or no fat, and only moderate amounts of sugar.

In most traditional fruit-based desserts, the biggest source of fat is the topping. It's not unusual for the cinnamon-flavored crumbs atop an apple crisp to contain as much as a full stick of butter! But fear not. By using the right ingredients, it's easy to greatly reduce the fat in fruit desserts without sacrificing the flavors and textures you love. In this chapter, the crisp and crumble toppings combine naturally sweet grain products like oats and whole wheat pastry flour with other wholesome ingredients, such as wheat germ, toasted nuts, and spices. Instead of the usual butter or margarine, small amounts of fruit juice concentrate, liquid sweeteners, and even nonfat margarine are used to moisten the toppings. Cobbler crusts combine unbleached flour and

oats or oat bran with nonfat dairy products. The result? Toppings so full of flavor that you will never miss the fat.

As for sugar, both the toppings and fillings in these confections contain only moderate amounts, making these desserts one of the more wholesome ways to satisfy a sweet tooth. Much of the sweetness in these luscious desserts comes from the fruit itself. The inclusion of juices and dried fruits also adds natural sweetness, while flavorings like cinnamon and orange rind further reduce the need for added sugar.

When creating desserts with fresh fruits, do be sure to use very ripe sweet produce, as this will insure a flavorful result. But don't think that cobblers and crisps can be made only during the summer months, when fresh fruits are most bountiful. Many of these recipes take advantage of frozen fruits and fruits canned in juice. Served hot from the oven, these heart-warming treats will provide your family with old-fashioned comfort all year long!

Summer Fruit Crisp

Yield: *8 servings*

4 cups sliced peeled peaches or nectarines (about 6 medium)

1 cup fresh or frozen (unthawed) blueberries, raspberries, or pitted sweet cherries

1/3 cup sugar

1 tablespoon cornstarch

TOPPING

1/4 cup plus 2 tablespoons quick-cooking oats

1/4 cup plus 2 tablespoons whole wheat pastry flour

1/4 cup plus 2 tablespoons light brown sugar

1/2 teaspoon ground cinnamon

2 tablespoons chilled tub-style nonfat margarine, or 3 tablespoons chilled reduced-fat margarine, cut into pieces

1/3 cup honey crunch wheat germ or chopped toasted pecans (page 167)

1. To make the filling, place the peaches or nectarines and the blueberries, raspberries, or cherries in a large bowl, and toss to mix well. Set aside.

2. Place the sugar and cornstarch in a small bowl, and stir to mix well. Sprinkle the mixture over the fruit, and toss to mix well. (If the fruit is tart, you may need to add another couple of tablespoons of sugar.) Coat a 9-inch deep dish pie pan with nonstick cooking spray, and spread the fruit mixture evenly in the pan. Set aside.

3. To make the topping, place the oats, flour, brown sugar, and cinnamon in a small bowl, and stir to mix well. Add the nonfat margarine, and stir until the mixture is moist and crumbly. (If you are using reduced-fat margarine, use a pastry cutter or 2 knives to cut the margarine into the oat mixture until it is moist and crumbly.) If the mixture seems too dry, add more margarine, 1/2 teaspoon at a time, until the proper consistency is reached. Stir in the wheat germ or pecans. Sprinkle the topping over the filling.

4. Bake uncovered at 375°F for 35 to 40 minutes, or until the filling is bubbly and the topping is golden brown. Cover loosely with aluminum foil during the last few minutes of baking if the topping starts to brown too quickly. Allow to cool at room temperature for at least 15 minutes, and serve warm or at room temperature.

NUTRITIONAL FACTS (PER SERVING)

Calories: 163 Carbohydrates: 37 g Cholesterol: 0 mg
Fat: 1 g Fiber: 3.4 g Protein: 3.2 g Sodium: 27 mg

You Save: Calories: 143 Fat: 13.2 g

Mini Blackberry Cobblers

For variety, substitute blueberries, raspberries, or diced peeled peaches for the blackberries.

1. To make the filling, place the blackberries in a large bowl. Set aside.

2. Place the sugar, cornstarch, and lemon or orange rind in a small bowl, and stir to mix well. Sprinkle the mixture over the fruit, and toss to mix well. (If the fruit is tart, you may need to add another couple of tablespoons of sugar.) Coat six 6-ounce custard cups with nonstick cooking spray, and divide the mixture evenly among the cups. Set aside.

3. To make the crust, place the flour, oats, sugar, baking powder, and salt in a medium-sized bowl, and stir to mix well. Using a pastry cutter or 2 knives, cut in the margarine or butter until the mixture resembles coarse crumbs. Add just enough of the milk to make a stiff dough, stirring just until the dough holds together and forms a ball.

4. Shape the dough into 6 balls. Using a rolling pin and working on a lightly floured surface, roll each ball into a 4-inch circle, and lay 1 crust over the fruit filling in each cup. Pinch the edges of each circle to make a decorative edge.

5. To glaze the crusts, brush each lightly with the egg substitute or egg white, and sprinkle with ¼ teaspoon of sugar. Using a sharp knife, cut 4 slits in the center of each crust to allow steam to escape during baking.

6. Place the cups on a baking sheet, and bake at 375°F for 30 minutes, or until the filling is bubbly and the crusts are lightly browned. Remove the cobblers from the oven, and allow to cool at room temperature for at least 10 minutes before serving warm.

Yield: *6 servings*

4 cups fresh or frozen (partially thawed) blackberries

¼ cup plus 2 tablespoons sugar

1 tablespoon cornstarch

¾ teaspoon dried grated lemon or orange rind, or 2¼ teaspoons fresh

CRUST

¾ cup unbleached flour

⅓ cup quick-cooking oats

1 tablespoon plus 1½ teaspoons sugar

½ teaspoon baking powder

⅛ teaspoon salt

2 tablespoons plus 1½ teaspoons chilled reduced-fat margarine or light butter

3 tablespoons evaporated skimmed milk

GLAZE

2 tablespoons fat-free egg substitute or 1 egg white, beaten

1½ teaspoons sugar

NUTRITIONAL FACTS (PER SERVING)

Calories: 215 Carbohydrates: 44 g Cholesterol: 0 mg
Fat: 3 g Fiber: 4.9 g Protein: 3.2 g Sodium: 86 mg

You Save: Calories: 94 Fat: 10.2 g

Biscuit-Topped Blueberry Cobbler

Yield: *8 servings*

5 cups fresh or frozen (partially thawed) blueberries

$1/4$ cup plus 2 tablespoons sugar

1 tablespoon plus $1/2$ teaspoon cornstarch

1 tablespoon plus 1 teaspoon frozen orange juice concentrate, thawed

BISCUIT TOPPING

$3/4$ cup plus 2 tablespoons unbleached flour

$1/4$ cup oat bran

$1/3$ cup plus $1 1/2$ teaspoons sugar, divided

$1 3/4$ teaspoons baking powder

$1/2$ cup plus 2 tablespoons nonfat or low-fat buttermilk

Pinch ground cinnamon

For variety, substitute blackberries or pitted sweet cherries for the blueberries.

1. To make the filling, place the blueberries in a large bowl. Set aside.

2. Place the sugar and cornstarch in a small bowl, and stir to mix well. Sprinkle the mixture over the fruit, and toss to mix well. (If the fruit is tart, you may need to add another couple of tablespoons of sugar.) Add the juice concentrate, and toss to mix well.

3. Coat a 2-quart casserole dish with nonstick cooking spray, and spread the fruit mixture evenly in the dish. Cover the dish with aluminum foil, and bake at 375°F for 30 to 40 minutes, or until hot and bubbly.

4. To make the biscuit topping, place the flour, oat bran, $1/3$ cup of the sugar, and the baking powder in a medium-sized bowl, and stir to mix well. Add just enough of the buttermilk to make a moderately thick batter, stirring just until the dry ingredients are moistened.

5. Drop heaping tablespoonfuls of the batter onto the hot fruit filling to make 8 biscuits. Combine the remaining $1 1/2$ teaspoons of sugar and the cinnamon in a small bowl, and stir to mix well. Sprinkle the mixture over the biscuit topping.

6. Bake uncovered at 375°F for 18 to 20 minutes, or until the biscuits are lightly browned. Allow to cool at room temperature for at least 10 minutes before serving warm.

NUTRITIONAL FACTS (PER SERVING)
Calories: 190 Carbohydrates: 46 g Cholesterol: 0 mg
Fat: 0.7 g Fiber: 3.2 g Protein: 3.1 g Sodium: 120 mg

You Save: Calories: 128 Fat: 12.2 g

GINGER BAKED PEACHES

This dessert is equally delicious when made with pears.

Yield: *6 servings*

1. To make the filling, place the wheat germ, brown sugar, flour, ginger, and cinnamon in a small bowl, and stir to mix well. Add the juice concentrate, and stir just until the mixture is moist and crumbly. (If the mixture seems too dry, add more juice concentrate, 1/4 teaspoon at a time, until the proper consistency is reached.) Stir in the pecans if desired. Set aside.

2. Peel the peaches. Then cut each in half lengthwise, and remove the pit. Cut a thin slice off the bottom of each peach half so that it will sit upright. Place a rounded tablespoon of the filling in the cavity of each peach half, mounding it up.

3. Pour the orange juice into the bottom of a 9-inch square pan, and arrange the peaches in the pan. Bake uncovered at 375°F for 25 to 30 minutes, or until the peaches are tender and the filling is golden brown. Cover the peaches loosely with aluminum foil during the last few minutes of baking if the filling starts to brown too quickly. Serve warm, accompanying each serving with a scoop of low-fat vanilla ice cream, if desired.

3 large fresh peaches (about 8 ounces each)

1/3 cup orange juice

3 cups nonfat or low-fat vanilla ice cream (optional)

FILLING

1/4 cup plus 1 tablespoon honey crunch wheat germ

1/4 cup plus 1 tablespoon light brown sugar

1/4 cup whole wheat pastry flour

1/4 teaspoon ground ginger

1/4 teaspoon ground cinnamon

1 tablespoon plus 1 teaspoon frozen orange juice concentrate, thawed

2 tablespoons chopped toasted pecans (below) (optional)

NUTRITIONAL FACTS (PER SERVING)

Calories: 116 Carbohydrates: 27 g Cholesterol: 0 mg
Fat: 0.7 g Fiber: 2.7 g Protein: 2.8 g Sodium: 3 mg

You Save: Calories: 91 Fat: 12.4 g

Getting the Most Out of Nuts

Nuts add crunch, great taste, and essential nutrients to all kinds of baked goods. Unfortunately, nuts also add fat. But you can greatly reduce the fat—without sacrificing flavor—by toasting nuts before adding them to your recipe. Toasting intensifies the flavor of nuts so much that you can often cut the amount used in half.

Simply arrange the nuts in a single layer on a baking sheet, and bake at 350°F for about 10 minutes, or until lightly browned with a toasted, nutty smell. Be sure to check the nuts often, as once they begin to turn color, they can quickly burn. (For sliced almonds or chopped nuts, bake for only 6 to 8 minutes.) To save time, toast a large batch and store leftovers in an airtight container in the refrigerator for several weeks, or keep them in the freezer for several months.

Blueberries and Dumplings

Yield: *6 servings*

¹/₄ cup plus 2 tablespoons sugar

1 tablespoon plus 1¹/₂ teaspoons cornstarch

¹/₄ cup orange or white grape juice

¹/₂ cup water

4 cups fresh or frozen (unthawed) blueberries, pitted sweet cherries, or blackberries

DUMPLINGS

³/₄ cup unbleached flour

¹/₄ cup sugar

1 teaspoon baking powder

2 tablespoons chilled reduced-fat margarine or light butter, cut into pieces

2 tablespoons fat-free egg substitute

2 tablespoons nonfat or low-fat buttermilk or plain nonfat yogurt

1. Place the sugar and cornstarch in a large nonstick skillet, and stir to mix well. (If the fruit is tart, you may need to add another couple of tablespoons of sugar.) Add the juice, and stir to dissolve the cornstarch. Stir in first the water, and then the fruit.

2. Place the skillet over medium heat, and cook, stirring constantly, for about 5 minutes, or until the mixture is thickened and bubbly. Remove the skillet from the heat while you prepare the dumplings.

3. To make the dumplings, place the flour, sugar, and baking powder in a small bowl, and stir to mix well. Using a pastry cutter or 2 knives, cut in the margarine or butter until the mixture is the consistency of coarse meal. Add the egg substitute and just enough of the buttermilk or yogurt to form a thick batter, stirring just until the dry ingredients are moistened.

4. Return the fruit mixture to the heat, and bring to a boil over medium-high heat. Then reduce the heat to medium-low. Drop heaping teaspoonfuls of the batter onto the simmering fruit to make 12 dumplings. Cover the skillet, and simmer without stirring for about 10 minutes, or until the dumplings are firm to the touch. (Adjust the heat if necessary to maintain a gentle simmer.) Remove the skillet from the heat, and allow to sit uncovered for 5 minutes before serving warm.

NUTRITIONAL FACTS (PER SERVING)
Calories: 222 Carbohydrates: 48 g Cholesterol: 0 mg
Fat: 2.2 g Fiber: 2.9 g Protein: 2.9 g Sodium: 126 mg

You Save: Calories: 101 Fat: 10.8 g

Variation

To make Peaches and Dumplings, substitute diced peeled fresh or frozen peaches for the blueberries. Add ¹/₄ teaspoon each cinnamon and nutmeg along with the cornstarch, and increase the water to ³/₄ cup.

Cherry-Vanilla Cobbler

1. To make the filling, place the cherries in a large bowl. Set aside.

2. Place the sugar and cornstarch in a small bowl, and stir to mix well. Sprinkle the mixture over the fruit. (If the fruit is tart, you may need to add another couple of tablespoons of sugar.) Toss to mix well. Add the juice, and toss to mix well.

3. Coat a 2-quart casserole dish with nonstick cooking spray, and spread the mixture evenly in the dish. Cover the dish with aluminum foil, and bake at 375°F for 30 to 40 minutes, or until hot and bubbly.

4. To make the biscuit topping, place the flour, oat bran, sugar, and baking powder in a medium-sized bowl, and stir to mix well. Add just enough of the yogurt to make a moderately thick batter, stirring just until the dry ingredients are moistened. Drop heaping tablespoonfuls of the batter onto the hot fruit filling to make 8 biscuits.

5. Bake uncovered at 375°F for 18 to 20 minutes, or until the biscuits are lightly browned. Remove the dish from the oven, and allow to cool at room temperature for at least 10 minutes before serving warm.

Yield: *8 servings*

5 cups fresh or frozen (partially thawed) pitted sweet cherries

1/3 cup sugar

1 tablespoon plus 1 teaspoon cornstarch

1/4 cup white grape juice

BISCUIT TOPPING

3/4 cup unbleached flour

1/3 cup oat bran

1/4 cup sugar

1 1/2 teaspoons baking powder

3/4 cup plus 1 tablespoon nonfat or low-fat vanilla yogurt

NUTRITIONAL FACTS (PER SERVING)

Calories: 198 Carbohydrates: 46 g Cholesterol: 1 mg
Fat: 0.9 g Fiber: 3.3 g Protein: 3.8 g Sodium: 108 mg

You Save: Calories: 108 Fat: 13.3 g

Peach-Almond Crisp

Yield: *8 servings*

5 cups sliced peeled peaches (about 7 medium)

1/4 cup golden raisins or chopped dates

1/3 cup sugar

2 teaspoons cornstarch

TOPPING

2 cups oat flake-and-almond cereal*

2 tablespoons whole wheat pastry flour

1/3 cup light brown sugar

1/4 teaspoon ground cinnamon

1/8 teaspoon ground nutmeg

1 tablespoon plus 1 teaspoon chilled tub-style nonfat margarine, or 2 tablespoons chilled reduced-fat margarine, cut into pieces

1/4 cup honey crunch wheat germ or sliced toasted almonds (page 167)

*Quaker Toasted Oatmeal and General Mills Oatmeal-Almond Crisp are good choices.

1. To make the filling, place the peaches and the raisins or dates in a large bowl, and toss to mix well. Set aside.

2. Place the sugar and cornstarch in a small bowl, and stir to mix well. Sprinkle the mixture over the fruit, and toss to mix well. Coat a 9-inch deep dish pie pan with nonstick cooking spray, and spread the fruit mixture evenly in the pan. Set aside.

3. To make the topping, place the cereal in a blender or food processor, and process into crumbs. Measure the crumbs. There should be 3/4 cup. (Adjust the amount if needed.)

4. Place the crumbs, flour, brown sugar, cinnamon, and nutmeg in a small bowl, and stir to mix well. Add the nonfat margarine, and stir until the mixture is moist and crumbly. (If you are using reduced-fat margarine, use a pastry cutter or 2 knives to cut the margarine into the oat mixture until it is moist and crumbly.) If the mixture seems too dry, add more margarine, 1/2 teaspoon at a time, until the proper consistency is reached. Stir in the wheat germ or almonds, and sprinkle the topping over the filling.

5. Bake uncovered at 375°F for 35 to 40 minutes, or until the filling is bubbly and the topping is golden brown. Cover loosely with aluminum foil during the last few minutes of baking if the topping starts to brown too quickly. Allow to cool at room temperature for at least 15 minutes, and serve warm or at room temperature.

NUTRITIONAL FACTS (PER SERVING)

Calories: 178 Carbohydrates: 42 g Cholesterol: 0 mg
Fat: 1 g Fiber: 3.1 g Protein: 3 g Sodium: 57 mg

You Save: Calories: 128 Fat: 13.2 g

Trimming the Fat From Crumb Toppings

Deliciously crisp and crunchy, the crumb toppings that adorn fruit crisps and crumbles are typically loaded with fat and calories. The reason? Often a full stick of butter or margarine is used to hold the crumbs together. But you can easily reduce or even eliminate the fat in these toppings by moistening the mixture with fruit juice concentrate; a liquid sweetener like maple syrup, honey, or fruit spread; reduced-fat margarine or light butter; or even nonfat margarine. The secret to using these low- and no-fat substitutes is to add only the amount needed to moisten the crumb topping mixture. If you use too much, the moisture in these fat substitutes will make your topping doughy instead of crisp or crumbly.

When mixing up no- and low-fat crumb toppings, start with only a tablespoon or two of your chosen fat substitute. Mix up the topping; if it seems too dry, add more fat substitute, a quarter to a half teaspoon at a time, until the mixture is moist and crumbly. If you are using a liquid sweetener as your fat substitute, reduce the sugar in the recipe accordingly to prevent the topping from being overly sweet. Sprinkle the topping over the fruit filling, and bake as usual. If the top starts to brown too quickly, cover it loosely with aluminum foil during the last few minutes of baking.

To save even more fat in crumb toppings, replace part or all of the nuts with honey crunch wheat germ or a barley nugget cereal like Grape-Nuts. Or toast the nuts using the directions on page 167, and reduce the amount by half. You will still get a nutty taste and a crunchy texture, but with a lot less fat and calories.

Mixed Fruit Crisp

Yield: *8 servings*

2 medium apples, peeled and
  sliced

2 medium pears, peeled and
  cut into ³⁄₄-inch chunks

2 medium unpeeled red plums,
  cut into ³⁄₄-inch slices

¹⁄₄ cup dark raisins or dried
  cranberries

¹⁄₃ cup sugar

1¹⁄₂ teaspoons cornstarch

TOPPING

4¹⁄₂ large (2¹⁄₂-x-5-inch) low-fat
  graham crackers

¹⁄₄ cup light brown sugar

¹⁄₄ teaspoon ground cinnamon

¹⁄₄ teaspoon ground ginger

1 tablespoon plus 1¹⁄₂
  teaspoons chilled tub-style
  nonfat margarine, or 2
  tablespoons plus 1 teaspoon
  chilled reduced-fat
  margarine, cut into pieces

¹⁄₄ cup honey crunch wheat
  germ or chopped walnuts

1. To make the filling, place the apples, pears, plums, and raisins or dried cranberries in a large bowl, and toss to mix well. Set aside.

2. Place the sugar and cornstarch in a small bowl, and stir to mix well. Sprinkle the mixture over the fruit, and toss to mix well. Coat a 9-inch deep dish pie pan with nonstick cooking spray, and spread the fruit mixture evenly in the pan. Set aside.

3. To make the topping, break the graham crackers into pieces, place in the bowl of a food processor, and process into crumbs. Measure the crumbs. There should be ³⁄₄ cup. (Adjust the amount if needed.)

4. Place the crumbs, brown sugar, cinnamon, and ginger in a small bowl, and stir to mix well. Add the nonfat margarine, and stir until the mixture is moist and crumbly. (If you are using reduced-fat margarine, use a pastry cutter or 2 knives to cut the margarine into the crumb mixture until it is moist and crumbly.) If the mixture seems too dry, add more margarine, ¹⁄₂ teaspoon at a time, until the proper consistency is reached. Stir in the wheat germ or walnuts. Sprinkle the topping over the filling.

5. Bake uncovered at 375°F for 35 to 40 minutes, or until the filling is bubbly and the topping is golden brown. Cover loosely with aluminum foil during the last few minutes of baking if the topping starts to brown too quickly. Allow to cool at room temperature for at least 15 minutes, and serve warm or at room temperature.

NUTRITIONAL FACTS (PER SERVING)
Calories: 177 Carbohydrates: 42 g Cholesterol: 0 mg
Fat: 1.3 g Fiber: 2.4 g Protein: 2 g Sodium: 81 mg

You Save: Calories: 154 Fat: 10.5 g

Spiced Peach Cobbler

For variety, substitute pears for the peaches.

1. To make the filling, place the cornstarch and 2 tablespoons of the nectar or juice in a small bowl, and stir to dissolve the cornstarch. Set aside.

2. Place the sugar and spices in a 3-quart pot, and stir to mix well. Add the remaining 1/2 cup of nectar or juice, and stir to mix well. Add the peaches, and bring to a boil over medium-high heat, stirring frequently. Reduce the heat to medium-low, cover, and simmer, stirring occasionally, for about 5 minutes, or just until the peaches are tender.

3. Stir the cornstarch mixture, and slowly pour it into the boiling peach mixture, stirring constantly. Cook and stir for another minute, or until the mixture has thickened. Remove the pot from the heat, cover, and set aside.

4. To make the biscuit topping, place the flour, oat bran, 1/4 cup of the sugar, and the baking powder in a medium-sized bowl, and stir to mix well. Add just enough of the yogurt to make a moderately thick batter, stirring just until the dry ingredients are moistened.

5. Coat a 2-quart baking dish with nonstick cooking spray, and spread the hot peach mixture evenly in the dish. Drop heaping tablespoonfuls of the batter onto the fruit filling to make 8 biscuits. Sprinkle the remaining 1 1/2 teaspoons of sugar over the biscuit topping.

6. Bake uncovered at 375°F for about 20 minutes, or until the biscuits are lightly browned. Allow to cool at room temperature for at least 10 minutes before serving warm.

1 tablespoon plus 1 1/2 teaspoons cornstarch

1/2 cup plus 2 tablespoons peach nectar or white grape juice, divided

1/4 cup plus 2 tablespoons sugar

1/4 teaspoon ground cinnamon

1/4 teaspoon ground allspice

1/4 teaspoon ground nutmeg

4 1/2 cups sliced peeled peaches (about 6 medium)

BISCUIT TOPPING

3/4 cup plus 2 tablespoons unbleached flour

1/4 cup oat bran

1/4 cup plus 1 1/2 teaspoons sugar, divided

1 3/4 teaspoons baking powder

1/2 cup plus 3 tablespoons nonfat or low-fat vanilla yogurt

NUTRITIONAL FACTS (PER SERVING)
Calories: 187 Carbohydrates: 45 g Cholesterol: 1 mg
Fat: 0.5 g Fiber: 2.5 g Protein: 3.6 g Sodium: 122 mg

You Save: Calories: 119 Fat: 13.7 g

Hawaiian Pineapple Crisp

Yield: *8 servings*

4 cups bite-sized pieces of fresh pineapple (about 1 medium)

¼ cup sugar

2 teaspoons cornstarch

⅛ teaspoon ground nutmeg

TOPPING

½ cup quick-cooking oats

¼ cup whole wheat pastry flour

⅓ cup light brown sugar

1 tablespoon plus 1½ teaspoons chilled tub-style nonfat margarine, or 2 tablespoons plus 1 teaspoon chilled reduced-fat margarine, cut into pieces

⅓ cup shredded sweetened coconut

3 tablespoons honey crunch wheat germ or chopped toasted macadamia nuts or almonds (page 167)

1. To make the filling, place the pineapple in a large bowl. Set aside.

2. Place the sugar, cornstarch, and nutmeg in a small bowl, and stir to mix well. Sprinkle the mixture over the fruit. (If the fruit is tart, you may need to add another couple of tablespoons of sugar.) Toss to mix well. Coat a 9-inch deep dish pie pan with nonstick cooking spray, and spread the fruit mixture evenly in the pan. Set aside.

3. To make the topping, place the oats, flour, and brown sugar in a small bowl, and stir to mix well. Add the nonfat margarine, and stir until the mixture is moist and crumbly. (If you are using reduced-fat margarine, use a pastry cutter or 2 knives to cut the margarine into the oat mixture until it is moist and crumbly.) If the mixture seems too dry, add more margarine, ½ teaspoon at a time, until the proper consistency is reached. Stir in the coconut and the wheat germ or nuts. Sprinkle the topping over the filling.

4. Bake uncovered at 375°F for 35 to 40 minutes, or until the filling is bubbly and the topping is golden brown. Cover loosely with aluminum foil during the last few minutes of baking if the topping starts to brown too quickly. Allow to cool at room temperature for at least 15 minutes, and serve warm or at room temperature.

NUTRITIONAL FACTS (PER SERVING)
Calories: 149 Carbohydrates: 31 g Cholesterol: 0 mg
Fat: 2.4 g Fiber: 2.2 g Protein: 2.3 g Sodium: 30 mg

You Save: Calories: 157 Fat: 12.8 g

Strawberry-Apple Cobbler

1. To make the filling, place the apples and strawberries in a large bowl, and toss to mix well. Set aside.

2. Place the sugar and cornstarch in a small bowl, and stir to mix well. Sprinkle the mixture over the fruit, and toss to mix well. Add the juice, and toss to mix well.

3. Coat a 2½-quart casserole dish with nonstick cooking spray, and spread the fruit mixture evenly in the dish. Cover the dish with aluminum foil, and bake at 375°F for 30 to 40 minutes, or until hot and bubbly.

4. To make the biscuit topping, place the flour, oats, ⅓ cup of the sugar, and the baking powder in a medium-sized bowl, and stir to mix well. Add just enough of the buttermilk to make a moderately thick batter, stirring just until the dry ingredients are moistened. Drop heaping tablespoonfuls of the batter onto the hot fruit filling to make 9 biscuits. Combine the remaining 1½ teaspoons of sugar and the cinnamon in a small bowl, stir to mix, and sprinkle over the biscuits.

5. Bake uncovered at 375°F for 18 to 20 minutes, or until the biscuits are lightly browned. Allow to cool at room temperature for at least 10 minutes before serving warm.

Yield: *9 servings*

4 cups sliced peeled apples (about 5½ medium)

2 cups sliced strawberries

½ cup sugar

1 tablespoon cornstarch

¼ cup apple juice

BISCUIT TOPPING

1 cup unbleached flour

⅓ cup quick-cooking oats

⅓ cup plus 1½ teaspoons sugar, divided

1½ teaspoons baking powder

½ cup plus 3 tablespoons nonfat or low-fat buttermilk

Pinch ground cinnamon

NUTRITIONAL FACTS (PER SERVING)

Calories: 206 Carbohydrates: 49 g Cholesterol: 0 mg
Fat: 0.7 g Fiber: 2.3 g Protein: 3 g Sodium: 112 mg

You Save: Calories: 118 Fat: 12.5 g

Trimming the Fat From Cobbler Toppings

Biscuit toppings add that down-home touch to cobblers. Unfortunately, they can also add a lot of fat. The good news is that it's a simple matter to reduce or even eliminate the fat in your biscuit toppings. Try replacing part or all of the butter, margarine, or other solid shortening in biscuit toppings with half as much nonfat or low-fat buttermilk or yogurt. (Replace oil with three-fourths as much buttermilk or yogurt.) Mix the batter just until the dry ingredients are moistened, being careful not to overmix. If the mixture seems too dry, add a bit more buttermilk or yogurt. For an extra-moist and tender texture, substitute oat bran or quick-cooking oats for a fourth of the flour in the recipe. Drop the biscuits onto your cobbler, bake as usual, and enjoy!

Another way to slash fat in your cobbler toppings is to substitute reduced-fat margarine or light butter for full-fat shortenings. See the inset on page 51 for tips on using these products.

Cherry-Apple Crisp

Yield: *8 servings*

3½ cups sliced peeled apples (about 4½ medium)

1½ cups fresh or frozen (unthawed) pitted sweet cherries

⅓ cup sugar

2 teaspoons cornstarch

TOPPING

4½ large (2½-x-5-inch) low-fat graham crackers

¼ cup light brown sugar

¼ teaspoon ground cinnamon

1 tablespoon plus 1½ teaspoons chilled tub-style nonfat margarine, or 2 tablespoons plus 1 teaspoon chilled reduced-fat margarine, cut into pieces

¼ cup honey crunch wheat germ or chopped toasted pecans (page 167)

1. To make the filling, place the apples and cherries in a large bowl, and toss to mix well. Set aside.

2. Place the sugar and cornstarch in a small bowl, and stir to mix well. Sprinkle the mixture over the fruit, and toss to mix well. Coat a 9-inch deep dish pie pan with nonstick cooking spray, and spread the fruit mixture evenly in the pan. Set aside.

3. To make the topping, break the graham crackers into pieces, place in the bowl of a food processor, and process into crumbs. Measure the crumbs. There should be ¾ cup. (Adjust the amount if needed.)

4. Place the crumbs, brown sugar, and cinnamon in a small bowl, and stir to mix well. Add the nonfat margarine, and stir until the mixture is moist and crumbly. (If you are using reduced-fat margarine, use a pastry cutter or 2 knives to cut the margarine into the mixture until it is moist and crumbly.) If the mixture seems too dry, add more margarine, ½ teaspoon at a time, until the proper consistency is reached. Stir in the wheat germ or pecans. Sprinkle the topping over the filling.

5. Bake uncovered at 375°F for 35 to 40 minutes, or until the filling is bubbly and the topping is golden brown. Cover loosely with aluminum foil during the last few minutes of baking if the topping starts to brown too quickly. Allow to cool at room temperature for at least 15 minutes, and serve warm or at room temperature.

NUTRITIONAL FACTS (PER SERVING)
Calories: 157 Carbohydrates: 36 g Cholesterol: 0 mg
Fat: 1 g Fiber: 2 g Protein: 1.9 g Sodium: 91 mg

You Save: Calories: 149 Fat: 13.2 g

Plum Delicious Crisp

1. To make the filling, place the plums in a large bowl. Set aside.

2. Place the brown sugar and cornstarch in a small bowl, and stir to mix well. Sprinkle the mixture over the fruit, and toss to mix well. (If the fruit is tart, you may need to add another couple of tablespoons of sugar.) Coat a 9-inch deep dish pie pan with nonstick cooking spray, and spread the fruit mixture evenly in the pan. Set aside.

3. To make the topping, place the oats, flour, brown sugar, and cinnamon in a small bowl, and stir to mix well. Add the maple syrup, and stir until the mixture is moist and crumbly. (If the mixture seems too dry, add more maple syrup, $\frac{1}{4}$ teaspoon at a time, until the proper consistency is reached.) Stir in the wheat germ or walnuts. Sprinkle the topping over the filling.

4. Bake uncovered at 375°F for 35 to 40 minutes, or until the filling is bubbly and the topping is golden brown. Cover loosely with aluminum foil during the last few minutes of baking if the topping starts to brown too quickly. Allow to cool at room temperature for at least 15 minutes, and serve warm or at room temperature.

Yield: *8 servings*

5 cups $\frac{3}{4}$-inch-thick slices unpeeled red or purple plums (about 10 medium)

$\frac{1}{3}$ cup light brown sugar

1 tablespoon cornstarch

TOPPING

$\frac{1}{2}$ cup quick-cooking oats

$\frac{1}{4}$ cup whole wheat pastry flour

$\frac{1}{3}$ cup light brown sugar

$\frac{1}{2}$ teaspoon ground cinnamon

2 tablespoons maple syrup

$\frac{1}{4}$ cup honey crunch wheat germ or chopped walnuts

NUTRITIONAL FACTS (PER SERVING)
Calories: 164 Carbohydrates: 37 g Cholesterol: 0 mg
Fat: 1.3 g Fiber: 3.2 g Protein: 2.9 g Sodium: 6 mg

You Save: Calories: 142 Fat: 12.9 g

Apple-Raisin Crisp

Yield: *8 servings*

4³/4 cups sliced peeled apples
 (about 6¹/2 medium)

¹/3 cup dark raisins

¹/3 cup light brown sugar

1¹/2 teaspoons cornstarch

2 tablespoons water

TOPPING

¹/4 cup plus 2 tablespoons
 quick-cooking oats

¹/4 cup plus 2 tablespoons
 whole wheat pastry flour

¹/3 cup light brown sugar

¹/2 teaspoon ground cinnamon

2 tablespoons frozen (thawed)
 apple juice concentrate or
 maple syrup

¹/3 cup honey crunch wheat
 germ, chopped toasted
 pecans (page 167), or
 chopped walnuts

For variety, substitute dates, dried pitted cherries, dried cranberries, or chopped dried apricots for the raisins.

1. To make the filling, place the apples and raisins in a large bowl, and toss to mix well. Set aside.

2. Place the brown sugar and cornstarch in a small bowl, and stir to mix well. Sprinkle the mixture over the fruit, and toss to mix well. (If the fruit is tart, you may need to add another couple of tablespoons of sugar.) Add the water, and toss to mix well. Coat a 9-inch deep dish pie pan with nonstick cooking spray, and spread the fruit mixture evenly in the pan. Set aside.

3. To make the topping, place the oats, flour, brown sugar, and cinnamon in a small bowl, and stir to mix well. Add the juice concentrate or maple syrup, and stir until the mixture is moist and crumbly. (If the mixture seems too dry, add more juice concentrate or maple syrup, ¼ teaspoon at a time, until the proper consistency is reached.) Stir in the wheat germ or nuts. Sprinkle the topping over the filling.

4. Bake uncovered at 375°F for 35 to 40 minutes, or until the filling is bubbly and the topping is golden brown. Cover loosely with aluminum foil during the last few minutes of baking if the topping starts to brown too quickly. Allow to cool at room temperature for at least 15 minutes, and serve warm or at room temperature.

NUTRITIONAL FACTS (PER SERVING)
Calories: 160 Carbohydrates: 37 g Cholesterol: 0 mg
Fat: 1 g Fiber: 2.8 g Protein: 2.7 g Sodium: 7 mg

You Save: Calories: 146 Fat: 13.2 g

CRANbERRY-PEAR CRumble

1. To make the filling, place the pears and cranberries in a large bowl, and toss to mix well. Set aside.

2. Place the brown sugar and cornstarch in a small bowl, and stir to mix well. Sprinkle the mixture over the fruit, and toss to mix. (If the fruit is tart, you may need to add another couple of tablespoons of sugar.) Coat a 9-inch deep dish pie pan with nonstick cooking spray, and spread the fruit mixture evenly in the pan. Set aside.

3. To make the topping, place the oats, flour, brown sugar, and cinnamon in a small bowl, and stir to mix well. Add the juice concentrate, and stir until the mixture is moist and crumbly. (If the mixture seems too dry, add more juice concentrate, 1/4 teaspoon at a time, until the proper consistency is reached.) Stir in the wheat germ or pecans. Sprinkle the topping over the filling.

4. Bake uncovered at 375°F for 35 to 40 minutes, or until the filling is bubbly and the topping is golden brown. Cover loosely with aluminum foil during the last few minutes of baking if the topping starts to brown too quickly. Allow to cool at room temperature for at least 15 minutes before serving warm.

NUTRITIONAL FACTS (PER SERVING)
Calories: 163 Carbohydrates: 38 g Cholesterol: 0 mg
Fat: 1.1 g Fiber: 3.8 g Protein: 2.9 g Sodium: 5 mg

You Save: Calories: 143 Fat: 13.1 g

Yield: *8 servings*

4 1/2 cups diced peeled pears (about 5 medium)

1/2 cup coarsely chopped fresh or frozen (unthawed) cranberries

1/3 cup light brown sugar

2 teaspoons cornstarch

TOPPING

1/4 cup plus 2 tablespoons quick-cooking oats

1/4 cup plus 2 tablespoons whole wheat pastry flour

1/3 cup light brown sugar

1/2 teaspoon ground cinnamon

2 tablespoons frozen orange juice concentrate, thawed

1/3 cup honey crunch wheat germ or chopped toasted pecans (page 167)

Cocoa Fruit Crisp

Yield: *8 servings*

4½ cups sliced peeled pears (about 4½ medium)

¼ cup plus 2 tablespoons dried pitted cherries

⅓ cup sugar

2 teaspoons cornstarch

TOPPING

⅓ cup quick-cooking oats

¼ cup whole wheat pastry flour

2 tablespoons plus 1½ teaspoons Dutch processed cocoa powder

¼ cup plus 2 tablespoons light brown sugar

2 tablespoons chilled tub-style nonfat margarine, or 3 tablespoons chilled reduced-fat margarine, cut into pieces

⅓ cup honey crunch wheat germ or chopped walnuts

1. To make the filling, place the pears and dried cherries in a large bowl, and toss to mix well. Set aside.

2. Place the sugar and cornstarch in a small bowl, and stir to mix well. Sprinkle the mixture over the fruit, and toss to mix well. (If the fruit is tart, you may need to add another couple of tablespoons of sugar.) Coat a 9-inch deep dish pie pan with nonstick cooking spray, and spread the fruit mixture evenly in the pan. Set aside.

3. To make the topping, place the oats, flour, cocoa, and brown sugar in a small bowl, and stir to mix well. Add the nonfat margarine, and stir until the mixture is moist and crumbly. (If you are using reduced-fat margarine, use a pastry cutter or 2 knives to cut the margarine into the oat mixture until it is moist and crumbly.) If the mixture seems too dry, add more margarine, ½ teaspoon at a time, until the proper consistency is reached. Stir in the wheat germ or walnuts. Sprinkle the topping over the filling.

4. Bake uncovered at 375°F for 35 to 40 minutes, or until the filling is bubbly and the topping is golden brown. Cover loosely with aluminum foil during the last few minutes of baking if the topping starts to brown too quickly. Remove the dish from the oven, and allow to cool at room temperature for at least 15 minutes. Serve warm or at room temperature.

NUTRITIONAL FACTS (PER SERVING)
Calories: 181 Carbohydrates: 42 g Cholesterol: 0 mg
Fat: 1.4 g Fiber: 4 g Protein: 2.7 g Sodium: 26 mg

You Save: Calories: 140 Fat: 13.5 g

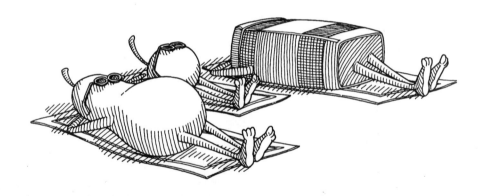

Top: Three-Fruit Cobbler (page 181)

Center Left: Cranberry-Pear Crumble (page 179)

Center Right and Bottom: Ginger Baked Peaches (page 167)

Center Left: Pear-Cranberry Bread (page 195)
Center Right: Fruit and Nut Bread (page 197)
Bottom: Golden Pumpkin Bread (page 193)

Three-Fruit Cobbler

1. To make the filling, drain the apricots, peaches, and oranges, reserving $3/4$ cup of the mixed juice. Cut the apricot halves in half. If the peach slices are large, cut them in half, also. Combine the fruits in a medium-sized bowl, and set aside.

2. Place the sugar, cornstarch, and cinnamon in a $2^{1}/_2$-quart pot, and stir to mix well. Add half of the reserved juice, and stir until the cornstarch is dissolved. Stir in the remaining juice.

3. Place the pot over medium heat, and cook, stirring constantly, for several minutes, or until thickened and bubbly. Add the fruit to the pot, and cook and stir for about 30 seconds to coat it with the juice mixture.

4. Coat a 10-inch pie pan with nonstick cooking spray, and spread the fruit mixture evenly in the pan. Set aside.

5. To make the crust, place the flour, oat bran, sugar, and baking powder in a medium-sized bowl, and stir to mix well. Using a pastry cutter or 2 knives, cut in the margarine or butter until the mixture resembles coarse crumbs. Add just enough of the buttermilk to make a stiff dough, stirring just until the dough holds together and forms a ball.

6. Turn the dough onto a floured surface, and pat into a 7-inch circle. Then, using a rolling pin, roll the dough into an 11-inch circle. Use a knife or pizza wheel to cut the circle into $1/2$-inch strips.

7. Arrange half of the strips over the filling, spacing them $1/2$-inch apart. Arrange the remaining strips over the filling in the opposite direction to form a lattice top. Trim the edges to make the dough conform to the shape of the pan.

8. To glaze the crust, combine the egg substitute and water in a small dish, and brush over the crust. Sprinkle the sugar over the crust.

9. Bake at 375°F for 25 to 30 minutes, or until the filling is bubbly and the crust is lightly browned. Allow to cool at room temperature for at least 10 minutes before serving warm.

Yield: *8 servings*

1 can (1 pound) apricot halves in juice, undrained

1 can (1 pound) sliced peaches in juice, undrained

1 can (10 ounces) mandarin orange segments in juice, undrained

$1/3$ cup sugar

1 tablespoon plus $1^{1}/_2$ teaspoons cornstarch

$1/4$ teaspoon ground cinnamon

CRUST

$3/4$ cup unbleached flour

$1/2$ cup oat bran

1 tablespoon sugar

$3/4$ teaspoon baking powder

3 tablespoons chilled reduced-fat margarine or light butter

3 tablespoons nonfat or low-fat buttermilk

GLAZE

2 teaspoons fat-free egg substitute

2 teaspoons water

1 tablespoon sugar

NUTRITIONAL FACTS (PER SERVING)
Calories: 183 Carbohydrates: 39 g Cholesterol: 0 mg
Fat: 2.4 g Fiber: 2.4 g Protein: 3 g Sodium: 88 mg

You Save: Calories: 120 Fat: 10.8 g

California Crumble

Yield: *6 servings*

1 can (1 pound) sliced peaches
   in juice, drained

1 can (1 pound) apricot halves
   in juice, drained

3 tablespoons light brown sugar

1/4 cup plus 1 tablespoon dark
   raisins, chopped dates, dried
   pitted cherries, or chopped
   pitted prunes

TOPPING

1/4 cup plus 2 tablespoons
   quick-cooking oats

1/4 cup plus 2 tablespoons
   whole wheat pastry flour

1/3 cup light brown sugar

1/2 teaspoon ground cinnamon

2 tablespoons chilled tub-style
   nonfat margarine, or 3
   tablespoons chilled
   reduced-fat margarine,
   cut into pieces

1/3 cup honey crunch wheat
   germ or chopped toasted
   almonds or walnuts (page
   167)

1. To make the filling, cut the peaches and apricots into bite-sized pieces, and place them in a large bowl. Add the brown sugar, and toss to mix well. Add the raisins, dates, cherries, or prunes, and toss to mix well.

2. Coat a 9-inch deep dish pie pan with nonstick cooking spray, and spread the fruit mixture evenly in the pan. Set aside.

3. To make the topping, place the oats, flour, brown sugar, and cinnamon in a small bowl, and stir to mix well. Add the nonfat margarine, and stir until the mixture is moist and crumbly. (If you are using reduced-fat margarine, use a pastry cutter or 2 knives to cut the margarine into the oat mixture until it is moist and crumbly.) If the mixture seems too dry, add more margarine, 1/2 teaspoon at a time, until the proper consistency is reached. Stir in the wheat germ or nuts. Sprinkle the topping over the filling.

4. Bake uncovered at 375°F for 30 to 35 minutes, or until the filling is bubbly and the topping is golden brown. Cover loosely with aluminum foil during the last few minutes of baking if the topping starts to brown too quickly. Allow to cool at room temperature for at least 15 minutes, and serve warm or at room temperature.

NUTRITIONAL FACTS (PER SERVING)
Calories: 186 Carbohydrates: 40 g Cholesterol: 0 mg
Fat: 1.3 g Fiber: 3.4 g Protein: 4.2 g Sodium: 38 mg

You Save: Calories: 143 Fat: 13.4 g

Very Blueberry Crisp

Yield: *6 servings*

1. To make the filling, place the blueberries in a large bowl. Set aside.

2. Place the sugar, cornstarch, and lemon rind in a small bowl, and stir to mix well. Sprinkle the mixture over the fruit, and toss to mix well.

3. Coat a 9-inch deep dish pie pan with nonstick cooking spray, and spread the fruit mixture evenly in the pan. Cover the dish with aluminum foil, and bake at 375°F for about 20 minutes, or until the berries start to soften and release their juices.

4. While the berries are cooking, place the oats, flour, brown sugar, and cinnamon in a small bowl, and stir to mix well. Add the nonfat margarine, and stir until the mixture is moist and crumbly. (If you are using reduced-fat margarine, use a pastry cutter or 2 knives to cut the margarine into the oat mixture until it is moist and crumbly.) If the mixture seems too dry, add more margarine, $1/2$ teaspoon at a time, until the proper consistency is reached. Stir in the wheat germ or nuts.

5. Sprinkle the filling over the hot berries, and bake uncovered for about 25 additional minutes, or until the filling is bubbly and the topping is golden brown. Cover loosely with aluminum foil during the last few minutes of baking if the topping starts to brown too quickly. Allow to cool at room temperature for at least 15 minutes, and serve warm or at room temperature.

4 cups fresh or frozen (partially thawed) blueberries

$1/3$ cup sugar

$2 1/2$ teaspoons cornstarch

$3/4$ teaspoon dried grated lemon rind, or $2 1/4$ teaspoons fresh

TOPPING

$1/4$ cup plus 2 tablespoons quick-cooking oats

$1/4$ cup plus 2 tablespoons whole wheat pastry flour

$1/3$ cup light brown sugar

$1/2$ teaspoon ground cinnamon

2 tablespoons chilled tub-style nonfat margarine, or 3 tablespoons chilled reduced-fat margarine, cut into pieces

$1/3$ cup honey crunch wheat germ or chopped toasted pecans or walnuts (page 167)

NUTRITIONAL FACTS (PER SERVING)

Calories: 206 Carbohydrates: 47 g Cholesterol: 0 mg
Fat: 1.5 g Fiber: 4.3 g Protein: 3.9 g Sodium: 40 mg

You Save: Calories: 143 Fat: 13.2 g

Cinnamon-Apple Cobbler

Yield: *9 servings*

2¹/₂ teaspoons cornstarch

³/₄ cup water or apple juice, divided

¹/₄ cup plus 3 tablespoons light brown sugar

³/₄ teaspoon ground cinnamon

6 cups sliced peeled apples (about 8 medium)

¹/₄ cup dark raisins

BISCUIT TOPPING

1 cup unbleached flour

¹/₃ cup quick-cooking oats

¹/₃ cup plus 1¹/₂ teaspoons sugar, divided

1¹/₂ teaspoons baking powder

¹/₂ cup plus 3 tablespoons nonfat or low-fat buttermilk

Pinch ground cinnamon

1. To make the filling, place the cornstarch and 2 tablespoons of the water or juice in a small bowl, and stir to dissolve the cornstarch. Set aside.

2. Place the brown sugar and cinnamon in a 3-quart pot, and stir to mix well. Add the remaining water or juice, and stir to mix well. Add the apples and raisins, and bring to a boil over medium-high heat. Reduce the heat to medium-low, cover, and cook, stirring occasionally, for about 5 minutes, or just until the apples are tender.

3. Stir the cornstarch mixture, and slowly pour it into the boiling apple mixture, stirring constantly. Cook and stir for another minute, or until the mixture has thickened. Remove the pot from the heat, cover, and set aside.

4. To make the biscuit topping, place the flour, oats, ¹/₃ cup of the sugar, and the baking powder in a medium-sized bowl, and stir to mix well. Add just enough of the buttermilk to make a moderately thick batter, stirring just until the dry ingredients are moistened.

5. Coat a 2¹/₂-quart baking dish with nonstick cooking spray, and spread the hot apple mixture evenly in the dish. Drop heaping table-spoonfuls of the batter onto the fruit filling to make 9 biscuits. Combine the remaining 1¹/₂ teaspoons of sugar and the cinnamon in a small bowl, stir to mix well, and sprinkle over the biscuit topping.

6. Bake uncovered at 375°F for about 20 minutes, or until the biscuits are lightly browned. Remove the dish from the oven, and allow to cool at room temperature for at least 10 minutes before serving warm.

NUTRITIONAL FACTS (PER SERVING)

Calories: 178 Carbohydrates: 42 g Cholesterol: 0 mg
Fat: 0.6 g Fiber: 2.1 g Protein: 2.7 g Sodium: 104 mg

You Save: Calories: 128 Fat: 12.6 g

Apricot-Ginger Crisp

For variety, substitute canned peaches or pears for the apricots.

Yield: *6 servings*

1. Cut the apricots into bite-sized pieces. Coat a 9-inch deep dish pie pan with nonstick cooking spray, and spread the apricots evenly in the pan. Set aside.

2. To make the topping, break the gingersnaps into pieces, place them the bowl of a food processor, and process into crumbs. Measure the crumbs. There should be ¾ cup plus 2 tablespoons. (Adjust the amount if needed.)

3. Place the crumbs and brown sugar in a small bowl, and stir to mix well. Add the nonfat margarine, and stir until the mixture is moist and crumbly. (If you are using reduced-fat margarine, use a pastry cutter or 2 knives to cut the margarine into the mixture until it is moist and crumbly.) If the mixture seems too dry, add more margarine, ½ teaspoon at a time, until the proper consistency is reached. Stir in the wheat germ or pecans. Sprinkle the topping over the filling.

4. Bake uncovered at 375°F for about 25 minutes, or until the filling is bubbly and the topping is golden brown. Cover loosely with aluminum foil during the last few minutes of baking if the topping starts to brown too quickly. Allow to cool at room temperature for at least 15 minutes, and serve warm or at room temperature.

2 cans (1 pound each) apricots in juice or light syrup, drained

TOPPING

14 low-fat gingersnaps

¼ cup plus 1 tablespoon light brown sugar

1 tablespoon plus ½ teaspoon chilled tub-style nonfat margarine, or 2 tablespoons chilled reduced-fat margarine, cut into pieces

⅓ cup honey crunch wheat germ or chopped toasted pecans (page 167)

NUTRITIONAL FACTS (PER SERVING)
Calories: 175 Carbohydrates: 36 g Cholesterol: 0 mg
Fat: 2.4 g Fiber: 2.3 g Protein: 3.3 g Sodium: 125 mg

You Save: Calories: 131 Fat: 12.8 g

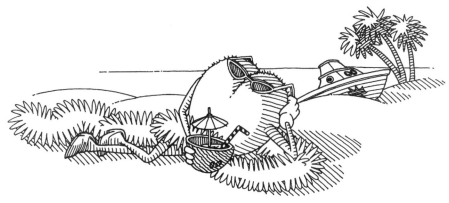

9

Delightful Dessert Breads

Quick breads and other sweet breads are among the most versatile of desserts. Served plain, with low-fat cream cheese, or with a glass of low-fat milk, they can double as nutritious breakfast breads or as great mid-morning or late-night snacks. Filled with fruits and topped with a temptingly sweet glaze, they can provide a glorious finale to even the most festive of meals.

As with most sweet baked treats, though, dessert breads are usually loaded with fat. Butter, margarine, and other shortenings are generally added to batters and doughs to impart moistness and tenderness. But as the recipes in this chapter show, delightfully moist and tender dessert breads can be made with no added fats at all. Instead, these recipes skillfully combine ingredients like whole wheat pastry flour, oat bran, and oats with fruit purées, juices, nonfat buttermilk, and other healthful fat substitutes. The result?

Delicious home-baked breads made with absolutely no oil, butter, or other fats.

What about sugar? While breads usually contain less sugar than cakes and other desserts, many include close to a full cup of sugar per loaf. But as you will see, sweet and delicious breads can be made with 25 to 50 percent less sugar. How? Sweet grains like oats and whole wheat pastry flour, naturally sweet fruits and juices, and sweet flavorings like vanilla and orange rind allow you to use only moderate amounts of sweetener, and still enjoy truly luscious results.

So whether you're looking for a warm fruit-filled yeast bread to serve with coffee or a whole wheat banana bread to accompany a late-night glass of milk, you need look no further. In this chapter you will find a wide variety of delightfully sweet treats that are special enough to fit any occasion, yet healthful enough to merit a regular place in your diet.

Brown Sugar Banana Bread

Yield: *16 slices*

2 cups whole wheat pastry flour

2 teaspoons baking powder

³/₄ teaspoon baking soda

¹/₄ teaspoon ground nutmeg

2 cups mashed very ripe
   banana (about 4 large)

¹/₂ cup plus 2 tablespoons light
   brown sugar

1 teaspoon vanilla extract

¹/₃ cup honey crunch wheat
   germ or chopped toasted
   pecans (page 167)

1. Place the flour, baking powder, baking soda, and nutmeg in a large bowl, and stir to mix well. Set aside.

2. Place the bananas and brown sugar in a medium-sized bowl, and stir until the brown sugar has dissolved. Add the banana mixture and vanilla extract to the flour mixture, and stir just until the dry ingredients are moistened. Fold in the wheat germ or pecans.

3. Coat an 8-x-4-inch loaf pan with nonstick cooking spray, and spread the mixture evenly in the pan. Bake at 325°F for about 55 minutes, or just until a wooden toothpick inserted in the center of the loaf comes out clean.

4. Remove the loaf from the oven, and let sit for 15 minutes. Invert the loaf onto a wire rack, turn right side up, and cool to room temperature. Wrap the loaf in plastic wrap or aluminum foil, and store for 8 hours or overnight before slicing and serving. (Overnight storage will develop the flavors and give the loaf a softer, moister crust.) Refrigerate any leftovers not eaten within 24 hours.

NUTRITIONAL FACTS (PER SLICE)

Calories: 107 Carbohydrates: 24.5 g Cholesterol: 0 mg
Fat: 0.6 g Fiber: 2.5 g Protein: 2.9 g Sodium: 123 mg

You Save: Calories: 65 Fat: 8.1 g

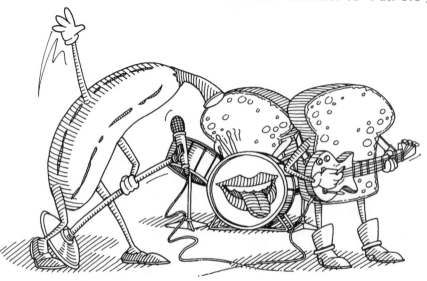

Carrot-Pineapple Bread

1. Place the flour, sugar, baking powder, and baking soda in a large bowl, and stir to mix well. Add the pineapple with its juice and the carrots, milk, and vanilla extract, and stir just until the dry ingredients are moistened. Fold in the dates or raisins and, if desired, the pecans.

2. Coat an 8-x-4-inch loaf pan with nonstick cooking spray, and spread the mixture evenly in the pan. Bake at 325°F for about 50 minutes, or just until a wooden toothpick inserted in the center of the loaf comes out clean.

3. Remove the loaf from the oven, and let sit for 15 minutes. Invert the loaf onto a wire rack, turn right side up, and cool to room temperature. Wrap the loaf in plastic wrap or aluminum foil, and store for 8 hours or overnight before slicing and serving. (Overnight storage will develop the flavors and give the loaf a softer, moister crust.) Refrigerate any leftovers not eaten within 24 hours.

Yield: *16 slices*

2 cups whole wheat pastry flour

1/2 cup sugar

2 teaspoons baking powder

3/4 teaspoon baking soda

1 can (8 ounces) crushed pineapple in juice, undrained

1 cup (packed) grated carrots (about 2 medium)

1/4 cup skim milk

1 teaspoon vanilla extract

1/3 cup chopped dates or golden raisins

1/3 cup chopped toasted pecans (page 167) (optional)

NUTRITIONAL FACTS (PER SLICE)

Calories: 98 Carbohydrates: 23 g Cholesterol: 0 mg
Fat: 0.3 g Fiber: 2.4 g Protein: 2.4 g Sodium: 114 mg

You Save: Calories: 72 Fat: 6.8 g

Fresh Pear Bread

Yield: *16 slices*

2 cups whole wheat pastry flour

1/2 cup sugar

2 teaspoons baking powder

3/4 teaspoon baking soda

1/4 teaspoon ground nutmeg

1/4 teaspoon ground cinnamon

3/4 cup pear nectar

1 teaspoon vanilla extract

1 1/3 cups finely chopped
    peeled pears (about 1 1/2
    medium)

1/4 cup plus 2 tablespoons
    dried currants or dark raisins

1/4 cup chopped walnuts
    (optional)

Make sure that the fresh pears you use for this recipe are perfectly ripe and sweet.

1. Place the flour, sugar, baking powder, baking soda, nutmeg, and cinnamon in a large bowl, and stir to mix well. Add the nectar, vanilla extract, and pears, and stir just until the dry ingredients are moistened. Fold in the currants or raisins and, if desired, the walnuts.

2. Coat an 8-x-4-inch loaf pan with nonstick cooking spray, and spread the mixture evenly in the pan. Bake at 325°F for about 45 minutes, or just until a wooden toothpick inserted in the center of the loaf comes out clean.

3. Remove the loaf from the oven, and let sit for 15 minutes. Invert the loaf onto a wire rack, turn right side up, and cool to room temperature. Wrap the loaf in plastic wrap or aluminum foil, and store for 8 hours or overnight before slicing and serving. (Overnight storage will develop the flavors and give the loaf a softer, moister crust.) Refrigerate any leftovers not eaten within 24 hours.

NUTRITIONAL FACTS (PER SLICE)
Calories: 93 Carbohydrates: 22 g Cholesterol: 0 mg
Fat: 0.4 g Fiber: 2.5 g Protein: 2.2 g Sodium: 121 mg

You Save: Calories: 65 Fat: 6.8 g

Applesauce-Oatmeal Bread

Yield: *16 slices*

1. Place the flour, oats, sugar, baking powder, baking soda, and cinnamon in a large bowl, and stir to mix well. Add the applesauce and vanilla extract, and stir just until the dry ingredients are moistened. Fold in the raisins or cranberries and, if desired, the nuts.

2. Coat an 8-x-4-inch loaf pan with nonstick cooking spray, and spread the mixture evenly in the pan. Bake at 325°F for about 45 minutes, or just until a wooden toothpick inserted in the center of the loaf comes out clean.

3. Remove the loaf from the oven, and let sit for 15 minutes. Invert the loaf onto a wire rack, turn right side up, and cool to room temperature. Wrap the loaf in plastic wrap or aluminum foil, and store for 8 hours or overnight before slicing and serving. (Overnight storage will develop the flavors and give the loaf a softer, moister crust.) Refrigerate any leftovers not eaten within 24 hours.

1 1/2 cups whole wheat pastry flour

3/4 cup quick-cooking oats

1/2 cup sugar

2 teaspoons baking powder

3/4 teaspoon baking soda

1/2 teaspoon ground cinnamon

1 1/2 cups unsweetened applesauce

1 1/2 teaspoons vanilla extract

1/4 cup plus 2 tablespoons dark raisins or dried cranberries

1/3 cup chopped toasted walnuts or pecans (page 167) (optional)

NUTRITIONAL FACTS (PER SLICE)
Calories: 97 Carbohydrates: 22.3 g Cholesterol: 0 mg
Fat: 0.5 g Fiber: 2.2 g Protein: 2.3 g Sodium: 121 mg

You Save: Calories: 69 Fat: 6.8 g

Mocha Banana Bread

Yield: *16 slices*

2 teaspoons vanilla extract

1/2 teaspoon instant coffee
   granules

1 3/4 cups whole wheat pastry
   flour

1/4 cup Dutch processed cocoa
   powder

1/2 cup plus 2 tablespoons
   sugar

2 teaspoons baking powder

3/4 teaspoon baking soda

1/2 teaspoon ground cinnamon

2 cups mashed very ripe
   banana (about 4 large)

1/2 cup chopped toasted
   pecans, almonds, or
   macadamia nuts (page 167)
   (optional)

1. Place the vanilla extract and coffee granules in a small bowl, and stir to mix well. Set aside.

2. Place the flour, cocoa powder, sugar, baking powder, baking soda, and cinnamon in a large bowl, and stir to mix well. Add the banana and the vanilla extract mixture, and stir just until the dry ingredients are moistened. Fold in the nuts, if desired.

3. Coat an 8-x-4-inch loaf pan with nonstick cooking spray, and spread the mixture evenly in the pan. Bake at 325°F for about 55 minutes, or just until a wooden toothpick inserted in the center of the loaf comes out clean.

4. Remove the loaf from the oven, and let sit for 15 minutes. Invert the loaf onto a wire rack, turn right side up, and cool to room temperature. Wrap the loaf in plastic wrap or aluminum foil, and store for 8 hours or overnight before slicing and serving. (Overnight storage will develop the flavors and give the loaf a softer, moister crust.) Refrigerate any leftovers not eaten within 24 hours.

NUTRITIONAL FACTS (PER SLICE)

Calories: 104 Carbohydrates: 24.8 g Cholesterol: 0 mg
Fat: 0.6 g Fiber: 2.6 g Protein: 2.4 g Sodium: 121 g

You Save: Calories: 68 Fat: 7.1 g

Golden Pumpkin Bread

1. Place the flour, baking powder, baking soda, and pumpkin pie spice in a large bowl, and stir to mix well. Set aside.

2. Place the pumpkin, orange juice, brown sugar, and vanilla extract in a medium-sized bowl, and stir to mix well and to dissolve the brown sugar. Add the pumpkin mixture to the flour mixture, and stir just until the dry ingredients are moistened. Fold in the wheat germ or pecans.

3. Coat an 8-x-4-inch loaf pan with nonstick cooking spray, and spread the mixture evenly in the pan. Bake at 325°F for about 55 minutes, or just until a wooden toothpick inserted in the center of the loaf comes out clean.

4. Remove the loaf from the oven, and let sit for 15 minutes. Invert the loaf onto a wire rack, turn right side up, and cool to room temperature. Wrap the loaf in plastic wrap or aluminum foil, and store for 8 hours or overnight before slicing and serving. (Overnight storage will develop the flavors and give the loaf a softer, moister crust.) Refrigerate any leftovers not eaten within 24 hours.

Yield: *16 slices*

2 cups whole wheat pastry flour

2 teaspoons baking powder

3/4 teaspoon baking soda

2 teaspoons pumpkin pie spice

1 1/4 cups mashed cooked pumpkin or canned pumpkin

3/4 cup orange juice

1/2 cup plus 2 tablespoons light brown sugar

1 1/2 teaspoons vanilla extract

1/3 cup honey crunch wheat germ or chopped toasted pecans (page 167)

NUTRITIONAL FACTS (PER SLICE)

Calories: 93 Carbohydrates: 20.7 g Cholesterol: 0 mg
Fat: 0.5 g Fiber: 2.5 g Protein: 2.9 g Sodium: 124 mg

You Save: Calories: 79 Fat: 9.2 g

PEACH PERFECTION BREAD

Yield: *16 slices*

1 can (1 pound) sliced peaches in juice, undrained

1/3 cup oat bran

1/2 cup light brown sugar

1 3/4 cups whole wheat pastry flour

2 teaspoons baking powder

3/4 teaspoon baking soda

1/4 teaspoon ground nutmeg

1/4 teaspoon ground cinnamon

1 1/2 teaspoons vanilla extract

1/4 cup plus 2 tablespoons chopped dried peaches, dark raisins, or golden raisins

1/3 cup honey crunch wheat germ or chopped toasted pecans (page 167)

1. Drain the peaches, reserving the juice. Place the drained peaches in a blender or food processor, and process until smooth. Pour the peach purée into a 2-cup measuring cup, and add enough of the reserved juice to bring the volume to 1 2/3 cups.

2. Place the oat bran and brown sugar in a medium-sized bowl, and add the peach purée. Stir with a wire whisk until well mixed, and set the mixture aside for at least 15 minutes to allow the oat bran to soften.

3. Place the flour, baking powder, baking soda, nutmeg, and cinnamon in a large bowl, and stir to mix well. Add the peach mixture and the vanilla extract to the flour mixture, and stir just until the dry ingredients are moistened. Fold in the dried fruit and the wheat germ or pecans.

4. Coat an 8-x-4-inch loaf pan with nonstick cooking spray, and spread the mixture evenly in the pan. Bake at 325°F for about 45 minutes, or just until a wooden toothpick inserted in the center of the loaf comes out clean.

5. Remove the loaf from the oven, and let sit for 15 minutes. Invert the loaf onto a wire rack, turn right side up, and cool to room temperature. Wrap the loaf in plastic wrap or aluminum foil, and store for 8 hours or overnight before slicing and serving. (Overnight storage will develop the flavors and give the loaf a softer, moister crust.) Refrigerate any leftovers not eaten within 24 hours.

NUTRITIONAL FACTS (PER SLICE)
Calories: 93 Carbohydrates: 21 g Cholesterol: 0 mg
Fat: 0.6 g Fiber: 2.6 g Protein: 2.9 g Sodium: 124 mg

You Save: Calories: 83 Fat: 9.9 g

Pear-Cranberry Bread

Yield: *16 slices*

1. Drain the pears, reserving the juice. Place the drained pears in a blender or food processor, and process until smooth. Pour the pear purée into a 2-cup measuring cup, and add enough of the reserved juice to bring the volume to 1⅔ cups.

2. Place the oat bran in a medium-sized bowl, and add the pear purée. Stir with a wire whisk until well mixed, and set the mixture aside for at least 15 minutes to allow the oat bran to soften.

3. Place the flour, sugar, baking powder, and baking soda in a large bowl, and stir to mix well. Add the pear mixture and the vanilla extract to the flour mixture, and stir just until the dry ingredients are moistened. Fold in the cranberries and the wheat germ or walnuts.

4. Coat an 8-x-4-inch loaf pan with nonstick cooking spray, and spread the mixture evenly in the pan. Bake at 325°F for about 45 minutes, or just until a wooden toothpick inserted in the center of the loaf comes out clean.

5. Remove the loaf from the oven, and let sit for 15 minutes. Invert the loaf onto a wire rack, turn right side up, and cool to room temperature. Wrap the loaf in plastic wrap or aluminum foil, and store for 8 hours or overnight before slicing and serving. (Overnight storage will develop the flavors and give the loaf a softer, moister crust.) Refrigerate any leftovers not eaten within 24 hours.

1 can (1 pound) pear halves in juice, undrained

⅓ cup oat bran

1¾ cups whole wheat pastry flour

½ cup sugar

2 teaspoons baking powder

¾ teaspoon baking soda

2 teaspoons vanilla extract

½ cup dried cranberries

⅓ cup honey crunch wheat germ or chopped walnuts

NUTRITIONAL FACTS (PER SLICE)
Calories: 107 Carbohydrates: 25 g Cholesterol: 0 mg
Fat: 0.6 g Fiber: 2.6 g Protein: 2.7 g Sodium: 122 mg

You Save: Calories: 81 Fat: 9.5 g

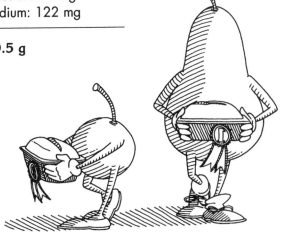

Getting the Fat Out of Your Favorite Quick Bread Recipes

Many traditional quick bread recipes are loaded with fat. This is a shame, because these sweet treats can often be made with no fat at all. And as the recipes in this chapter show, just about any moist ingredient can replace the fat in quick breads. Applesauce and fruit purées perform especially well as fat substitutes in quick breads, but mashed cooked pumpkin and sweet potatoes, Prune Purée (page 131), and nonfat or low-fat buttermilk and yogurt can also act as fat substitutes. Use the following tricks of the trade to insure success when eliminating the fat from your favorite quick bread recipes.

☐ *Replace the desired amount of butter, margarine, or other solid shortening with half as much fat substitute.* For instance, if you are omitting 1/2 cup of butter from a recipe, replace it with 1/4 cup of fruit purée, nonfat buttermilk, mashed cooked pumpkin, or other fat substitute. If the recipe calls for oil, substitute three-fourths as much fat substitute. Mix up the batter. If it seems too dry, add a little more fat substitute. For extra flavor and tenderness, try substituting fruit purée or nonfat buttermilk for the recipe's liquid, as well.

☐ *Eliminate only half the fat in a recipe at first.* The next time you make the recipe, try replacing even more fat. Continue reducing fat until you find the lowest amount that will give you the desired results. Realize that as you remove more and more fat from a recipe, the following tips—for using low-gluten flours and eliminating eggs, for instance—become even more important.

☐ *Use low-gluten flours.* Wheat flour contains proteins that, when mixed with liquid into a batter, form tough strands called gluten. Fat tenderizes baked goods by interfering with this process—which is why removing the fat from baked goods often makes them tough or rubbery. The good news is that you can leave out the fat and still have a tender texture if

you use a low-gluten flour like whole wheat pastry flour in your fat-free quick breads. (Read more about whole wheat pastry flour on page 13.) Ingredients such as oats, bran, cornmeal, and cocoa powder also form little or no gluten, making them ideal ingredients for use in fat-free quick breads.

☐ *Minimize mixing.* Stirring batter excessively develops gluten and toughens the texture of baked goods. Stir only enough to mix well.

☐ *Avoid overbaking.* Reduced-fat baked goods tend to bake more quickly than do those made with fat, and if left in the oven too long, they can become dry. To prevent this, bake fat-free quick breads at 325°F to 350°F, and check the product for doneness a few minutes before the end of the usual baking time.

☐ *Eliminate the eggs.* You may have noticed that none of the fat-free quick breads in this book contains any eggs. Why? Fat adds tenderness to baked goods. Eggs, on the other hand, toughen the structure of baked goods as their proteins coagulate during baking and bind the batter together. For this reason, fat-free quick breads that contain too many eggs can have a tough texture. For maximum tenderness, substitute 2 tablespoons of your chosen fat substitute for each whole egg in your recipe.

☐ *Increase the leavening if necessary.* Fat lubricates batters and helps quick breads rise better. When fats are creamed with sugar, they also incorporate air into the batter, which further aids rising. For these reasons, when you eliminate the fat from your quick bread recipe, your bread might not rise as well. If this happens, try adding a little extra baking soda to your recipe, starting with 1/4 teaspoon. (Alternatively, add a teaspoon of baking powder.) For each cup of acidic liquid—fruit purée or buttermilk, for instance—avoid using more than 1 teaspoon of baking soda, as more soda might cause the product to take on a bitter or soapy taste.

Fruit and Nut Bread

1. Place the flour, sugar, and baking soda in a large bowl, and stir to mix well. Add the buttermilk, honey, and vanilla extract, and stir to mix well. Fold in the fruits and nuts.

2. Coat four 1-pound cans with nonstick cooking spray. Divide the batter among the cans, and bake at 300°F for about 45 minutes, or just until a wooden toothpick inserted in the center of a loaf comes out clean.

3. Remove the bread from the oven, and let sit for 15 minutes. Invert the loaves onto a wire rack, turn right side up, and cool to room temperature. Wrap the loaves in aluminum foil or plastic wrap, and let sit overnight before slicing and serving. (Overnight storage will develop the flavors and give the loaves a softer, moister crust.) Refrigerate any leftovers not eaten within 24 hours.

Yield: *32 slices*

3 cups whole wheat pastry flour

1/2 cup sugar

1 teaspoon baking soda

1 3/4 cups nonfat or low-fat buttermilk

1/4 cup honey

2 teaspoons vanilla extract

1/2 cup dried cranberries or dried pitted cherries

1/2 cup chopped dried apricots or pineapples

1/2 cup dark raisins

1/2 cup golden raisins

2/3 cup chopped toasted pecans (page 167)

NUTRITIONAL FACTS (PER SLICE)

Calories: 104 Carbohydrates: 21 g Cholesterol: 0 mg
Fat: 2 g Fiber: 1.9 g Protein: 2.4 g Sodium: 55 mg

You Save: Calories: 59 Fat: 6.9 g

Baking Festive Round Loaves

Any quick bread recipe can be used to make festive round loaves by baking the batter in cans instead of loaf pans. These loaves can then be wrapped in colored plastic wrap, tied on top with a ribbon, and given as gifts during the holiday season or at any time of year.

Simply coat three or four 1-pound food cans with nonstick cooking spray, and divide the batter evenly among the cans, filling each half to two-thirds full. Bake at 300°F for about 45 minutes, or just until a wooden toothpick inserted in the center of a loaf comes out clean. Cool the bread in the cans for 10 to 15 minutes, remove the loaves from the cans, and cool completely before wrapping.

A word of caution is in order regarding the cans used to make these loaves. When choosing cans for baking, be sure to avoid those that have been lead-soldered. Lead is a toxic metal that can leach into foods during baking. Food cans produced in this country do not contain lead solder, as the United States canning industry eliminated this process in 1991. Some labels even state that the can is lead-free. Imported foods, however, may still be packaged in soldered cans.

To be safe, avoid baking bread in all cans with pronounced seams—a sign of possible lead soldering—and in all imported food cans. You will then be sure that your festive breads are as healthy as they are delicious.

OATMEAL RAISIN-NUT BREAD

Yield: *28 slices*

3/4 cup quick-cooking oats

2 cups nonfat or low-fat buttermilk

2 1/4 cups whole wheat pastry flour

3/4 cup sugar

1 teaspoon baking soda

1 teaspoon dried grated orange rind, or 1 tablespoon fresh

2 teaspoons vanilla extract

1 1/4 cups dark raisins

1/2 cup chopped toasted pecans (page 167)

For variety, substitute chopped dates, chopped dried apricots, dried pitted cherries, or dried cranberries for the raisins.

1. Place the oats and buttermilk in a medium-sized bowl, and stir to mix well. Set aside for at least 10 minutes.

2. Place the flour, sugar, baking soda, and orange rind in a large bowl, and stir to mix well. Add the buttermilk mixture and the vanilla extract to the flour mixture, and stir to mix well. Fold in the raisins and pecans.

3. Coat four 1-pound cans with nonstick cooking spray. Divide the batter among the cans, and bake at 300°F for about 45 minutes, or just until a wooden toothpick inserted in the center of a loaf comes out clean.

4. Remove the bread from the oven, and let sit for 15 minutes. Invert the loaves onto a wire rack, turn right side up, and cool to room temperature. Wrap the loaves in aluminum foil or plastic wrap, and let sit overnight before slicing and serving. (Overnight storage will develop the flavors and give the loaves a softer, moister crust.) Refrigerate any leftovers not eaten within 24 hours.

NUTRITIONAL FACTS (PER SLICE)

Calories: 102 Carbohydrates: 20 g Cholesterol: 0 mg
Fat: 1.9 g Fiber: 1.7 g Protein: 2.6 g Sodium: 65 mg

You Save: Calories: 48 Fat: 6.6 g

Zucchini-Spice Bread

1. Place the flour, sugar, baking powder, baking soda, cinnamon, lemon rind, and nutmeg in a large bowl, and stir to mix well. Add the zucchini, milk, and vanilla extract, and stir just until the dry ingredients are moistened. Fold in the raisins or walnuts.

2. Coat an 8-x-4-inch loaf pan with nonstick cooking spray, and spread the mixture evenly in the pan. Bake at 325°F for 50 to 55 minutes, or just until a wooden toothpick inserted in the center of the loaf comes out clean.

3. Remove the loaf from the oven, and let sit for 15 minutes. Invert the loaf onto a wire rack, turn right side up, and cool to room temperature. Wrap the loaf in plastic wrap or aluminum foil, and store for 8 hours or overnight before slicing and serving. (Overnight storage will develop the flavors and give the loaf a softer, moister crust.) Refrigerate any leftovers not eaten within 24 hours.

Yield: *16 slices*

2 cups whole wheat pastry flour

2/3 cup sugar

2 1/2 teaspoons baking powder

1/2 teaspoon baking soda

1 teaspoon ground cinnamon

1 teaspoon dried grated lemon rind, or 1 tablespoon fresh

1/2 teaspoon ground nutmeg

1 1/4 cups (packed) shredded unpeeled zucchini (about 1 medium-large)

3/4 cup skim milk

1 1/2 teaspoons vanilla extract

1/2 cup dark raisins or chopped walnuts, or 1/4 cup each raisins and walnuts

---

NUTRITIONAL FACTS (PER SLICE)
Calories: 103 Carbohydrates: 23 g Cholesterol: 0 mg
Fat: 0.3 g Fiber: 2.2 g Protein: 2.8 g Sodium: 123 mg

You Save: Calories: 72 Fat: 9 g

CINNAMON-APPLE CHOP BREAD

Yield: *8 servings*

DOUGH

1³/₄ cups plus 2 tablespoons unbleached flour

¹/₄ cup plus 2 tablespoons quick-cooking oats

¹/₄ cup sugar

2 teaspoons Rapid Rise yeast

¹/₄ teaspoon salt

¹/₂ cup plus 2 tablespoons skim milk

1 teaspoon lemon juice

2 teaspoons skim milk

FILLING

1¹/₂ cups chopped peeled apples (about 2 medium)

¹/₄ cup dark raisins

1 tablespoon sugar

¹/₂ teaspoon ground cinnamon

GLAZE

¹/₂ cup powdered sugar

2¹/₂ teaspoons skim milk

¹/₂ teaspoon vanilla extract

1. To make the dough, place ³/₄ cup of the flour and all of the oats, sugar, yeast, and salt in a large bowl, and stir to mix well. Set aside.

2. Place the milk in a small saucepan, and heat until very warm (125°F to 130°F). Add the milk to the flour mixture, and stir for 1 minute. Stir in the lemon juice. Stir in enough of the remaining flour, 2 tablespoons at a time, to form a soft dough.

3. Sprinkle 2 tablespoons of the remaining flour over a clean dry surface, and turn the dough onto the surface. Knead the dough for 5 minutes, gradually adding just enough of the remaining flour to form a smooth, satiny ball.

4. Coat a large bowl with nonstick cooking spray, and place the dough in the bowl. Cover the bowl with a clean kitchen towel, and let rise in a warm place for about 40 minutes, or until doubled in size.

5. To make the filling, place the apples, raisins, sugar, and cinnamon in a small bowl, and toss to mix well. Set aside.

6. Place the dough on a large floured cutting board, and pat it into a 10-inch circle. Pile the apple mixture on top of the dough, and draw the dough up and around the apple mixture so that the edges of the dough meet in the middle, completely covering the apple filling. Flatten the dough into an 8-inch circle.

7. Using a large sharp knife, slice the mound 5 times in one direction, cutting through to the board. Then slice 5 times in the other direction to form pieces of dough that are about 1¹/₂ inches square. Use the knife to gently mix the dough and apple mixture by lifting the mixture from the bottom and piling it back on top.

8. Coat a baking sheet with nonstick cooking spray, and gently mound the dough onto the sheet. Using your hands, gently shape the dough into an 8-inch circle, making sure that most of the apple mixture is touching pieces of dough. (This will insure that the dough holds together as it bakes.)

9. Cover the dough with a clean kitchen towel, and let rise in a warm place for about 30 minutes, or until nearly doubled in size. Brush the top lightly with the 2 teaspoons of skim milk Bake at 350°F for about 23 minutes, or until the bread is light golden brown and puffy. Remove the bread from the oven, and allow to cool for 3 to 5 minutes.

10. To make the glaze, place all of the glaze ingredients in a small bowl, and stir until smooth. Drizzle the glaze over the warm loaf. Immediately cut into wedges, or simply pull off chunks and serve warm.

NUTRITIONAL FACTS (PER SERVING)
Calories: 194 Carbohydrates: 44 g Cholesterol: 0 mg
Fat: 0.4 g Fiber: 1.4 g Protein: 4.1 g Sodium: 78 mg

You Save: Calories: 60 Fat: 8 g

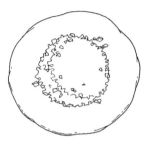

a. Pile the filling on the circle of dough.

b. Draw the dough up and around the filling.

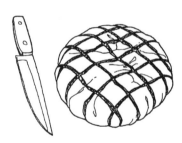

c. Slice the dough-wrapped mound 5 times in each direction.

d. Use a knife to gently mix the dough and the filling.

Making Cinnamon-Apple Chop Bread.

Time-Saving Tip

To make the dough for Cinnamon-Apple Chop Bread in a bread machine, simply place all of the dough ingredients except for ¼ cup of the flour in the machine's bread pan. (Do not heat the milk.) Turn the machine to the "rise," "dough," "manual," or equivalent setting so that the machine will mix, knead, and let the dough rise once.

Check the dough about 5 minutes after the machine has started. If the dough seems too sticky, add more of the remaining flour, a tablespoon at a time. When the dough is ready, remove it from the bread machine and proceed to shape, fill, and bake it as directed in the recipe.

CHERRY-CHEESE LOAF

Yield: *14 slices*

1 recipe Whole Wheat Sweet Dough (page 204)

2 teaspoons skim milk

2 tablespoons chopped toasted almonds, pecans, walnuts, or hazelnuts (page 167)

FILLING

1 block (8 ounces) nonfat cream cheese, softened to room temperature

1/4 cup sugar

2 tablespoons fat-free egg substitute, or 1 egg white

2 tablespoons unbleached flour

1 teaspoon vanilla extract

1 cup canned light (reduced-sugar) cherry pie filling

GLAZE

1/2 cup powdered sugar

2 1/2 teaspoons skim milk

1/2 teaspoon vanilla extract

1. To make the filling, place the cream cheese and sugar in a medium-sized bowl, and beat with an electric mixer until smooth. Add the egg substitute or egg white, flour, and vanilla extract, and beat until smooth. Set aside.

2. Place the dough on a lightly floured surface, and, using a rolling pin, roll it into a 10-x-14-inch rectangle. Coat a large baking sheet with nonstick cooking spray, and transfer the dough to the sheet.

3. Using a sharp knife, make 3 1/4-inch-long cuts at 1-inch intervals on both of the 14-inch sides. Spread the cheese filling down the center third of the dough; then cover the cheese mixture with the cherry pie filling. Fold the strips diagonally over the filling, overlapping them to create a braided look.

4. Cover the loaf with a clean kitchen towel, and let rise in a warm place for about 45 minutes, or until doubled in size.

5. Lightly brush the top of the loaf with the skim milk. Bake at 350°F for about 22 minutes, or until the loaf is lightly browned. Remove the loaf from the oven, and set aside while you prepare the glaze.

6. To make the glaze, place all of the glaze ingredients in a small bowl, and stir until smooth. Drizzle the glaze over the loaf, and sprinkle with the nuts. Let sit for 10 minutes before slicing and serving warm.

NUTRITIONAL FACTS (PER SERVING)
Calories: 165 Carbohydrates: 34 g Cholesterol: 2 mg
Fat: 0.9 g Fiber: 1.3 g Protein: 6 g Sodium: 158 mg

You Save: Calories: 118 Fat: 13.1 g

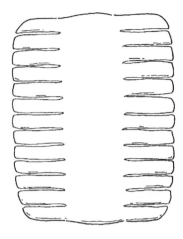

a. Make 3¼-inch-long cuts at
   1-inch intervals on each side
   of the dough.

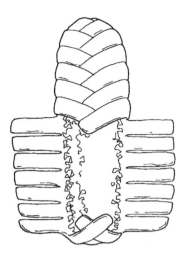

b. Fold the dough strips
   diagonally over the filling.

c. Continue folding the strips to
   create a "braided" loaf.

Making Cherry-Cheese Loaf.

A Dough for All Seasons

Warm, fragrant, and delicious, sweet yeast breads, cakes, and buns are always a special treat. And with just one recipe, you can make an infinite number of tantalizing baked goods. Use Whole Wheat Sweet Dough to prepare some of the yeast dessert breads presented in this chapter, or draw upon your imagination to create your own cinnamon rolls, coffee cakes, buns, and breads.

If the thought of making yeast dough from scratch scares you, fear not. This recipe is easily mixed by hand. Or, if you own a bread machine, follow the simple instructions provided at the end of the recipe to prepare this versatile dough with a minimum of fuss.

WHOLE WHEAT SWEET DOUGH

Yield: *about 1 pound,*
or 16 servings

¼ cup warm water
(105°F–115°F)

2 teaspoons Rapid Rise yeast

⅓ cup sugar, divided

2 cups unbleached flour

¾ cup whole wheat pastry
flour

½ teaspoon salt

½ cup plus 2 tablespoons
nonfat or low-fat buttermilk,
warmed to room
temperature

1. Place the water, yeast, and 1 teaspoon of the sugar in a small bowl, and stir to dissolve the yeast. Set aside.

2. Place the remaining sugar, ¾ cup of the unbleached flour, and all of the whole wheat flour and salt in a large bowl, and stir to mix well.

3. Add the yeast mixture and the buttermilk to the flour mixture, and stir for 1 minute. Stir in enough of the remaining unbleached flour, 2 tablespoons at a time, to form a soft dough.

4. Sprinkle 2 tablespoons of the remaining unbleached flour over a dry surface, and turn the dough onto the surface. Knead the dough for 5 minutes, gradually adding just enough of the remaining flour to form a smooth, satiny ball.

5. Coat a large bowl with nonstick cooking spray, and place the dough in the bowl. Cover the bowl with a clean kitchen towel, and let rise in a warm place for about 1 hour, or until doubled in size. Then proceed to shape, fill, and bake the dough according to recipe directions.

NUTRITIONAL FACTS (PER SERVING)

Calories: 89 Carbohydrates: 19 g Cholesterol: 0 mg
Fat: 0.3 g Fiber: 1.1 g Protein: 2.5 g Sodium: 77 mg

You Save: Calories: 45 Fat: 5 g

Time-Saving Tip

To make Whole Wheat Sweet Dough in a bread machine, simply place all of the dough ingredients except for ⅓ cup of the unbleached flour in the machine's bread pan. (Do not heat the water.) Turn the machine to the "rise," "dough," "manual," or equivalent setting so that the machine will mix, knead, and let the dough rise once.

Check the dough about 5 minutes after the machine has started. If the dough seems too sticky, add more of the remaining flour, a tablespoon at a time. When the dough is ready, remove it from the machine and proceed to shape, fill, and bake it as directed in the recipe of your choice.

Apple Streusel Loaf

1. Place the dough on a lightly floured surface, and, using a rolling pin, roll it into a 10-x-14-inch rectangle. Coat a large baking sheet with nonstick cooking spray, and transfer the dough to the sheet.

2. Using a sharp knife, make 3¼-inch-long cuts at 1-inch intervals on both of the 14-inch sides. Spread the pie filling down the center third of the dough. Fold the strips diagonally over the filling, overlapping them to create a braided look. (See the figure on page 203.)

3. Cover the loaf with a clean kitchen towel, and let rise in a warm place for about 45 minutes, or until doubled in size.

4. To make the streusel topping, place the flour, brown sugar, and cinnamon in a small bowl, and stir to mix well. Add the nonfat margarine, and stir until the mixture is moist and crumbly. (If you are using reduced-fat margarine, use a pastry cutter or 2 knives to cut the margarine into the flour mixture until it is moist and crumbly.) If the mixture seems too dry, add more margarine, ¼ teaspoon at a time, until the proper consistency is reached. Stir in the wheat germ and the pecans or walnuts.

5. Lightly brush the top of the loaf with the skim milk. Sprinkle with the streusel topping.

6. Bake at 350°F for about 22 minutes, or until the loaf is lightly browned. Remove from the oven, and let sit for 3 minutes before adding the glaze.

7. To make the glaze, place all of the glaze ingredients in a small bowl, and stir until smooth. Drizzle the glaze over the loaf. Let the loaf sit for 5 minutes before slicing and serving warm.

Yield: *14 servings*

1 recipe Whole Wheat Sweet Dough (page 204)

1 can (20 ounces) light (reduced-sugar) apple pie filling

2 teaspoons skim milk

STREUSEL TOPPING

3 tablespoons whole wheat pastry flour

3 tablespoons light brown sugar

¼ teaspoon ground cinnamon

2 teaspoons chilled tub-style nonfat margarine, or 1 tablespoon chilled reduced-fat margarine, cut into pieces

2 tablespoons honey crunch wheat germ

2 tablespoons chopped toasted pecans or walnuts (page 167)

GLAZE

⅓ cup powdered sugar

1½ teaspoons skim milk

¼ teaspoon vanilla extract

⅛ teaspoon ground cinnamon

NUTRITIONAL FACTS (PER SERVING)
Calories: 162 Carbohydrates: 35 g Cholesterol: 0 mg
Fat: 1 g Fiber: 1.7 g Protein: 3.5 g Sodium: 111 mg

You Save: Calories: 62 Fat: 7.3 g

Cinnamon-Raisin Ring

Yield: *16 servings*

1 recipe Whole Wheat Sweet Dough (page 204)

2 teaspoons skim milk

FILLING

2 tablespoons tub-style nonfat margarine, or 3 tablespoons reduced-fat margarine or light butter, softened to room temperature

2 tablespoons sugar

¾ teaspoon ground cinnamon

½ cup dark raisins

⅓ cup chopped toasted pecans or walnuts (page 167) (optional)

GLAZE

½ cup powdered sugar

⅛ teaspoon ground cinnamon

2½ teaspoons skim milk

½ teaspoon vanilla extract

1. Place the dough on a lightly floured surface, and, using a rolling pin, roll it into an 11-x-16-inch rectangle. Place the margarine, sugar, and cinnamon in a small dish, stir to mix well, and spread the mixture over the dough to within ¼ inch of the edges. Sprinkle the raisins and, if desired, the nuts over the margarine mixture. Roll the rectangle up jelly roll-style, beginning at the long end.

2. Coat a 14-inch pizza pan or a large nonstick baking sheet with nonstick cooking spray, and place the roll on the pan, bringing the ends around to form a circle. Using scissors, cut almost all of the way through the dough at 1-inch intervals. Twist each 1-inch segment to turn the cut side up. Cover with a clean kitchen towel, and let rise in a warm place for 35 to 45 minutes, or until doubled in size.

3. Lightly brush the top of the ring with the 2 teaspoons of skim milk, and bake at 350°F for about 15 minutes, or until lightly browned. Remove from the oven, and allow to cool for 3 minutes.

4. To make the glaze, place all of the glaze ingredients in a small bowl, and stir until smooth. Drizzle the glaze over the warm ring, and serve immediately.

NUTRITIONAL FACTS (PER SERVING)
Calories: 118 Carbohydrates: 27.5 g Cholesterol: 0 mg
Fat: 0.3 g Fiber: 1.1 g Protein: 2.6 g Sodium: 89 mg

You Save: Calories: 56 Fat: 7 g

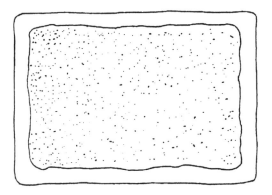

a. Spread the filling over the dough.

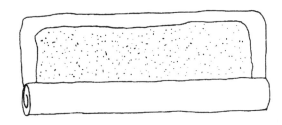

b. Roll the dough up jelly-roll style.

c. Bend the roll into a ring, and cut almost all the way through at 1-inch intervals.

d. Twist each 1-inch segment to turn the cut side up.

Making Cinnamon-Raisin Ring.

Cherry-Almond Ring

Yield: *16 servings*

1 recipe Whole Wheat Sweet Dough (page 204)

2 teaspoons skim milk

2 tablespoons sliced toasted almonds

FILLING

1 cup chopped pitted fresh or frozen (unthawed) cherries

1/4 cup sugar

3 tablespoons white grape juice, divided

1 tablespoon cornstarch

GLAZE

1/2 cup powdered sugar

2 1/2 teaspoons skim milk

1/4 teaspoon vanilla extract

1/4 teaspoon almond extract

1. To make the filling, place the cherries, sugar, and 2 tablespoons of the juice in a 1-quart pot, and bring to a boil over medium-high heat, stirring constantly. Reduce the heat to low, cover, and simmer for about 4 minutes, or until the cherries are soft.

2. Place the remaining tablespoon of juice and the cornstarch in a small bowl, and stir to dissolve the cornstarch. Add the cornstarch mixture to the cherries, and cook and stir for another minute or 2, or until the mixture is thick and bubbly. Remove the pot from the heat, and allow the mixture to cool to room temperature.

3. Place the dough on a lightly floured surface, and, using a rolling pin, roll it into an 11-x-16-inch rectangle. Spread the cherry filling over the dough to within 1/2 inch of the edges. Roll the rectangle up jelly roll-style, beginning at the long end.

4. Coat a 14-inch pizza pan or a large nonstick baking sheet with nonstick cooking spray, and place the roll on the pan, bringing the ends around to form a circle. Using scissors, cut almost all of the way through the dough at 1-inch intervals. Twist each 1-inch segment to turn the cut side up. (See the figure on page 207.) Cover with a clean kitchen towel, and let rise in a warm place for 35 to 45 minutes, or until doubled in size.

5. Lightly brush the top of the ring with the 2 teaspoons of skim milk, and bake at 350°F for about 15 minutes, or until lightly browned. Remove from the oven, and allow to cool for 3 minutes.

6. To make the glaze, place all of the glaze ingredients in a small bowl, and stir until smooth. Drizzle the glaze over the warm ring, sprinkle the almonds over the top, and serve immediately.

NUTRITIONAL FACTS (PER SERVING)
Calories: 125 Carbohydrates: 27 g Cholesterol: 0 mg
Fat: 0.6 g Fiber: 1.2 g Protein: 2.9 g Sodium: 78 mg

You Save: Calories: 60 Fat: 7.2 g

Resource List

Most of the ingredients used in the recipes in this book are readily available in any super-market, or can be found in your local health foods or gourmet shop. But if you are unable to locate what you're looking for, the following list should guide you to a manufacturer who can either sell the desired product to you directly or inform you of the nearest retail outlet.

Whole Grains and Flours

Arrowhead Mills, Inc.
Box 2059
Hereford, TX 79045
(800) 749-0730

Whole wheat pastry flour, oat flour, and other flours and whole grains.

The Baker's Catalogue
PO Box 876
Norwich, VT 05055-0876
(800) 827-6836

King Arthur white whole wheat flour, whole wheat pastry flour, unbleached pastry flour, and other flours, whole grains, and baking products.

Mountain Ark Trading Company
PO Box 3170
Fayetteville, AR 72702
(800) 643-8909

Whole grains and flours, unrefined sweeteners, dried fruits, fruit spreads, and a wide variety of other natural foods.

Walnut Acres Organic Farms
PO Box 8
Penns Creek, PA 17862-0800
(800) 433-3998

Whole wheat pastry flour, unbleached pastry flour, unbleached flour, and other flours. Also whole grains, unrefined sweeteners, dried fruits, and a wide variety of other organic and natural foods and baking products.

Sweeteners

Advanced Ingredients
331 Capitola Avenue, Suite F
Capitola, CA 95010
(408) 464-9891

Fruit Source granulated and liquid sweeteners.

Sucanat North America
Corporation/Wholesome Foods
525 Fentress Boulevard
Daytona Beach, FL 32114
(904) 258-4708

Sucanat granulated sweetener.

Vermont Country Maple, Inc.
76 Ethan Allen Drive
South Burlington, VT 05403
(800) 528-7021

Maple sugar, maple syrup, and other maple products.

Dutch Processed Cocoa Powder

The Baker's Catalogue
PO Box 876
Norwich, VT 05055-0876
(800) 827-6836

Hershey's Chocolate World
(800) 544-1347

Metric Conversion Tables

Common Liquid Conversions

Measurement	=	Milliliters
$1/4$ teaspoon	=	1.25 milliliters
$1/2$ teaspoon	=	2.50 milliliters
$3/4$ teaspoon	=	3.75 milliliters
1 teaspoon	=	5.00 milliliters
$1^1/4$ teaspoons	=	6.25 milliliters
$1^1/2$ teaspoons	=	7.50 milliliters
$1^3/4$ teaspoons	=	8.75 milliliters
2 teaspoons	=	10.0 milliliters
1 tablespoon	=	15.0 milliliters
2 tablespoons	=	30.0 milliliters

Measurement	=	Liters
$1/4$ cup	=	0.06 liters
$1/2$ cup	=	0.12 liters
$3/4$ cup	=	0.18 liters
1 cup	=	0.24 liters
$1^1/4$ cups	=	0.30 liters
$1^1/2$ cups	=	0.36 liters
2 cups	=	0.48 liters
$2^1/2$ cups	=	0.60 liters
3 cups	=	0.72 liters
$3^1/2$ cups	=	0.84 liters
4 cups	=	0.96 liters
$4^1/2$ cups	=	1.08 liters
5 cups	=	1.20 liters
$5^1/2$ cups	=	1.32 liters

Converting Fahrenheit to Celsius

Fahrenheit	=	Celsius
200—205	=	95
220—225	=	105
245—250	=	120
275	=	135
300—305	=	150
325—330	=	165
345—350	=	175
370—375	=	190
400—405	=	205
425—430	=	220
445—450	=	230
470—475	=	245
500	=	260

Conversion Formulas

LIQUID When You Know	Multiply By	To Determine
teaspoons	5.0	milliliters
tablespoons	15.0	milliliters
fluid ounces	30.0	milliliters
cups	0.24	liters
pints	0.47	liters
quarts	0.95	liters

WEIGHT When You Know	Multiply By	To Determine
ounces	28.0	grams
pounds	0.45	kilograms

Index

Almond Meringue Tart Shells, 74
Ambrosia Tapioca Pudding, 101
Apple butter, 14
Apple Cheesecake Parfaits, 108
Apple Streusel Loaf, 205
Apple-Raisin Crisp, 178
Apple-Raisin Risotto, 109
Apples, for use in pies, 84
Applesauce-Oatmeal Bread, 191
Applesauce-Spice Snack Cake, 61
Apple-Topped Cheesecake, 21
Apricot Custard Tart, 85
Apricot-Almond Drops, 123
Apricot-Apple Turnovers, 94–95
Apricot-Ginger Crisp, 185

Baked Brown Rice Pudding, 114
Banana Pudding Parfaits, 105
Banana-Fudge Crumb Cake, 44
Biscotti
    Cinnamon-Raisin, 137
    Triple Chocolate, 138
Biscuit-Topped Blueberry Cobbler, 166
Black Forest Crumb Cake, 44
Black Forest Pudding, 107
Blueberries and Dumplings, 168
Blueberry Swirl Cheesecake, 40–41

Breads. *See* Dessert breads.
Brown rice syrup, 14
Brown Sugar Banana Bread, 188
Brownies
    Cream Cheese Marble, 143
    Moist and Chewy Fudge, 141
    trimming the fat from your favorite
        recipes, 142–143
Busy Day Strawberry Cheesecake, 24
Butter, light, 10
    baking with, 51
    using in brownies, 142
    using in puddings, 111
Buttermilk, 6–7

Cake frostings
    Fluffy Cream Cheese, 48
    Pudding Perfection, 49
    Yogurt Fluff, 48
Cakes
    Applesauce-Spice Snack, 61
    Black Forest Crumb, 44
    Caramel-Apple Coffee, 55
    Cherry Tunnel, 65
    Chocolate Cream Cake Roll, 62
    Chocolate Ice Cream, 161
    Cinnamon-Mocha Fudge, 50

Citrus Carrot, 46
Citrus Pound, 51
Cranberry-Pear Coffee, 57
eliminating the fat from your favorite, 66–67
Fudge Marble, 63
Glazed Pineapple, 45
Heavenly Lemon, 58
Lemon Cream, 53
Mocha-Zucchini Snack, 60
Piña Colada, 52
Royal Raspberry, 54
Sour Cream Fudge, 56
Sour Cream-Coconut Bundt, 47
toppings, 46, 48–49
Tunnel of Fudge, 59
California Crumble, 182
Calories, 6
Cappuccino Cheesecake, 38–39
Caramel-Apple Coffee Cake, 55
Carbohydrates, 3
Carrot-Pineapple Bread, 189
Cereal, barley nugget, 16
Cheese. *See* Cottage cheese; Cream cheese;
  Farmer cheese; Neufchâtel cheese; Ricotta
  cheese; Yogurt cheese.
Cheesecakes
    Apple-Topped, 21
    Blueberry Swirl, 40–41
    Busy Day Strawberry, 24
    Cappuccino, 38–39
    Chocolate Swirl, 32–33
    Citrus Chiffon, 26
    Classic Berry-Topped, 27
    Coconut-Key Lime, 30
    getting the fat out of your favorite, 34–35
    Lite and Luscious Lemon, 20
    No-Bake Cherry, 36
    No-Bake Mocha Mousse, 37
    No-Bake Pineapple, 25
    Peach-Amaretto, 29
    tips for making perfect fat-free, 28
    Vanilla Yogurt, 22
Cherry Chiffon Pudding, 102
Cherry Tunnel Cake, 65
Cherry-Almond Ring, 208
Cherry-Apple Crisp, 176
Cherry-Cheese Loaf, 202–203

Cherry-Vanilla Cobbler, 169
Chewy Chocolate Chip Cookies, 130
Chewy Chocolate-Chocolate Chip Cookies, 132
Chocolate, replacing in puddings, 111
Chocolate Cream Cake Roll, 62
Chocolate flavor, low-fat, 64
Chocolate Ice Cream Cake, 161
Chocolate Jumbles, 128
Chocolate Swirl Cheesecake, 32–33
Chocolate-Hazelnut Mousse, 112
Cholesterol, 4
Cinnamon-Apple Chop Bread, 200–201
Cinnamon-Apple Cobbler, 184
Cinnamon-Mocha Fudge Cake, 50
Cinnamon-Raisin Biscotti, 137
Cinnamon-Raisin Ring, 206–207
Citrus Carrot Cake, 46
Citrus Chiffon Cheesecake, 26
Citrus Pound Cake, 51
Citrus Sugar Cookies, 134
Clafouti, Creamy, 119
Classic Berry-Topped Cheesecake, 27
Cobblers
    Biscuit-Topped Blueberry, 166
    Cherry-Vanilla, 169
    Cinnamon-Apple, 184
    Mini Blackberry, 165
    Spiced Peach, 173
    Strawberry-Apple, 175
    Three-Fruit, 181
    trimming the fat from toppings, 175
    See also Crisps.
Cocoa powder, 64
Cocoa Fruit Crisp, 180
Coconut, using in low-fat recipes, 31
Coconut Crunch Pie Crust, 71
Coconut-Key Lime Cheesecake, 30
Cookies
    Apricot-Almond Drops, 123
    Chewy Chocolate Chip, 130
    Chewy Chocolate-Chocolate Chip Cookies,
      132
    Chocolate Jumbles, 128
    Cinnamon-Raisin Biscotti, 137
    Citrus Sugar, 134
    Fat-Free Marshmallow Treats, 126
    keeping soft and moist, 133

Maple Oatmeal, 129
Maple Snickerdoodles, 136
Maple-Date Drops, 122
Mocha Meringues, 139
Mocha Oatmeal, 127
Molasses Spice, 135
Orange Oatmeal, 133
Peanut Butter Marshmallow Treats, 126
Peanutty Chocolate Jumbles, 128
Toasted Coconut Meringues, 140
trimming the fat from your recipes, 124–125
Triple Chocolate Biscotti, 138
Cool Chocolate-Raspberry Torte, 156–157
Cool Peach Melba, 158
Cornmeal, 12
Cottage cheese, 7
using in cheesecakes, 34
Cranberry-Pear Coffee Cake, 57
Cranberry-Pear Crumble, 179
Cream, replacing in puddings, 110
Cream cheese, 7
using in cheesecakes, 34
using in frostings and fillings, 61
using in puddings, 110
Cream Cheese Marble Brownies, 143
Creamy Clafouti, 119
Creamy Lemon Pie, 78
Creamy Tapioca Pudding, 100
Crème Caramel, 115
Crisps
Apple-Raisin, 178
Apricot-Ginger, 185
Cherry-Apple, 176
Cocoa Fruit, 180
Hawaiian Pineapple, 174
Mixed Fruit, 172
Peach-Almond, 170
Plum Delicious, 177
Summer Fruit, 164
Very Blueberry, 183
See also Cobblers.
Crumb crusts, making in a snap, 71
Crumb toppings, trimming the fat from, 171
Crunchy Nutty Pie Crust, 72

Dessert breads
Apple Streusel Loaf, 205

Applesauce-Oatmeal Bread, 191
baking festive round loaves, 197
Brown Sugar Banana Bread, 188
Carrot-Pineapple Bread, 189
Cherry-Almond Ring, 208
Cherry-Cheese Loaf, 202–203
Cinnamon-Apple Chop Bread, 200–201
Cinnamon-Raisin Ring, 206–207
eliminating the fat in your favorite quick
bread recipes, 196
Fresh Pear Bread, 190
Fruit and Nut Bread, 197
Golden Pumpkin Bread, 193
Mocha Banana Bread, 192
Oatmeal Raisin-Nut Bread, 198
Peach Perfection Bread, 194
Pear-Cranberry Bread, 195
Zucchini-Spice Bread, 199

Egg substitutes, 10–11
using in puddings, 111
Egg whites, 10–11
Eggs, 10

Farmer cheese, 8
using in cheesecakes, 35
Fat, 3–5, 18
budgeting, 5
halving in baking recipes, 56
monounsaturated, 4
polyunsaturated, 4
saturated, 4
substitutes, 8–10
Fat-Free Marshmallow Treats, 126
Flaky Oat Pie Crust, 73
Flaky Phyllo Tart Shells, 76–77
Flan, Spiced Pumpkin, 117
Flour
barley, 11
brown rice, 12
oat, 12
unbleached, 12–13
white whole wheat, 13
whole grain pastry, 13
whole wheat, 13
whole wheat pastry, 13
Fluffy Cream Cheese Frosting, 48

Fresh Mango Sorbet, 147
Fresh Pear Bread, 190
Frostings. *See* Cake frostings.
Frozen desserts
    Chocolate Ice Cream Cake, 161
    Cool Chocolate-Raspberry Torte, 156–157
    Cool Peach Melba, 158
    Fresh Mango Sorbet, 147
    Frozen Mocha Pie, 160
    Fruitful Frozen Yogurt, 150
    Ice Cream With Cherry-Amaretto Sauce, 159
    Light Ice Cream Sandwiches, 155
    making in your freezer, 150
    Mocha Meringue Tarts, 159
    Presto Peach Ice Cream, 151
    Simple Apricot Sorbet, 152
    Strawberry Angel Parfaits, 154
    Strawberry-Cheesecake Sherbet, 148
    Tangy Peach Sherbet, 146
    Tiramisu Sundaes, 154
    Tropical Breeze Freeze, 149
    Very Cranberry Granita, 153
    Very Strawberry Ice Cream, 151
Frozen Mocha Pie, 160
Fruit and Nut Bread, 197
Fruit juice concentrates, 15
Fruit preserves, 15
Fruit purées, 9
Fruit Source, 15
Fruit spreads, 15
Fruitful Frozen Yogurt, 150
Fruits, dried, 16
Fudge Marble Cake, 63

Gelatin mixes, 17
Ginger Baked Peaches, 167
Glazed Pineapple Cake, 45
Golden Pumpkin Bread, 193
Graham crackers, low-fat, 17
Grains, whole, 11
Granola, fat-free, 16
Greek Custard Tarts, 92

Harvest Pear Pie, 83
Hawaiian Pineapple Crisp, 174
Heavenly Lemon Cake, 58
Honey, 15

Hydrogenation, 4

Ice Cream
    with Cherry-Amaretto Sauce, 159
    Chocolate Ice Cream Cake, 161
    Light Ice Cream Sandwiches, 155
    Presto Peach, 151
    Very Strawberry, 149

Jams, 15

Key Lime Cheese Pie, 79

Lemon Cream Cake, 53
Lemon-Raspberry Tarts, 89
Light Ice Cream Sandwiches, 155
Linoleic acid, 4
Linolenic acid, 4
Lite and Luscious Key Lime Pie, 81
Lite and Luscious Lemon Cheesecake, 20
Lite Graham Cracker Pie Crust, 70

Maple Oatmeal Cookies, 129
Maple Snickerdoodles, 136
Maple syrup, 15
Maple-Date Drops, 122
Margarine, 10
    baking with reduced-fat, 51
    using in brownies, 142
    using in puddings, 111
Measuring techniques, 12
Meringue, making foolproof, 75
Meringue Tart Shells, 74
Meringues
    Mocha, 139
    Toasted Coconut, 140
Milk, 7–8
    evaporated skimmed, 7
    nonfat dry, 8
    skim, 7
    sweetened condensed, 8
    using in puddings, 110
    whole, 7
Mini Blackberry Cobblers, 165
Mini Cherry Strudels, 90–92
Mixed Fruit Crisp, 172
Mocha Banana Bread, 192

Mocha Meringue Tarts, 159
Mocha Meringues, 139
Mocha Oatmeal Cookies, 127
Mocha-Zucchini Snack Cake, 60
Moist and Chewy Fudge Brownies, 141
Molasses, 15
Molasses Spice Cookies, 135
Mousse, Chocolate-Hazelnut, 112

Neufchâtel cheese, 7
    using in cheesecakes, 34
No-Bake Cherry Cheesecake, 36
No-Bake Mocha Mousse Cheesecake, 37
No-Bake Pineapple Cheesecake, 25
Nutritional analysis of recipes, 18
Nuts, 17
    toasting, 167

Oat bran, 12
Oatmeal Raisin-Nut Bread, 198
Oats, 12
Oil, replacing solid shortenings with, 56
Orange Oatmeal Cookies, 133

Parfaits
    Apple Cheesecake, 108
    Banana Pudding, 105
    Strawberry Angel, 154
    Tapioca Pudding, 100
Peach Bavarian, 104
Peach Noodle Pudding, 118
Peach Perfection Bread, 194
Peach Streusel Pie, 82
Peach Trifle, Delightful, 113
Peach-Almond Crisp, 170
Peach-Amaretto Cheesecake, 29
Peaches, Ginger Baked, 167
Peaches and Dumplings, 168
Peanut Butter Marshmallow Treats, 126
Peanutty Chocolate Jumbles, 128
Pear Phyllo Pie, 86–87
Pear-Cranberry Bread, 195
Pie crusts
    Coconut Crunch, 71
    Crunchy Nutty, 72
    Flaky Oat, 73
    Lite Graham Cracker, 70

Pie fillings, 17
Pies
    Creamy Lemon, 78
    Frozen Mocha, 160
    Harvest Pear, 83
    Key Lime Cheese, 79
    Lite and Luscious Key Lime, 81
    Peach Streusel, 82
    Pear Phyllo, 86
    Praline Pumpkin, 96
    Pumpkin Cheese Pie, 93
    Razzleberry, 80
    Sour Cream Apple, 84
Piña Colada Cake, 52
Pineapple Tapioca Pudding, 101
Plum Delicious Crisp, 177
Polenta Pudding, 116
Praline Pumpkin Pie, 96
Presto Peach Ice Cream, 151
Prune Purée, 131
Pudding mixes, 17
Pudding Perfection Frosting, 49
Puddings
    Ambrosia Tapioca, 101
    Baked Brown Rice, 114
    Banana Pudding Parfaits, 105
    Black Forest, 107
    Cherry Chiffon, 102
    Creamy Tapioca, 100
    Peach Noodle, 116
    Pineapple Tapioca, 100
    Polenta, 116
    Rum-Raisin Bread, 99
    Sour Cream and Apple Bread, 98
    Tapioca Pudding Parfaits, 100
    trimming the fat from your favorite, 110–111
Pumpkin Cheese Pie, 93

Quick breads. *See* Dessert breads.

Raspberry Angel Tarts, 88
Razzleberry Pie, 80
Ricotta cheese, 8
    using in cheesecakes, 34
Royal Raspberry Cake, 54
Rum-Raisin Bread Pudding, 99
Salt, 17–18

Sherbet
    Strawberry-Cheesecake, 148
    Tangy Peach, 146
Simple Apricot Sorbet, 152
Sorbet
    Fresh Mango, 147
    Simple Apricot, 152
Sour cream, 8
    using in puddings, 110–111
Sour Cream and Apple Bread Pudding, 98
Sour Cream Apple Pie, 84
Sour Cream Fudge Cake, 56
Sour Cream-Coconut Bundt Cake, 47
Spiced Peach Cobbler, 173
Spiced Pumpkin Flan, 117
Strawberries n' Cream, 103
Strawberry Angel Parfaits, 154
Strawberry Angel Tarts, 88
Strawberry-Apple Cobbler, 175
Strawberry-Cheesecake Sherbet, 148
Sucanat, 16
Sugars
    brown, 14–15
    comparison of, 16
    date, 15
    maple, 15
    refined white, 14
Sugarcane syrup, 16
Summer Fruit Crisp, 164
Sweeteners, 14–16
Syrup
    brown rice, 14
    maple, 15
    sugarcane, 16

Tangy Peach Sherbet, 146
Tapioca Pudding, Ambrosia, 101
Tapioca Pudding, Creamy, 100
Tapioca Pudding, Pineapple, 101

Tapioca Pudding Parfaits, 100
Tart shells
    Flaky Phyllo, 76
    Meringue, 74
Tarts
    Apricot Custard, 85
    Greek Custard, 92
    Lemon-Raspberry, 89
    Mocha Meringue, 159
    Strawberry Angel, 88
Three-Fruit Cobbler, 181
Tiramisu Sundaes, 154
Tiramisu Treats, 106
Toasted Coconut Meringues, 140
Toasting nuts, 167
Trans-fatty acids, 4
Triple Chocolate Biscotti, 138
Tropical Breeze Freeze, 149
Tunnel of Fudge Cake, 59
Turnovers, Apricot-Apple, 94–95

Vanilla Yogurt Cheesecake, 22
Very Blueberry Crisp, 183
Very Cranberry Granita, 153
Very Strawberry Ice Cream, 149

Wheat germ, 17
Whipped topping, nonfat, 17
    using in puddings, 111
Whole Wheat Sweet Dough, 204

Yogurt, 8
Yogurt cheese, 8
    as a frosting, 46
    making and using, 23
    using in cheesecakes, 23, 35
Yogurt Fluff Frosting, 48

Zucchini-Spice Bread, 199

Other Exciting Avery Low-Fat Cookbooks

Most recipes have less than 1 gram of FAT per serving

SECRETS OF FAT-FREE BAKING

Over 130 low-fat & fat-free recipes for scrumptious and simple-to-make cakes, cookies, brownies, muffins, pies, breads, plus many other tasty goodies

SANDRA WOODRUFF, RD

240 pages • ISBN 0-89529-630-6 • $13.95

A GUIDE TO LOW-FAT & NO-FAT CHEESECAKE RECIPES

HEALTHY GOURMET CHEESECAKES

SIMPLE RECIPES FOR SENSATIONAL CHEESECAKES

KRIS ERICKSON

324 pages • ISBN 0-89529-783-3 • $14.95

INCLUDES FAT-FREE RECIPES, TACTICS FOR EATING OUT,
SHOPPING TIPS, FAT-BURNING EXERCISES & MUCH MORE

Secrets of
LIVING FAT-FREE

Hints, tips, recipes, and
strategies for losing
weight and feeling great

SANDRA WOODRUFF, RD

FROM THE BEST-SELLING AUTHOR OF SECRETS OF FAT-FREE COOKING

208 pages • ISBN 0-89529-787-6 • $9.95

LESS FAT, GREAT TASTE

GLORIA'S GOURMET LOW-FAT MUFFINS

Easy-to-Make
Easy-to-Bake

HEALTHY GOURMET
R·E·C·I·P·E·S

GLORIA AMBROSIA
BESTSELLING AUTHOR OF GLORIA'S GLORIOUS MUFFINS

256 pages • ISBN 0-89529-732-9 • $10.95

200+ Delicious Quick & Easy Recipes Without Added Fat, Sugar or Salt

LOW-FAT COOKING FOR GOOD HEALTH

A HEALTHFUL
COLLECTION
OF LOW-FAT,
WHOLESOME,
AND DELICIOUS
KITCHEN-TESTED
RECIPES THAT
HELP REDUCE
YOUR FAMILY'S
RISK OF CANCER,
DIABETES,
HEART DISEASE,
HIGH
CHOLESTEROL,
HYPERTENSION,
AND MORE

GLORIA ROSE
Director of the Gourmet Long Life Cooking Schools

384 pages • ISBN 0-89529-686-1 • $14.95

Most recipes have less than **1** gram of **FAT** per serving

SECRETS OF FAT-FREE COOKING

Over 150 fat-free and low-fat recipes from breakfast to dinner—appetizers to desserts

SANDRA WOODRUFF, RD

FROM THE BESTSELLING AUTHOR OF SECRETS OF FAT-FREE BAKING

192 pages • ISBN 0-89529-668-3 • $13.95

Most recipes have less than **1** gram of **FAT** per serving

SECRETS OF FAT-FREE INDIAN COOKING

Over 150 low-fat and fat-free traditional and contemporary recipes—corn curry to chicken vindaloo

PRIYA KULKARNI
ANITA RANADE

224 pages • ISBN 0-89529-805-8 • $14.95

Most recipes have less than **1** gram of **FAT** per serving

SECRETS OF FAT-FREE KOSHER COOKING

Over 150 low-fat and fat-free traditional and contemporary recipes—from matzoh balls to kugel

DEBORAH BERNSTEIN, M.D.

196 pages • ISBN 0-89529-806-6 • $14.95

240 pages • ISBN 0-89529-748-5 • $14.95

192 pages • ISBN 0-89529-735-3 • $14.95

Most recipes have less than **1** gram of **FAT** per serving

FAT-FREE HOLIDAY RECIPES

Low-fat and fat-free meal plans for traditional family celebrations and get-togethers including Christmas, Thanksgiving, New Year's Day, Easter, Hanukkah, Passover, and much more

SANDRA WOODRUFF, RD
FROM THE BEST-SELLING AUTHOR OF *SECRETS OF FAT-FREE BAKING*

240 pages • ISBN 0-89529-629-2 • $13.95

Most recipes have **80% LESS FAT** than standard versions

Brand Name Fat-Fighter's
C·O·O·K·B·O·O·K

OVER 150 LOW-FAT AND FAT-FREE RECIPES FROM BREAKFAST TO DESSERT USING BRAND NAME PRODUCTS

Sandra Woodruff, R.D.

384 pages • ISBN 0-89529-687-X • $13.95

DELIGHTFULLY DELICIOUS DISHES FROM AMERICA'S LOW-FAT, NO-FAT EXPERT

LOW FAT NO FAT

COOKBOOK

KAREN BELLERSON

FROM THE AUTHOR OF AMERICA'S BEST SELLING FAT COUNTER
—*THE COMPLETE & UP-TO-DATE FAT BOOK*

A TEMPTING COLLECTION OF OVER 190 CONTEMPORARY & TRADITIONAL RECIPES

250 pages • ISBN 0-89529-782-5 • $14.95